TRIALS ELSEWHERE
Stories of Life and Development in West Africa

By

R. Matthias

Anywhere But Here Publications

aBHp

Cover photo by R.Matthias
Cover design © 2015 by Evan Wainio-Woldanski

ISBN: 978-0-9948164-0-5
ISBN (ebook): 978-0-9948164-2-9

For Mom and Dad

Author's Note

The names of the people and organizations have been changed. All the people in this book are wonderful and have left a positive impact on my life and the places they reside. Although there were ups and downs as there is with any relationship, it is not my intention to besmirch the reputation of anyone or any organization mentioned.

— R.Matthias

Acknowledgements

This book could never have happened without the constant encouragement of many, many people including, Ken Hernden, Michael DiSanto, Tracy Spurway, Craig Peaker, Richard Herrington, Mathew Gilmore, Tara Isard, Nicole Isard my editor Jena Schmitt, and of course my beautiful wife Donna and our wonderful son, Evan.

TABLE OF CONTENTS

Doing a stupid thing

Washington, D.C., June 2003, at work

My phone rang — again.

The reason most IT departments don't seem to get anything done is because the staff is constantly on the phone; my personal best is having four lines going at once.[1] If you're in IT, you know the drill. Someone's raving, threatening to gut the richest man in the world because of the seemingly terrible software he practically forces you to buy, but since he's not available, you'll have to do. I say "seemingly terrible" because in my experience, when computers crash, it's usually for the same reason planes crash: pilot error.

But the truth hurts, so you never actually reveal this fact to the hapless end user/layman. Instead, you imply it: "Are you sure the machine is plugged in?"[2] End users usually react to this apparent shot at their competence with a bizarre game of one-upmanship, as if they're going to

---

1   Five actually, if you count the guy at my desk trying to talk to me at the same time, apparently oblivious to the handset pushed to my ear.

2   It isn't unreasonable to ask either. During my time as help desk administrator, I was responsible for monthly stats, and noted, on average, 20 percent of the problems in any given month had to do with something not being plugged in properly. So there.

equal the score for all who've been wronged by a computer, anywhere, ever. Yes, computers are a plague that you — the help desk guy — have personally bestowed upon the professional classes of the world, and they're going to *make you pay*. You endure this, like the guy who's supposed to get wet at the dunk tank. You watch with fascination while normal, average professionals try for hernias with the frantic need to bring you down, hoping their next verbal shot — the scorn in their voice — will send you splashing into the water, vindicating themselves and scoring a point: "Ha, ha! One for our team!" It's bizarre because the tank's rigged, and by their age, they should know it.

They can't possibly win, and it should be obvious the instant they launch their first broadside. Computer people/the Elect can play hide-and-seek inside jargon for days. Some of it isn't even real, created only for the amusement of the clergy: "Sir, this problem was clearly the result of an ID-10-T. Just reboot your machine and it'll be fine."[3] Of course, such extremes are for emergencies only. Most people are civil and understanding, and you feel good helping them. But the number of people who call, or stop you in the hall, or go looking for you on your lunch break just to bully you into admitting it's your fault and not theirs, creates a real "them against us" attitude. They're few but aggressive, like terrorists. Over time, they wear you down. You feel hunted. After awhile you keep your jargon locked and loaded, even when you're just having a cigarette.

My phone was ringing. It was midafternoon on a long day at the dunk tank. Before picking up, I cleared my throat and readied my hard-done-by voice, a quiet, polite, tired whisper that says, *Happy to help, but man, I'm beat, so don't*

---

3 To decode, simply replace the one and the zero with the letters of the alphabet they most closely resemble.

ask for too much. I whispered into the phone, "Hello, ITS,[4] what can I do for you?" The voice on the other end was that of a young woman, university age, confident, bubbly. It was obvious she had exciting news.

"Hello! Is this Robin Matthias?"

"Yup."

"Hi! I work for Human Rights Internet and I was wondering if you'd like to go to the Republic of the Gambia and work to help promote human rights in Africa!"

"Sure."

"Uh, maybe you might want to *think* about that?" About a year after my arrival in the Gambia, I was sitting at a bar with a young, wide-eyed intern who stared at me while I told stories about how my friends and I ended up in a tribal court upcountry. When I finished, she paused for a breath and said, "Wow, I hope I have an adventure like that while I'm here."

"Oh, that's easy. Just do something stupid." I guess that's the essence of it: do something stupid. Don't all adventures or at least interesting stories start that way? They sure don't start due to the motive power of "good clean living." Carrying the Ring into Mordor wasn't calculated to increase Frodo's "health and wellness." Heroes of the stage and screen have higher causes — or at least coercion — forcing them to do asinine things: love, blackmail, God and country, whatever. There's always some cause, some purpose or power that allows us, the viewers, to forgive the hero for making what's really just a jackass move.

I had no lofty reason, no higher cause. My only defence for agreeing in three seconds to quit my job, strap myself to an airplane and hurtle myself across the Atlantic to a country I'd never heard of, for an organization I hardly knew of, comes down to the fact that I was tired and feeling a bit daffy.

---

4 Information and Telecommunication Services.

The woman on the other end of the phone had gotten my resume from a Canadian government program called NetCorps, or Cyberjeunes in French, which I'd applied to over a year before. Its purpose was to send young Canadians to the developing world to help build IT capacity and infrastructure. A successful candidate might find himself doing computer training in Peru, building a government website in the Philippines, or acting as IT support for a local NGO. I'd applied on a whim after a friend of mine, who knew how badly I wanted to travel, suggested it. The cut-off age was 30 and I was 28 when I completed the application. I got the call just months from my 30th birthday. It'd been so long, I'd totally forgotten about it.

NetCorps took the applicants and farmed them out to various Canadian NGOs who would do the nuts and bolts of liaising with various organizations overseas. The Corps had given me to Human Rights Internet, and they were going to give me to the Centre for Human Rights in Africa, in the Republic of the Gambia.

A little bit of research revealed the centre specialized in teaching African lawyers the intricacies of bringing cases before the African Commission on Human and Peoples' Rights (ACHPR). The ACHPR was a kind of continental Supreme Court for human rights abuse. If you felt your rights had been trampled in Mauritania and the Mauritanian government couldn't or wouldn't give you justice, you could take your complaint to the ACHPR. However, the procedures for tabling a complaint were complicated. Enter the centre. It held workshops to teach lawyers how to navigate the Byzantine waters of the ACHPR, ensuring they'd make the best use of their time in front of the commission.

The centre and ACHPR were based in the Republic of the Gambia, a small country in West Africa bounded on three sides by its neighbour, Senegal, and the Atlantic Ocean to the west. The predominate geographic feature is the Gambia River, which runs down the middle of the country. The country's about 600 km long and about 60 km at its widest. On a map, it literally looks like a thorn in the side of Senegal. Its borders follow the turns in the waterway, and there's a legend that when the British took control of the place, they sailed a gunboat down the river, firing cannons as they went; where the balls landed, so lay the border. Although clearly untrue, it gives an idea of the country's small size.

The Gambia is one of those places that's seemingly always been owned by someone else. By 1965, the year of its independence from the British Empire, the Gambia had been part of the Ghanaian Empire, the Songhai Empire and the Mali Empire. It was a Muslim country; West Africa being an early convert to Islam, taking up the Koran almost 1,000 years ago. Eventually, the Europeans arrived, and after dividing up the African cake, the English found the slice that included the Gambia on their plate, and they promptly dragged away approximately three million locals to serve their enlightened endeavours. Slavery died hard in the Gambia. Even after it was abolished in the rest of the British Empire, it wouldn't be abolished in the Gambia until 1906.

In 1965, the Gambia became an independent country within the British Commonwealth. Stable following independence, a coup was attempted in the 1980s, which was put down by the Senegalese at the invitation of the Gambian president, Sir Dawda Kairaba Jawara. In 1994, Lieutenant Yahya Jammeh succeeded where others had failed and took the presidency by force, promptly ending all democratic activity. Faced with international pressure to re-establish democratic government, Jammeh allowed himself to be elected president in 1996. The elections were considered dubious by international observers, but in another set of elections in 2001, which were understood by the international community to be fair, he was re-elected president with a 53 percent majority.

This is all I knew about Gambia before leaving, truly not very much indeed. I didn't want to know more though. Travel was something I'd wanted to do my whole life, and I didn't want to expose myself to festering doubts, the kinds of thoughts I could use to talk myself out of going. Folly kicked me out the door, and I wanted to keep the momentum up. Common sense was the enemy, and knowledge was the font of common sense. Common sense tells you, "There's a huge AIDS epidemic over there," or, "They speak a different language over there," or, "Hey, they're Muslims and the Western world just declared war on the whole lot." I didn't want to know the facts. Mysteries entice, facts dismay. The Gambia was a mystery, and I wanted to keep it that way. At least until my feet touched the ground.

In the month or so following the phone call, while I wrapped things up in D.C., I spent a lot of time trying to work out why I was so obsessed with travelling. I'm considered a creature of common sense by my peers,[5] and those last months were surreal, like watching yourself do something you wouldn't actually do. Deep down though, I was preparing myself to leave for years.

Reading never came to me naturally. I grew up in a house of readers, so books were in my blood, but due to my poor reading skills, I stuck to the picture books, but the only ones my family had around were atlases. My first love was a huge *The Times Historical Atlas of the World*. History from Biblical times to the present was logged in this huge 800-page coffee table book. I'd pull it down every day and flip through it when I got home from school, some part of my mind captivated by the way the pictures — the changing borders — told the story. The brief captions hooked my interest, and soon words like *Abyssinia*, *Thebes* and *Holy Roman Empire* were floating around in my head, and not long afterwards, I wanted to know more. I wanted to know what made the lines move.

In addition to being a household of readers, we were a household of immigrants. My mother was Guyanese and her family would always talk

---

5   For awhile in high school I was even known as "the voice of reason."

about the old days in the old country. My father's side brought the Canadiana, and they were no slouches in the story telling game either. I can remember Christmas dinners lasting all day. Everyone would be in the kitchen cooking and drinking and nibbling — but mostly talking. Dinner itself could be up to three hours long, the dinner and desert courses devolving into long chats over wine and liquor around the table. I just sat there with my chin in my hands, listening, oblivious to the fact I was breaking a cardinal rule by putting my elbows on the table. The interesting thing for me was the way in which my relatives spoke. There wasn't a lot of short sharp talk, what people usually call "banter". When someone spoke it was at length. They spoke long-form, for minutes at a time. Whatever they said would have a story arc, complete with moments of humour and emotive highs and lows.

During the last few years of high school, I made peace with the written word and went to university to study history. I dedicated four years to the study of places and people that, absurdly, I'd never seen, having neither time nor inclination as a student. Over the years, I'd come close to visiting Europe a couple of times, but my better judgment kept getting in the way. "It's so expensive. Do I *really* need to go to Europe? How will I get by? I don't even speak French. I should just stay and look for a job." Common sense always found me something more practical to do. When Human Rights Internet called, things were different. I was older and so less wise. As I'd matured, my infatuation with doing the right thing waned. I'd made enough mistakes to realize that almost anything could be survived; the common sense values of my youth felt like a child's security blanket. It was time for a change.

But diving headfirst down life's "reckless behaviour" slide wasn't the only reason for agreeing to go. I also wanted to test a theory. When my undergraduate degree ended, I staggered away with the rest of the survivors and took stock of what I'd learned. What lessons had I dragged from the trenches? Among other things, I learned that universities work a lot like a Moroccan bazaar. Each department is trying to sell its point of view to the students milling around campus. For example, you can ask why the Roman Empire collapsed and almost every discipline in the academy has a weighty opinion on offer. Economists say the imperial economy was in shambles; political scientists see the rise of praetorianism as the problem; environmentalists point to a global drop in temperature, which allowed screaming bands of Germans to come charging across the frozen Rhine. Everything from lead pipes to poor family values can be found on sale by someone looking to get a dissertation published.

After sampling some other disciplines, I finally became a loyal customer of the history department. Its way of explaining things appealed to me. Psychology explains the human experience as a function of behaviour, sociology as a function of social interaction, economics in terms of production and consumption. History explains the human experience in terms of our passage through time, and the narrative aspect intrigued me. I'm not suggesting it's superior to any other discipline; they've all got their ups and downs, but for a boy who'd been brought up in a family of readers and storytellers, history had an intuitive familiarity.

As a story lover you might have guessed English to be my first choice, but history's story is pragmatic, and as a child of the "make a difference generation," the old adage about repeating the past resonated with me.[6] I highly recommend the in-depth study of the past for any young idealists out there with pretensions to changing the world. Studying history lets you sit over the shoulder of some of the greatest and worst problem solvers who ever lived, and watch how they got things done or how they

---

6   I can still remember the endless assemblies in school about "thinking globally but acting locally," and the *carpe diem* T-shirts that were popular even in the last years of my undergraduate. It's the only Latin most of my generation knows.

didn't. There's hardly a contemporary situation or event for which you can't look back in time for advice or inspiration about. Some people look at Iraq and see Munich, 1938; others look and see the Vietnam War. Right or wrong, some people refract the present through the past, and I've got to admit, I'm one of them.

Every profession has hazards, and reading history at the undergraduate level is no exception. There's the occasional allergic reaction to red rot,[7] the occasional skirmish with a psychotic who daylights as a history professor, but the real hazard is a particular form of neurosis. History goes to your head. It's inevitable. One morning you wake up with the sudden and profound understanding that you're smarter than Napoleon or Winston Churchill or George Washington, or whomever it is whose exploits you routinely follow. One morning you wake up and say, "*I* wouldn't have sent that second-rater Grouchy[8] to cover my back with the Prussians. What the hell was Nappy *thinking*?" Hubris is the disease of people who read a lot about getting things done but never actually have to get things done. You become judgmental. You forget hindsight really is 20/20. You become a know-it-all. You become one of those people who listen to someone's wacky "look what happened to me" story and rather than see the humour, shake your head at their pathetic problem-solving skills. You think you're special because you know Gandhi's real name and can pronounce *Kapital* with a German accent. In other words, you wake up one morning and you're an asshole.

The cure is simple, though: try your hand at real life. Make your own

---

7   Red rot is the decay of leather that's been vegetable-tanned. Prolonged exposure to moisture and other irritants can cause the leather to decompose. A book cover that's fallen prey to red rot leaves a trace of red dust on your fingers (or more likely the white cotton gloves the archivist makes you wear to handle any book that old).

8   Emmanuel de Grouchy, Marquis de Grouchy, one of Napoleon's marshals during the Hundred Days campaign, and largely seen as a key reason Napoleon lost.

plans for invading Russia and see how you do. Why not? It's the "make a difference" age, after all. Aren't we all supposed to be out there pushing the world in some new direction? Making something (anything) happen? Aren't we all supposed to have a plan to burn Moscow?

I realized early on the first step was to ditch history. Not reading it, but pursuing it academically. History makes at least one thing clear: historians don't make history.[9] This glimmer of enlightenment revealed itself to me while in my history MA. Academic history didn't agree with me back in those days. The professionals didn't read the record the way I did, rather they saw the past as the past — a museum diorama you tinkered with but never actually emulated: "No, the Persians used their spears in an overhead thrusting motion, not under-handed." People have written whole articles about the intricacies of Persian spear work, and reading, debating and finally adding your own scholarly contribution to the Persian martial arts debate is the province of academic history. You aren't supposed to try and actually *use* the Persian spear.

I dropped out and enrolled in a Masters of Library and Information Science (MLIS) program. Like any geeky kid whose formative years saw the advent of *Pac-Man* and *Missile Command*, I'd always been interested in computers. I still remember my first program, which I wrote in Grade 10 using BASIC on a Commodore 64. It was a Christmas tree, rendered with big square blocks, and it looked like a cross-section of a pine tree built with Lego. Some of the blocks blinked different colours for lights. It was beautiful. Changing the world via Commodore 64 might seem a bit of a stretch, but again, I was a child of the information revolution, and despite the information revolution still being in diapers when I was coming up, there was much hope and optimism surrounding the whole adventure.[10] The

---

9   With the possible exception of Karl Marx.

10 I remember when computers didn't have mice but did have a B: drive, and when one

information revolution was going to save the world via unprecedented levels of efficiency, and getting things done would be easier than ever before. For aspiring movers and shakers, the golden age had arrived.

There was no way I was going to sign on for another four-year tour starting from scratch with a computer science degree, not when real life was so close. The MLIS degree was perfect: it refined my computer knowledge, stamped it with a master's credential, taught me useful things about how humans interact with information, provided the basics for becoming a crack IT manager and it was only two years long — a real bargain. It paid off quickly. Within months of graduating, I was already on my way to Washington, D.C., to help save the world. I took a job at the public library to help "bridge the digital divide," to help "provide access to information" and to help "build capacity in socioeconomically underprivileged groups." I had skills. I had knowledge. I had gumption. What could go wrong?

Well, all kinds of things could go wrong, actually. There was the time I surprised (and was surprised by) a crackhead smoking up behind the building while I wheeled out a load of discards.[11] There were the strange (and occasionally threatening) bathroom incidents, and naturally, the parade of homeless (and sometimes very disturbed) people who are a fixture in all public libraries.[12] "Bridging the digital divide" wasn't always fun and games,

---

megabyte of RAM made the front page.

11 Discards are library books that are to be thrown out. Yes, librarians throw out thousands of library books every year. This always shocks people, which, in turn, shocks me. They must notice how a library keeps getting new books, but at the same time, the library's walls are fixed. The building doesn't expand to make extra space. Where do they think yesterday's pulp fiction goes? Sell it? Sure, some titles with a market value get sold. Send them to schools in Africa? Not a chance. Books are heavy and so the cost of shipping them en masse to anywhere, much less Africa, is mind-blowing.

12 A colleague of mine in my MLIS who'd formally worked in the mental health industry, told me it was usual policy to send less extreme cases to the local public library for an unsupervised day out. The idea was that the public library was "safe" and "quiet."

though. The old expression, "long hours of drudgery punctuated by moments of sheer terror," usually applied to sailing ships, also applied to development work in North America. Some of the incidents I've listed above provided the terror, the following illustrates the boredom, the day-to-day grind, the reason you end the day asking, "What am I doing here? I've got *two* degrees, for Christ's sake."

It was the day Human Rights Internet had called and my phone was ringing. Again. I was working the late shift, covering the help desk until 9 p.m., one of the worst jobs you can imagine. Had Dante known about computers, he'd have included late-night help desk in *Inferno*.[13] Nevertheless, the call I'd received that afternoon left me spinning in my chair and smiling like a fool as I worked on my entity-relationship diagrams and occasionally searched Google for "the Gambia." I picked up and answered enthusiastically, "Hello, help desk. This is Robin, what can I do to—"

"You have to come upstairs right now!"

"Who is this?"

"You have to come *now*! It's Biography!"[14]

"What's—"

"We have a situation here and we need you guys *now*!" He hung up. Curious. The caller sounded unusually panicked. It's normal for callers to be angry, and sure, there's a certain amount of panic whenever someone loses control of a computer, but this was different. With great foreboding I pulled myself up and headed for the elevator. The biography division was three

---

Sure, except for all the other outpatients.

13 You get the worst of the day on that shift. By the time you get to work, everyone else is already moving at warp speed and angry people are already stamping their feet. You haven't even had a coffee yet. There's usually a list of complaints the morning people have rolled over to you because they know you're coming in late, and that between their lunch and you settling in, they'll likely be heading home by the time you notice.

14 DCPL was organized along subject divisions. Biography was the reading room with stacks specializing in biographies and autobiographies.

floors above the IT digs in the basement.

Maybe the closest elevator would be working today. It wasn't. I'd have to use the one in the far corner of the building, on the other side of The Cage. Behind the black-steel grating that made up the walls of The Cage, books were stacked to the roof on old shelves, like the kind you see in high-school libraries, bowed under the weight. Some were in boxes stacked all over the place, others were dumped on the floor. I wish I could say The Cage was a graveyard for old books, the ones with olive-drab or fire-engine-red covers, but the truth is that after five years at the library, I had no idea what The Cage was for. I'd never even seen anyone in there. In five years, no one I asked seemed to know either. Looking at it that night, I just felt depressed.

Turning right from the elevator, I approached Biography, and through the glass walls I could see two security guards and an African-American man, the latter waving his finger at the former two. His eyes were bugging out of his head in agitation. I couldn't hear what he was saying, but he was clearly yelling, and the person sitting at the public computer looked to be yelling back. A few feet away stood the librarian who had called. What now? I pulled open the heavy glass door, and the screaming inside was loud and piercing. I quietly slipped around to the librarian. "So Ben, what's going on?"

It turned out Finger Waver wanted to use the public machine, but the man currently using it still had some time left on his session. Ben had signed the guy up to be next, but he wanted it *now*. "Is there anything wrong with the computers?"

"This is *about* the computers," Ben answered.

"This is *about* security. There's nothing wrong with the machines, is there? Why did you call the help desk?"

"This is about the computers!" Ben insisted. No point in arguing. It seemed to be a security problem, and I had no idea why the two officers hadn't done anything about it. From a distance I could see the computer monitor — only about 10 minutes left. I walked over to the guy yelling. His pants were too big and new-looking, probably a donation from a shelter. His button-down shirt was clean but too big as well, and his French cuffs were frayed. The sole of one filthy sneaker flapped loose at the front. He carried a plastic shopping bag full of papers. He was the aggressive type.

"What seems to be the problem, sir?"

Turning to face me was an event: dead silence, back straight, pivot of the heel, the expression on his face saying, "How *dare* you interrupt me." He practically spit: "I don't need help from *you* people." I'd lived in D.C. long enough to know "you people" meant "whitey."

"Well, sir, I'm the head of intranet development and I'm here to make sure you get the service you deserve." My title was more descriptive than authoritative, but dropping it had the desired effect. He started talking and I encouraged him. "To really get to the bottom of this sir, I need you to start at the beginning, and please, give me every detail." I motioned him over to a table and told the gentleman using the machine to continue working while I sorted it out.

My new friend was there to do research, but he wouldn't tell me a thing about it except how important it was.[15] He'd come into the library around four that afternoon and checked his Hotmail in the business division. Next, he'd gone to Popular Library[16] to use the computers to design some fliers. Following that, he went to Black Studies and told me how irritated he was because the librarian kept asking after the details of his research. He was sure they were going to steal his idea. He didn't trust her. I asked for a detailed description of the librarian; he obliged. I asked him

---

15 This was typical. A lot of "researchers" in public libraries are there pursuing their pet conspiracy theory.

16 Popular Library was the name given to the division that specialized in paperback fiction. Tom Clancy, Daphne du Maurier and such.

again, after getting Ben to get me a piece of paper[17] on which to copy the details down. I promised to look into it. Feeling harassed in Black Studies,[18] he'd signed up to use another computer — this one in Biography — and, having an hour to spare before it was available, left the library to print his fliers. He held up and waved his bag around, which contained, among other documents, a stack of hot-pink paper. On returning, he headed straight to the machine he'd been assigned and the guy sitting here now was already at work. Sure, he'd missed his reservation, but he was a busy man; the library should factor busy people like him into its systems. Happily, the other patron was getting up now, and so I wouldn't have to extend the interview with a more-detailed-than-you-could-possibly-imagine explanation of the library's computer use policy.

He had his computer. Catastrophe diverted. I was free to leave, my spirits utterly deflated. I asked the two guards why they hadn't thrown the guy out, he was causing a disturbance. The problem had to do with the computers — and that wasn't their department; their union told them so. They were there in case "something went wrong." I let it go, threw my notes from the interview into the recycling bin and gave Ben all the Hell I could muster, at that time of night. I made my way back down to the quiet of the basement.

The incident wasn't remarkable, but it left me more discouraged and tired than usual. It was still on my mind a couple of hours later when I shut down the office and climbed the wide concrete stairwell to the first floor. Security was still there, manning the airport metal detector and x-ray machine that all people, including staff, had to pass through to get into the library. Unlike the bag checkers at most airports, the ones here carried guns

---

17 Apologizing, of course, for not being better prepared.
18 As you can guess by the name, Black Studies was the division for African-American history and literature. And yes, the official name was Black Studies.

and handcuffs.

I pushed through the heavy glass door and stopped a moment to look back at the library. As usual, piles of blankets were lined up against the wall. If you only passed the library occasionally, you wouldn't know each pile contained a human being trying to get some sleep; the blankets pulled up over their heads, although sometimes a grimy foot or hand poked out. There was usually over a dozen or so, maybe 20. Sometimes, when the air was still, you could smell them from across the street. A soup kitchen was right beside the library and these guys wanted first crack. "Godspeed, boys," I whispered quietly to myself. They'd need all the help they could get. In Biography, it'd taken a reference librarian, a systems librarian and two security guards to sort out a 10-minute scheduling blip. With public servants like that, I figured the guys in the homemade sleeping bags didn't have a chance. I guess I was more than ready to go. An act of whimsy had kicked the blocks out from under the car, but now it was rolling free, and not a moment too soon.

First Impressions

Senegambia Beach Hotel, three days after arrival

The pool looked great, right out of a Club Med promotional. Big and blue, shaded by palm trees, it was fantastic to sit by its side, slumped in my chair, legs crossed, cigarette drooping from my mouth, drinking my beer and feeling like James Dean behind my shades. The centre's workshop was in full swing; I'd arrived in the middle of it and was put to work instantly.

"Work" consisted of hooking up projectors to various laptops and making sure the printer and dialup connection in the hotel's secretariat were working. In other words, with my experience, the workday consisted of tanning poolside. I'd arrived three days before and was still living in the hotel, so I didn't even have a commute. Every couple of hours a speaker would finish, the delegates would take a break and I'd rig the conference room for the next presentation, in total about 10 minutes' effort. After that, I was free to do as I would, and so I did.

Sitting by the pool, I could feel my confidence surging. It was stupid. All I'd done was get on an airplane, but for whatever reason, I felt I had control, like I could get what I wanted if I tried. I was just an intern but had six months to get my foot in the door. Six months to get my dream job: doing IT for international development. I'd been in-country for three days and had been lucky enough to land in a workshop filled with very connected

19

development people. True, they were human rights defenders, not known for their IT passion, but it was a place to start. I finished my beer and went to the conference room; they were due for a break any minute.

Manoeuvring around the finger foods, I did my best to mingle. I'd managed a few conversations with some of the participants and the speakers. I'd already met the staff of the centre as well, 10 in all.

Five of the 10 were lawyers who made the place go. After the director — Samantha — came Idrissa, a burly Senegalese man in his early 40s standing head and shoulders over me with a deep, menacing voice. Some people referred to him as Shaka Zulu, though never to his face. Janet was young, mid-20s and Congolese. She was very smart, very competent and very pretty. Working under Janet were Muhammad and Madeleine. Muhammad was a young Liberian, about 30. He was a quiet guy with a big smile; he kept his hands perpetually clasped behind his back and his head bowed in thought, nodding thoughtfully in conversation, every inch the Mandarin. Madeleine was Malian, educated in Paris and very French, right down to the giggle. She'd just finished her law degree. Together, Janet, Muhammad and Madeleine were the bread-and-butter staff responsible for the workshops and other legal work at the centre. Everyone else was support: secretaries, gofers and interns. With the exception of Samantha, I received a very measured welcome. I wouldn't call it cold, but certainly an atmosphere that seemed to say, "has anyone sniffed the new fish?" filled the secretariat when Samantha introduced me.

The participants in the workshop — about 25 of them — were lawyers from across Africa. They were friendly in a polite and proper sort of way. Africa is a very formal place; relaxed buddy-buddy interactions have no place there, except between the closest of friends. Almost all the participants had studied in Europe or America for some portion of their degree, but even still, there was a premium on prim. People always shook hands when greeting, even if they'd already greeted each other that morning. Always

20

looking their best, even for the workshop, the participants usually wore suits or traditional dress. The North American image of a civil rights defender — a university student with a bandanna and Birkenstocks — was definitely not the look here. In fact, after asking one of the participants from Uganda what he thought about the Peace Corps, he admitted he didn't know much about them except that they looked "dirty." Being from North America, specifically post-punk-rock North America, I found the manners and formality strange but not necessarily bad. These guys were pros. They walked with straight backs but a relaxed step. Their attitude and professionalism really inspired me. My time in D.C. had embittered me to "do good" organizations because the ones I'd interacted with felt like hippy halfway houses. These guys were different. No join-the-march-smoke-a-joint-and-we've-done-our-bit types here, just real professionals; well-disciplined soldiers trying to get things done on the front line. After all, Martin Luther King and Thurgood Marshall wore suits too.

The workshops themselves were pretty boring. Not because of my wonderfully sharp legal mind, but because I already knew most of the content. It was all basic stuff, or stuff you could find out about on the Internet. When I mentioned this to one of the participants, he just gave me a long, sarcastic look and said, "the Internet?" Yeah, point taken, but the comment made me feel pretty good, reinforcing my conviction that IT was of importance in the world of development.

Beer by the pool and occasionally fixing a computer was how I spent the first three days. I hadn't really left the hotel, being too tired on one hand, and too intimidated on the other; my airport experience — a confused tug of war between baggage handlers with myself playing the rope — still resonated Nevertheless, I hadn't come this far to be intimidated by a few dozen yards of road. I reconciled myself to have dinner out that night.

During the daylight hours, the main strip outside — all two or three hundred feet of it — resembled a roadside watering hole in Arizona. The kind of place you'd stop at for gas: windswept, dust-filled and lonely. Standing at the hotel's entrance at 9 p.m., however, I could hear music and laughter in restaurants up the street. With no streetlights, a 20-metre chasm of dark separated me from the ambient light of the restaurants and taxis. Standing there, in the last pool of light the hotel had to offer, I could see silhouettes across the street, mostly lanky young guys loitering on the low concrete wall opposite the hotel. They seemed to be looking in my direction. I glanced at the security guard sitting on a bench by the hotel entrance, an older gentleman in a uniform two sizes too big. He shrugged sympathetically. We didn't speak, but his look said it all: "Sorry, Boss Man, my jurisdiction ends with the light."

I trudged out into the void, hoping for the best. About halfway across, I noticed in my peripheral vision a tall loping form, bobbing its way in my direction. It was alleyway dark, the kind of dark you avoided at all costs in D.C. I picked up the pace and added some lateral to my gait, trying to open the gap. It didn't help. Too afraid of looking too afraid, my side step was too subtle to escape. He cut me off in a flash, rounding up so close I had to step back. "How *de* evening?"

"It's fine, thank you."

"That's fine, boss, fine. You remember me? I'm Lamin from the hotel."

"Sorry?"

"You must remember! I'm the gardener from the hotel!" The suddenness of the meeting left me off-balance. I didn't know what to make of the guy. He was taller than me, even stooped, but incredibly thin. He wore a Rastafarian hat, jeans and a Bob Marley T-shirt. I really couldn't tell who he was in the dark. "How are you?" I asked.

"Not fine. Not fine, boss."

"Really, that's too bad," and I started moving off. He stepped in front of me.

"Excuse me! Excuse me! Can I speak with you? You know prices have gone up, but the pay, it stay the same." He started groping for my arm and I stepped back to keep it out of his reach.

"Sorry you're having a rough time, but I gotta go."

"You know, boss, the children. I just need a little for the milk."

"Milk?"

"Boss Man, you know, the pay, it's low, my *childrens*, they need the milk."

"How much is milk?"

"Just need 50, boss, just for the *childrens*. I'm an honest man, just need a bit — it's not easy — just need a can of milk."

As my night vision adjusted, I started to get a better sense of my surroundings. With a certain amount of alarm, I noticed we weren't alone. We were only feet away from the low cinderblock wall by the edge of the street. I could see the silhouettes of several young men; I couldn't make their faces out, but no doubt they were looking right at us.

The guy I was speaking with was young and still smiling despite the sob story. I didn't know what to make of him. Sure, he was pushy, but he looked to be in earnest, and either way I was afraid of what might happen if I pushed my way past him; a good 10 metres separated me from the light, and a lot can happen in 10 metres. Nevertheless, I could feel my back stiffening. I don't like being threatened. But despite my brewing temper, I was a stranger and didn't know the rules. More importantly, what if his story was true? What if I bumped into him by the pool tomorrow, on his knees in the sun with a trowel, working for milk? The guilt would be enormous. Quietly, emphatically, he whispered, "Come, Boss Man. It's for the *childrens!*" his face twisted up, displaying their agony. I'd filled my pocket before leaving, having no idea how much it would cost to eat dinner out, and I so reached in, hoping for a small bill.

"Here you go." I slapped a note into his palm. He rolled his hand around, trying to capture some light. It was 50 dalasis. "Look, this is all I've got. Gotta go." While he studied the note, I started moving fast, which caught him off-guard. His feeble protest trailed off behind me — so did laughter. The lights were ahead and I just kept moving.

I didn't slow down until I was engulfed by the flood of florescent light covering the street. I took a seat on the concrete patio of the first eatery in my path, Ali Baba's. Flopping down at one of the plastic tables, I pulled out a cigarette, ordered the local lager, *Joyful JulBrew*,[19] flipped through the menu and considered events.

My time in D.C. had left me with a certain amount of skill in dealing with panhandlers and other street denizens. My job had taken me to the roughest parts of the inner city, and the inner city of the "murder capital of America" at that. Sure, there had been some scary moments: the day I got stuck on a street corner with a couple thousand dollars' worth of computer equipment. The presence of a white boy in the middle of the "hood" with monitors and CPUs stacked at his feet immediately attracted the attention of 10 or 12 "local youths." With the branch library closed behind me, the 40 minutes it took a library van to arrive were touch and go. I negotiated the situation and made it out with life, limb and computer equipment intact, not to mention a bolstered impression of my own street savvy.

Other situations over the years helped reinforce that impression. Situations including teenage prostitutes turning tricks in the bathroom, completely naked men (not even socks) admiring themselves in bathroom mirrors, librarians being attacked by the public, the public being attacked by librarians, gang members and crackheads doing their thing, flagrant racism, the ubiquitous masturbators. Through it all, I was also trying to do my job.

Our small IT staff of about 10 was tasked with bringing the library's

---

19 Brewed by Muslims for sinning Christians.

IT infrastructure into the new millennium, no easy task considering most divisions were still using rotary telephones and typewriters when I'd shown up. Management upheavals[20], fending off hostile takeover attempts by other agencies,[21] hostile budget meetings, hostile press, hostile librarians, hostile public, political infighting, overblown needs assessments and vendor contract negotiations were all just a "part of the job." When I showed up in Africa, I felt like I'd seen it all, both on the street and in the boardroom. And yet I hadn't been out of the hotel for two minutes before getting fleeced.

I sipped my beer. It was silly to assume the same rules applied here. The guy was a *bumpster*. I'd been warned about these guys: young men on the make, trying to get money any way they could. In D.C. people used veiled threats to get your money; here, they used confidence games like the one I'd just encountered. All smiles, full of good will, trying to win my sympathy, it caught me completely off-guard. Sure, his "milk" angle seemed lame, and I would've laughed it off in D.C., but in the context of "poor Africa," it gained a measure of credibility. Just enough sympathy to make me hand over the money. I don't think I would have otherwise, despite the boys sitting on the wall. In fact, the guys on the wall almost blew it. Having come from D.C., I was ready for confrontation, not guilt. It was clever. All these tourists, used to pushing and being pushed, melted when someone got in their face with a sob story, a big smile and "no hard feelings." People want to help a baby or hand out lollies and then go home and tell their friends, "In my small way, I made a difference." The *bumpsters* understood this, and looking around, I could see them at work in the restaurant.

At the table opposite me, a British couple sat with a young Gambian,

---

20 We changed managers faster than the Late Roman Empire changed emperors.
21 Our most generous opponent was OCTO: Office of the Chief Technology Officer. OCTO was the D.C. government's citywide IT department, and they felt strongly that the library's IT should fall under them. Fending them off was a constant chore.

not unlike the man I'd paid a few minutes before. Maybe in his 50s, the Englishman's shirt was wide open, revealing a beach-ball gut, round and red, dwarfing his stick legs, faded green tattoos on his arms. His wife had the same body, topped with frizzy peroxide hair. They were being entertained by a young Gambian guy who was all smiles. They looked to be enjoying themselves, and the bottle in the plastic wine bucket probably helped. The Gambian kid — a good Muslim — would only take Fanta.[22] It looked innocent enough, but the longer you lived there, the more you'd learn.

Eventually, I'd know guys who made their living by "being friendly." Maybe acting as an impromptu tour guide, picking up a free meal along the way, happy to stay in touch when their "friends" left and soon collecting regular sums via Western Union. Personable guys, but in the end, I was worn down by their callousness. Watching them in restaurants, always smiling, always sober and acting like young Horatio Algers became irritating. I'd run into them later in the week, catastrophically drunk and stoned, doubled over with laughter at the stupidity of their sponsors. Not every tour guide was on the make, but the fact that the "official tour guides" had to wear uniforms and badges to try and separate themselves from the majority, told the story.

I'd been told the number one *bumpster* gambit was romancing old foreign women. According to the interns, the Gambia was the male prostitution capital of West Africa. When I was told this, I didn't really know what to make of it. It was such a strange thing to be told, just like that, over lunch. The kind of casual comment that makes people chew their food a moment longer than they should. As surprising as it was to hear at lunch, it seemed innocuous enough to see at dinner. In fact, it took me awhile to zero in on it at first.

---

22 Fanta is a Coca-Cola product line that sells fruit-flavoured drinks. It was founded in Germany in the 1940s due to the difficulty of importing Coke into Nazi Germany. The most common flavour in the Gambia was orange, which tasted something like Orange Crush.

A lot of people were there, a fair mix of tourists and Gambians, but eventually, as I ate my dinner, I started to notice. An old lady, very thin, the over-tanned skin on her face cracked like leather, sat to my right, feeding cigarettes and beer into her face, big gold bracelets sliding up and down liver-spotted arms with each puff and swig. But she wasn't alone. Her companion, with an exaggerated "gangsta rappa" slouch, was a young Gambian man, maybe 20 years old. Built like a Hollywood movie star, huge and cut, he displayed himself in a see-through red, yellow and green tank top, complete with a cannabis crest decorating its chest. I could just make out his eyes under the bangs of his dreads, slow and heavy, just a little beyond relaxed. One of his massive arms was thrown across the table and she was squeezing his hand and chatting enthusiastically. He acknowledged her with a goofy grin. I couldn't hear what they were saying because the place was loud, but occasionally his mouth would move a little, his head floating on the end of its neck with the effort, and she'd pitch her head back and laugh ridiculously.

It looked like bad TV. Apparently, these women came from places like Germany, Holland, the U.K. and Sweden with the express purpose of picking up these young men. After being around awhile, I'd see these couples everywhere, sitting in restaurants or on the beach, smoking and drinking, holding hands as they walked down the street. It was so common, a young Gambian friend of mine asked me to edit a play he'd written for a youth group. He'd authored a morality play about the evils of *bumpsting* because he wanted "something everyone could relate to." [23]

This wasn't a 10-bucks-a-pull sort of affair; these women looked more interested in companionship. They'd take their "boy" out to restaurants no Gambian could afford, buy them clothes and send money after they'd gone home. It was all out in the open, no dark streets with idling

---

23 He was part of a Red Cross youth education program.

cars. For all the sordidness this openness seemed to purge — and it did purge a good portion of it — the handholding only added to the bleakness. At first impression, it looked pathetic, these women taken in by good-looking beach bums and their "easy, easy, just relax, *mon*" attitude.

On the other hand, one reason people holidayed in a place like the Gambia was to escape the realities of the developed world, to live a life only dreamed of in their two-room Glasgow flats. The soap opera lifestyle Hollywood sends you to bed with doesn't necessarily have to be a wet dream. In a poor country like the Gambia, even a mechanic can be a king. Seize the day! Buy the ticket! If you want to do all the stuff you can't back home, like walk around topless, just go to someone else's country. Out in "unpretentious Africa" — so close to nature, so *real* — no need to worry about social expectations or cultural roles. Who cares what other people think? After all, aren't vacations a time to relax, to let your hair down, to do what you want without worrying what the boss or the neighbours think? Want to show off pictures of yourself with an arm around the unpretentious local guy selling coconuts on the beach? The developing world can oblige. If you want to be desirable and aren't too picky about why, you can have that too. All you need is money. If you have enough, no one will remind you the place you're in actually has more rules than the place you left, that walking around topless in a Muslim country, or chugging beers as fast as you can during Ramadan, is offensive to the locals. Paradise can be complicated, mostly because we think it isn't.

While I ate, another presence announced itself over my shoulder. He was complaining in a heavy German accent about his beer being too warm. His voice was carrying, and it didn't hold any concern for the young guy trying to serve him. "Yes, boss! I tell them the beer is warm, but we have no current now. Sorry!"

"No power?" he grunted with disgust. "You don't have a generator? How can you be serving food and not have a generator?"

"Sorry, sorry! Maybe I can get some ice."

"Ice? You don't put ice in beer! Forget it, just get me my food," and he waved the kid away. In North America, in the eyes of someone prone to making these kinds of judgments, this guy would've been nothing but white trash, right down to his mullet, but here he was, pushing this kid around like he was head of his own plantation. He wasn't a tourist, because every time the kid came to the table, he kept going on about the pristine condition he kept his own generator in. Then it occurred to me he probably *was* the owner of his own plantation — or something like it. He looked like a plumber, but here, a plumber's wage could buy you a big house, with land and servants to go with it. I wondered how much the ticket cost that brought him there. Whatever the cost, in his mind it was probably the best money he had ever spent.

In due fairness to my dining companions, they found themselves dissatisfied and did something about it. I had to respect their gumption, or whatever it was that brought them there. Was it courageous or cowardly? It took guts to leave everything you knew, your friends and family. But maybe these guys were booze hounds who couldn't hold down jobs, an embarrassment to their family, a joke to their friends. Either way, they'd made their move. "Go West, young man," that's what they used to say. Go West and stake your claim; find your fortune. That's how my country came to be, after all. I knew too, from my education, that most of the early settlers in Canada and America weren't much better than that abusive German.

I wondered how my own goals and wishes fit into the scene. All around me I saw conquistadors, people I imagined would have "just so much to talk about" over dinner with Hernán Cortés or Juan Ponce de León. As I made my way out of the place, I imagined myself as one of the good guys. Sure, I had goals; I was here for my own purposes, but my goals dovetailed with those of the locals. That's what I told myself as I got up. Thinking about it a bit more, I guessed working for human rights defenders

29

made me a 21st century clergyman: a missionary of the moral majority. Missionaries were not the most savoury image from my perspective, but it did feel good to be among the righteous. I left a big tip.

I'd taken about two steps out of Ali Baba's when I heard someone yell my name. At another restaurant across the street I could see an African man waving at me from a patio table that seated about 12. I recognized him immediately, one of the workshop participants. Everyone at the table was from the workshop. I walked over smiling, making the rounds, people getting half out of their chairs to shake my hand. They invited me to sit and eat with them. I'd already eaten but was happy to join them for a drink. Frantic shuffling of chairs as everyone insisted I sit with them. Finally, wedged into a corner between a man from Nigeria and a woman from Kenya, polite questions and warm smiles were thrown my way. What do you think of the workshop? Where did you eat? Was it good? What would you like to drink? Almost everyone took a turn to ensure my arrival at their table was a warm one, and then, greetings over, they returned to their conversation.

A man at the table resumed telling his story: "So I went back to the bar and showed it to him. He just looked at me. I told him I wasn't going to drink it, and he'd best give me another one. I tell you, he just stared at me. Didn't have enough brains to reply! I tell you, he said he would ask the manager. Now my friend," he yelled theatrically at the man sitting opposite him, "do you need to *ask* your manager to give me a new bottle of water? Really? This country!" Rounds of approving laughter followed. The man sitting next to me filled in the details. Apparently, the poor victim had gotten a bottle of water during the workshop and there had been a bit of dirt in it. I was aware of the incident: the intern from Rwanda had talked about it all afternoon. The Gambian staff at the centre hadn't said a word, though. People started sounding off as soon as he'd finished his story.

"The service here is terrible. Really!"

"How long have we been waiting for our food? Boy, boy! Where is our food? We've been waiting for nearly an hour. You can't expect us to pay for this?" The waiter ran off to the kitchen.

"They don't know anything here. Just a bunch of farmers."

"I know. This place really is unimaginable."

I asked the woman next to me what she thought: did she like the Gambia? "Oh yes, it's so rural. So *African.*"

"What do you mean? Is it different in Kenya?"

She laughed: "You must be joking. You don't see places like this anymore."

"Like what?"

"They don't even have buildings here. Where's the city? Being here is like being in the middle of the countryside. But I do like it. We're so much more European in East Africa. This is like the *real* Africa."

It was reassuring to hear something positive about the Gambia, because for the next 20 minutes, no doubt goaded on by liquor, the table went on a vicious and emotional rant about the stupidity of Gambians. It was depressing. Every person there was sub-Saharan African, except me.[24] Making matters worse was the sense of imperiousness, of gentility, they assumed because they were human rights defenders. They were educated and wanted everyone to know it. They were acting like young lawyers and congressional aides at a D.C. happy hour. Compared to them, the odious German was tame. Our table was a lot louder, and things were getting worse. Some of the men were becoming indiscreet, eyes lingering a bit too long at women in the street. Baiting the waiter was turning into a sport and everyone

---

24 "Sub-Saharan African" is the modern politically correct way to refer to black Africans in Africa. The African states north of the Sahara are generally Arabic, North Africa having been an early conquest of the newly converted Islamic armies pouring out of the Arabic peninsula in the 7th century. They're still Africans, though. Africa is a place, not an ethnicity.

was taking turns. I knew the next hour (it would be impolite to leave sooner) was going to hurt. These educated African human rights defenders were talking the way racist white guys do in the movies. Not like rednecks, but like aristocrats, shrill with contempt. I felt passers-by would assume I, the token white guy, would be the instigator. I spent the time trying to make eye contact with our beleaguered waiter, giving him hopeful smiles and wishing I was wearing an "I'm not with stupid" T-shirt.

An hour passed, and I made my exit, heading for home. The guy who'd hassled me earlier had moved on. I passed through the dark without incident. One or two guys hanging by the wall got up to try and intercept, but I was too annoyed to take notice and they backed off.[25] I was annoyed by the participants: human rights defenders by day, the worst kind of tourists by night. Sure, you had a right to be proud of your education, your achievements, but to wield them in the face of the less fortunate, almost sadistically, didn't line up with my Canadian sense of rights, fraternity or equality. How do you get anywhere when the human rights defenders look down on the less fortunate?

The workshop came to an end. I managed to conceal my feelings, a task made easier by a couple of participants who felt the same way I did. We'd commiserated quietly over the last couple of days. On the last day, it had been arranged to take everyone to the market in Banjul for some shopping. Banjul was the capital city, and it was miles away from the Senegambia region. The interns had arranged a couple of Volkswagen minivans to make the trip. I quickly grabbed a window seat and tuned out the chatter in the van, focusing on the road to Banjul.

---

25 Inadvertently, I'd hit on a key survival skill: never make eye contact. Eye contact or a polite smile meant "come on over." As aggressive as these boys were, often trailing you literally for hours, they wouldn't even start if you weren't friendly and easygoing — at least not in the Gambia. Senegal and Ethiopia were different stories altogether.

The trip to the capital was about a half an hour. We left the hotel and rejoined the highway I'd come down from the airport, except we turned in the other direction. Within minutes of leaving Senegambia, we passed a large sandy area filled with cars painted yellow. About a dozen were arrayed in the lot, their drivers sitting on shaded benches surrounding the trunk of a huge tree. No two cars matched and none looked to be in a decent state of repair. An old Peugeot sat with a 20-degree list. An ancient Mercedes — filled with people swaying back and forth in unison — rolled along, pushed by a group of guys, a dust cloud rising with their effort. This was the local taxi stand.

The local taxis were painted yellow and were for the conveyance of the local people. Inside Senegambia, on the main strip, the taxis were painted green and called tourist taxis. The local taxis weren't allowed inside Senegambia — that was tourist taxi territory.[26] The price difference between the two was enormous. Apparently, the green taxis had special licences and kept their cars up to a higher standard. As a result, they were allowed first crack at the tourists in Senegambia, and they charged accordingly. Twenty-five dalasis' worth of ride in a yellow taxi cost 350 if the car was painted green. The green taxis guarded their tourist-rich patch with vigilance. God help the local driver who turned into Senegambia. I once heard Samantha describe the tourist taxis as "practically a mafia."

Farther along, the sea was visible a kilometre to the left, blue and twinkling in the sunlight. Green fields of vegetation and small rice patties stretched out, covering the gentle gradient between the highway and the sea. Hundreds of palm trees dotted the landscape, their trunks all leaning the same way, heads bouncing in unison with the wind. Beyond the stretch of green, along the water's edge, sat several large hotels. Groups of tightly packed bungalows, nuzzled comfortably beside the sea, hidden under the

---

26 Say that five times fast.

palms. Only the occasional glimpse could be seen from the highway. Hundreds of snow-white bedsheets suspended between the trees flapped in the breeze.

The other side of the road was lined with low concrete walls about seven feet high. Some were decorated with extravagant hanging plants and flowers. Most had broken bottles sticking out of the top.[27] You could see houses poking up over the top of the walls, some two stories high. They looked modern, European-style collections of boxes arranged asymmetrically with clean lines, wide balconies and painted almost universally bright white, yellow or salmon.

We soon arrived at the intersection where the Atlantic Highway[28] met Kairaba Avenue. Kairaba — I would one day learn — was the main commercial area for the well-to-do locals, sporting electronics stores, cellphone companies, Internet service providers, gas stations and even a couple of North American-style grocery stores with North American-style goods. Kairaba also boasted *the light*.

Where the Atlantic Highway and Kairaba intersected stood the only traffic light in the Gambia. It was a simple four-way stop. The intern acting as our tour guide, a young local woman, said it had been donated to the government, but she didn't know by whom.

Not far through the light, our two-lane highway became four lanes (at least it looked like four lanes — there were no lines down the middle) and we picked up speed. Mangroves and tall grass intersected by blue streams stretched out on both sides. The highway was built on top of some

---

27 This was a common feature of local compounds. When the compound wall was finished, a layer of cement was smoothed over the top, and into it the broken bottles were set, pointy side up. The idea was to discourage the curious and the mischievous from popping over the wall.

28 Also know as the "Atlantic Road," although while I was there "Atlantic Highway" was a more common usage.

kind of bank or high ground. We arrived at a bridge. Modest, it was like a large Bailey bridge. Police hovered around the approach. Off to the left, a small shack sat near a large tree, a couple of AK-47s propped up against the trunk. A group of men in sloppy green fatigues were crowded onto a small bench, enjoying the shade of the tree. They never took their eyes off us. A cop stuck his head through the driver's window, quickly surveyed the van, and yanked it back out. He had a few words with the driver before waving us on. Crossing the bridge gave a view of a small marina to the right. Long thin boats like 30-foot bananas painted all kinds of colours drifted quietly around their moorings. Some were pulled up onto the muddy shore.

Banjul was just around the corner. Dead ahead, I could see the Arch 22 monument. This was a '70s home decor version of a Roman triumphal arch, built to celebrate the coup of '94 (which was on July 22, hence the name). We circled the roundabout in front of the arch, in the middle of which stood a golden statue of a soldier with a child in one arm and a rifle slung over his shoulder. His other arm was raised as if demanding someone to stop. He looked like a Styrofoam gold-lamé-dressed crossing guard. The arch itself was made of concrete, tinted a light pink. It looked like the profile of a house supported on four columns. You could see the imperfections: the subtle undulations in what should have been straight columns, the cracks in the surface, the boarded-up drinks stand behind the statue, the unkempt lawn around the monument's base. The whole thing looked like a Disney theme park fallen into disrepair.

Winding through the streets on our way to the market, I got my first look at Banjul. Most of the buildings were about three stories, made of cinderblocks and fitted with large, open-air staircases going up the front. Laundry was washed and hung to dry from these impromptu verandas. Smoke from coal and gas stoves drifted from them too, staining the sides of the buildings. Single-story dwellings huddled around the feet of the taller apartment blocks, and every roof in the city had thickets of antennas growing out of them. Some buildings had over a dozen poking crookedly into the air on iron, steel or bamboo poles, even broomsticks. Every type of antenna you can imagine, from rusting satellite dishes to Yagis.[29] It looked as if the West's pre-cable TV antennas had been harvested from suburbs and dumped here.

Some of the buildings were clearly from a different time: huge, massive stone blocks instead of concrete, grand curving stairways carved out of granite, coats of arms cut in relief over huge symmetrical doorways. These were the monuments left by the British. Derelict imperialism.

We pulled over into a street and the message was passed that we'd arrived. The streets were filled. Banjul — unlike other Gambian towns — had sidewalks and paved roads. The sidewalks were covered in merchandise while people generally walked in the street, sharing it with cars, goats, cows, chickens and feral dogs. Men pouring with sweat as if someone had dumped a bottle of water over them pushed wheelbarrows stacked to their chins with sacks of grain, cloth and watermelons. Handcarts were everywhere, dodging around the dilapidated cars and trucks with horns that never seemed to stop. The traffic wasn't much past two miles an hour. The trucks were from another time, with a 1950s look to them. The exhausts of most were at street level, and hot black clouds of diesel smoke made you gag. The garbage in the street made you gag too. The streets were the gutter, and I'm not being metaphorical. Garbage seemed to cling to everything. There were no waste bins. I remember the shock of watching one of the participants — a young woman from the Sudan — casually drop her empty Coke can at the feet of an ancient-looking woman sitting on the curb by a big basket of smoked

---

29 Yagi-Uda antennas (usually just called Yagis) are probably one of the most distinctive antennas ever invented. Yagis were those strange arrays every house in North America had on its roof before the advent of cable television. They look like a set of grey metal bars of descending size, arranged smallest to largest. They're named after the Japanese engineers who invented them in the 1920s, Shintaro Uda and Hidetsugu Yagi.

fish. The legion of flies covering the fish jumped into the air, some settling on the old woman. Neither woman noticed because they were distracted by more interesting things.

There were Arabs everywhere. In fact, most of the vendors were annoyed-looking Arabs. Inquiring about this, I was told Banjul was practically a Mauritanian colony, but no one knew why.[30] Their shops were on the first floor of the old warehouse buildings lining the street. Some of the warehouses had old electric signs, broken and caked in dirt. Perhaps the legacy of a better day. The shops were like small garages that spilled out onto the sidewalks. Imagine every garage sale you've ever been to lining one street, squished together, not a blade of grass between one driveway and the next. The shops were lined with all kinds of merchandise: cheap ghetto-blasters with monster-size speakers and ridiculously exaggerated controls, cellphones, rusted tools and finished clothing, mostly cheap knock-offs of high-quality items — *Gasio* watches, *Royban* sunglasses and *Nykor* cameras.

Browsing with my group, it was obvious the hot ticket item was cloth. Shop after shop was literally filled to the rafters with bolts of it. Any possible way the human mind could contrive to combine colours and patterns could be had. As in North America, people there loved clothes, and as in North America, there were finished clothes available for purchase. But here the quality of the cloth was all-consuming. If you didn't want to wear Western clothes like t-shirts and jeans, style options were limited. Basically, there were about three or four traditional outfits for men and women. In terms of cut or shape, dressing was a pretty conservative affair. So you showed your style and your individuality via the colours and patterns of the fabric, and apparently Banjul market's selection was fantastic. The participants ignited into a "shop till you drop" frenzy. We were practically

---

30 After being there for awhile, it was made clear to me that the Gambia enjoyed close relations with Mauritania because they shared a common enemy, Senegal.

running from one stall to the next, looking for the best patterns, trying to cover as much ground as possible. I didn't buy anything, being too absorbed in the sights and sounds, but the participants showered me with cloth-buying advice anyway. The best fabrics came from Mali. Never buy cloth with a waxy feel. Cloth with a salty taste is the highest quality.

"How do you know it's salty?"

"Salty, yes!" and the young human rights defender from Uganda immediately started licking the corner of a bolt he'd pulled out. (He decided he didn't like the taste and left it in the end.) The cloth merchants were almost universally Mauritanians of Moorish decent. They wore long, flowing "nightshirts" reaching down below the knees, complete with baggy pants and sandals, and often topped off with a small round skullcap. Called a *boubou* by the locals, it was the standard male dress of the West African region, despite some local variations.[31]

The Mauritanian merchants invariably sat inside their stalls in the shade at the back, doing the books at small desks and sipping strong cups of tea. Sometimes they sat in the back on bales of fabric, cuddling together. It didn't take long to realize the standards of male affection here were very different from what I was used to. It wasn't unusual to see two men sprawled out together, one preening the other's hair, or to see two men walk down the street hand in hand. I remember the first time a man grabbed my hand as we walked along. I had been there for about a year; he was a client, educated in the U.K., and we were walking out to his warehouse where he wanted to have a Wi-Fi connection installed. It was a strange thing. He did it absent-mindedly, playing with my fingers while listening intently to what I was saying, and then we were suddenly holding hands. It never bothered me, and amongst my friends it became a good test of new interns' cultural

---

31 The Mauritanian shirt had Western-style collars and cuffs, while the Gambian version had shorter sleeves and an open V-neck.

sensitivity. Even the most self-assured "world traveller" types, displaying all kinds of bravado in terms of food and customs, would panic when you reached across the dinner table and started stroking their hand. One guy even threatened to hit me.

While I wandered, I saw a young man carrying a tray on his head of sandwich bags, each filled with about a cup of water and knotted at the top. People would buy a bag, tear off a corner and suck on it to refresh themselves. But it was his T-shirt that caught my attention. It was black with a picture of the Twin Towers on the front. One was burning, and a plane was frozen near the second tower, moments from impact. In the foreground, an image of Osama bin Laden stared heroically into the distance. Flying off the page in comic book font were the words *Freedom Fighter*. During the course of the day I saw more shirts and paraphernalia like this, with subtle variations, on sale and on people. This was the land of Islam and people weren't afraid to fly the flag. Having just come from Washington, D.C., the invasion of Iraq only months old, seeing the T-shirt put me in an instantaneous state of shock, just a second long but palpable.

The few hours we spent in Banjul market left my head spinning. It shook some reality back into my gung-ho attitude. Pretending to be James Bond back by the pool in Senegambia was easy. Life outside of Senegambia, outside the tourist district, was humbling, worse than anything I'd seen, and really, I hadn't seen much. And yet I'd seen some things during my first week: male prostitutes who specialized in the over-60 crowd, human rights advocates who didn't seem to care about the common people, the casual commercialization of terrorism. All these things floated around in my head while I tried to sleep that night.

I started to question my desire to try and "make a difference." I didn't feel qualified. As a professional problem solver, the most baffling issue of the day — the thing that really got my mind racing — was the litter. Poverty, bigotry and strife were things I'd expected. Seeing and smelling it

39

in person caught me a little off-guard, but these weren't surprises. They were problems we still had in the West. These problems never got "solved," they just got managed. Furthermore, the list of devices, techniques and philosophies one could use to manage them was long, tried and comprehensive. The trash in the streets of Banjul was different. You expect to see economic strife everywhere in the world, but not trash: it's just too easy to deal with. You don't need a World Bank loan or expensive consultants or the Enlightenment to prop up a few hundred drums on the streets of Banjul and have them carted to the dump a couple of times a week.

They had everything they needed — bins, pickups, dumps and the idle soldiery necessary to get the job done. This was a problem that could get solved in very short order. It would take time for people to get used to using bins because habits die hard, but people would come around. Who wanted to live in a street filled with garbage? I mean, the whole development gig seemed to pinion on certain assumptions. People want good hospitals. People want affordable food. People want clean water. Shouldn't *people want clean streets* be on the list too? If it wasn't, what did that mean about other assumptions westerners were making?

There'd be plenty of time to agonize over saving the world though. A more pressing problem needed solving sharpish: I had to find a place to live. The centre was supposed to provide me with a place to stay, but it hadn't, which I didn't know until I'd landed. All I really knew was I didn't want to live in a Banjul apartment block. How did renting work here? I doubted there was a Landlord-Tenant Act.

Money

One week after arriving

I found a place to live and a roommate too, just a day after the workshop. His name was Robel, and I knew him from my brief two weeks of training in Canada. We'd been catapulted to Gambia by the same organization, and we made contact via email during the workshop. I hardly knew him. We hadn't spent much time hanging around during our training, but I knew he'd be arriving a few days after me, and I hoped we'd connect quickly.

We arranged to meet at the cybercafé in Senegambia. In a long rectangular concrete box of a building, halfway up the strip, about five computers were available for about two dollars an hour. When I discovered the place, I was shocked. I'd developed an impression of Africa before coming, derived mostly from TV commercials featuring hard-up children and news footage of the latest famine. The café just didn't fit. In fact, Senegambia didn't fit at all. It was a long way from nice, but it was a long way from a refugee camp too. On the other hand, Banjul market had left more impact than a lifetime of Save the Children ads, and I'd only been there two hours.

I was walking up from my hotel when I saw Robel standing in front of the café. A Canadian citizen but Ethiopian by birth, his parents had been protesters in the old country, leaving as refugees during a government

41

crackdown. They'd lived awhile in Kenya and then immigrated to Canada while Robel was still a kid. From there, he'd found his way into the computer science department at the University of Toronto, and as a new graduate, found his way into the NetCorps program to get some job experience. Now, here he was. Extremely thin, his oversized button-down — which would have been large on my 200-pound frame — flapped like laundry drying in the wind, and his pants bunched up on his boots. Robel was partial to smiling, and I clearly remember his huge white grin and large, sleepy eyes as I greeted him. "So what do you make of this place, man?"

"This place is *crazy*!"

"I know it! Have you been to Banjul market yet?"

"No, but my hotel's a dump and expensive to boot. I'm out of money." Money was a problem. The centre had brokered a deal for my room in the hotel, but I was still paying out of pocket. I mentioned the obligation to billet new interns to the financial officer of the centre, a Gambian named Mamadou, and he told me there used to be a place. Unfortunately, the last intern had gone out and found his own accommodation because he wanted to live "closer to the people." Without an occupant, the centre couldn't justify keeping an intern house. I was on my own.

I was dumbfounded. One intern, around for only six months, wanted to — as Muhammad put it — "bang on a drum with the natives" and so they liquidate a major asset? Sure, they saved some money, but it was money they'd been prepared to spend anyway.[32] What about the future? Weren't they planning to get more interns? Of course they were, Mamadou assured me. I guess the idea was to save now and worry about a new place later. Now it was later, and they'd left it to the last minute and couldn't find a place, which was both a problem for me and the centre. Every intern reported back to their home organization and rated their experience. A bad

---

32 They hadn't planned to sell the place; they only did so after the intern moved out.

review could end in disaster, depriving them of critical support. Interns didn't just fetch coffee, for example, shortly after I left they wanted to create a short movie about human rights to distribute on DVD across Africa and in Europe. The idea was to remind the world of the shocking human rights scene all over Africa in a the way only moving pictures could. A good idea, but only an idea. To make it reality, specific skills were required. Enter the interns.

In addition to special projects, "intern power" made IT work, and because everything done at the centre revolved around the Internet, this was no laughing matter. The Internet kept them in touch with human rights defenders across Africa and the world. They also used it as their primary research tool. Without Internet access, they couldn't have performed the workshops or any legal work at all. There were no libraries; it cost too much to call another lawyer, even a local one, to consult over work. Bottom line: no Internet, no centre. If our connection went down for more than an hour, people went home. They couldn't even get news. Alienating the IT guy was not a "play to win" management move, but I was determined to make a go of it, so I decided not to red-flag the place in my first review home.

I wanted answers, though. Why play Russian roulette with your organization over six months' rent you're willing to spend anyway? Although it was never made explicit, as I subtly probed the issue over the next six months, a certain theme kept coming up: when the last IT intern decided he wanted to live "closer to the people," he really annoyed the staff at the centre. It was considered a slight because they'd provided a nice place and he'd turned it down. There were niceties, a decorum. You accepted generosity with grace — whether you wanted it or not. Turning the place down was like being invited to dinner, surveying the table and announcing you weren't hungry.

The whole notion of "closer to the people" begged the question: What does he think of us? We're people, aren't we? I never met the guy, but

I always wondered what he meant by that. I'd meet young Westerners while I was there, and they'd often talk about "the real Gambia" and "real Gambians." The staff at the centre seemed real. True, they were lawyers and accountants, but they still considered themselves "real people." Their annoyance was palpable whenever "closer to the people" came up. Most of the kids I met looking for the "real Gambia" were actually looking for a particular subculture. Usually, they were very heavily into the music scene back home and naturally enough wanted to explore the music scene in the Gambia. They had no more interest in the lawyers, engineers or doctors they worked with in the Gambia than they did with the ones back home. Fair enough, but back home you'd never say over the lunch table how much you'd like to meet some "*cool* people — no offence, anyone," so why would you do it there?[33] It became obvious during my time at the centre that respect mattered more than money.

But for now, Robel and I were caught in the same vice grip; his organization had assured him a place would be found "soon," but hadn't offered too many more details. In the meantime, he was staying in a hotel at his own expense. Since he was about to be turned out into the street, and the human rights defenders he was here to help didn't seem too worried about it, it made sense for us to room together. Together *where* was the next question, and a troubling one too, because neither of us had the slightest idea where to start. We didn't know the language or even anyone we could ask about renting except our new colleagues, and they were tepid at best. We had no idea how to determine a "good" neighbourhood from a "bad"

---

33 Another common attitude I found among some of the younger interns was the strange notion that the "real people" all lived in rural villages. Good thing we don't make the same assumptions about North Americans, since almost all those drum-banging hippies were city kids. Strangely, none of them seemed to have visited farms back home. I know, because I always asked. No one could explain to me why the rural scene was so much hipper in Gambia than the one back home. Weird.

one, how much was too much, or what kinds of questions were appropriate to ask and how to go about it: "So, yeah, you actually have a flush john here or what? You know, Euro style?" We had no idea how anything worked, and it kept us up at night.

The stress made it great to talk to Robel. We didn't even know each other's last names, but our looming homelessness bound us together, and our meeting sounded like best friends exchanging spring break stories and backslaps. Although happier and more enthusiastic than our acquaintance dictated, the feelings were sincere. There's nothing like finding someone who shares the same miseries you do. Robel had other problems as well. Despite the fact he'd been scheduled to show up for months, no one had thought to provide the IT intern with a computer. New ones had been purchased, but they'd gone to management. Robel was left to redesign their website — the stated purpose of his internship — with paper and pencil.[34]

The centre staff hadn't been forthcoming about rentals when I'd initially made inquiries: another aftereffect of the incident with the last intern, I later discovered. So I was shocked to hear Muhammad say the day following the workshop that he'd spoken to his landlord and the compound next door to him was available at what he considered a reasonable price. A very relieved *fantastic* was my first thought, which was immediately followed by, *What the hell is a compound?* Would I be paying for a whole house? Then again, did I really care as long as it was less than a hotel? One of the interns, a Rwandan who'd already put five months in, was still living in a hotel. I couldn't afford that. Muhammad assured me that splitting the rent would cost less than six months in a hotel, and it was only a short walk from the centre. The place had three bedrooms, but another intern from Canada was

---

34 Eventually, we'd get a broken one going, but I had to bankroll the project, paying for parts myself because Robel was flat broke. We also had to go into Serekunda market on our own time to find what we needed.

due to arrive in a month, and in the meantime, the Rwandan was happy to room with us because she only had a month left. It was perfect. I loved the place and I hadn't even seen it yet. It felt like I'd just left the doctor's office with good news. I enthusiastically accepted the offer to check the place out, and after lunch, Muhammad and I did just that.

It was a 10-minute drive in the direction of the airport. We arrived at a roundabout, turned right and drove a short distance past some corrugated iron huts, then turned left into a small, suburb-like place. Little houses, white with Spanish tile roofs, each surrounded by a concrete wall — it looked like a tiny Arizona subdivision dropped in the desert. It was all new: no landscaping, just sand-filled yards littered with construction jetsam. We slowed by one of the houses. A couple of men dressed in *boubous* stood around a white Mercedes, looking bored, sweating behind big aviator shades. Muhammad pulled his hatchback up behind the Benz, we jumped out and crunched across the gravel to chat with the gentlemen impatiently waiting for us. Introductions were brief. A stocky guy with a soccer ball belly was introduced as the landlord, and he quickly removed the padlock on a red metal gate set in a yellow concrete wall.

The wall fenced off a compound about the size of a small plot in a North American suburb. Discarded cinderblocks and other bits of debris were scattered around, half buried by the windswept sand filling the yard. In the middle of the sand and rubble, trying to maintain its dignity, sat a tiny, whitewashed bungalow, its neat lines a stark contrast to the chaos of the yard. The house looked like it might have been stolen from somewhere else and gently placed there by helicopter. It had a simple peaked roof, a veranda off the front door running half the length of the house, and double windows on the veranda looking in on the living room, kind of like a smaller, cement facsimile of a North American bungalow. The copy had flaws besides its size: the banister surrounding the veranda was intended to have an old European carved stone look, but the bits of cement hanging off the posts revealed them to be moulded concrete; single streaky coats of white paint covered the iron window frames, most of which were warped; the concrete driveway was permanently scarred by the sloppy rake work used to smooth it. All in all, it was beautiful. Looking at it, Banjul market felt a million miles away. While Muhammad chatted with the landlord, I let myself in for a quick walk-through.

The double door consisted of glass panes held in a heavy-duty iron frame. The lock was a massive piece of steel, the only steel in the whole house. It felt peaceful inside; the harsh sunlight outside was softened indoors, similar to a quiet spring afternoon. It was cool and my eyes relaxed as I poked around. The stillness was destroyed when I moved around, the blue tile floor and white concrete walls amplifying every step harshly. The bathroom was a walk-in, no tub, no shower stall, just a drain in the floor and a showerhead. There was a flush toilet and sink. It was all working; there was water. The kitchen was bare except for an aluminium basin still covered in construction dust. The three bedrooms were a decent size and one had a full bathroom. Barring the kitchen, all the rooms had working lights.

I was sold. In fact, I was damn near enthusiastic. The price still needed sorting, but considering some of the dumps I'd lived in, I felt like I was standing in the lap of luxury. I left home when I was 18. Here I was in the Gambia, just shy of 30, and the string of hovels, couches and floors I'd stretched out on between now and then could've formed a comprehensive treatise on student living. In D.C., working as a successful professional, I'd considered myself lucky because my apartment had a separate kitchen. Here, I was strolling around the grounds, taking in the air, surveying *my* quarter acre. It was a glorified sand dune, but it was *my* sand dune. Suddenly, the annoying German in the restaurant made a bit more sense, which was an uncomfortable thought because I was sure we had nothing in common. I pushed the thought out of my mind.

"How much?" I asked after rejoining Muhammad and the landlord

47

outside.

"Two thousand five hundred," the landlord replied, big smile.

"I see. Right. And that's for how long?"

"Each month."

"So, for six months?"

"Fifteen thousand. Pay immediate."

"What?"

Muhammad broke in: "He means only that the total sum is payable upon the signing of the lease."

"Yes, it's true," added the landlord.

"Uh, that's dalasis, right?"

"Yes, yes, of course."

Well, thank God for that. One American dollar was worth about 29 dalasis, so I'd have to come up with about $520 USD. We agreed to meet in a day's time to complete the transaction.

That evening, I emailed Robel and we agreed to split the cost. He'd come up with his end after we got our second pay instalment from Human Rights Internet in a couple of months. The issue was getting the balance for tomorrow. There was no such thing as Visa or MasterCard in the Gambia. Credit simply didn't exist. There was a bank in Senegambia, the Standard Bank, and it had an ATM that worked for some cards, including, happily, mine. Unfortunately, I'd passed by on my way back from the house and a group of hostile-looking tourists were gathered around. The man standing at the machine jerked his card out of the slot and dropped his heavy fist on the counter's edge. He announced to the crowd, in a heavy English accent, that "the fuckn' thing still don't work!" I went into the bank to ask when the ATM would be fixed. They had no idea. With the candid, good-natured customer-service enthusiasm people new to the service industry exhibit when someone asks them a question they can actually answer, the manager explained it was completely possible for the machine to be out of action for over a week. Oh yes, very common. All the machines in the country (there were five he said) frequently went down at the same time due to a problem with their central computer. I asked pointedly how it affected tourism. Wasn't this the only ATM in the tourist area? How were tourists supposed to spend money if they couldn't get any? Senegambia clientele was a hard-drinking bunch, not the kind to cash traveller's cheques and stick to a budget. Day or night, someone was always standing in front of the ATM. Didn't the government have something to say about the quality of the service? Wasn't tourism one of the most important sources of revenue for the country? Well, it sure was, but the young manager in his stylish but far too big suit apologized: "Easy, easy. What can be done?"[35]

Fortunately, I was the kind of guy to carry traveller's cheques and stick to a budget. Nevertheless, it gave me pause when I considered these were my financial reserves, my backup plan, and I was dipping into them less than a week after arriving. Retrieving them from my room, I returned to the bank, passed a new crowd of disgruntled tourists, and presented myself to the counter with $600 in U.S. traveller's cheques. Six-hundred dollars translated into about 17,000 dalasis. They paid me in hundreds and fifties — mostly fifties. The counting machine was broken, so two tellers counted it out by hand, binding each stack of a thousand. I watched the two bored women work with a sense of shocked fascination. They weren't really going to hand me a huge grocery bag of cash, were they? Twenty minutes later, 17 bricks of wrinkled notes arranged in six stacks — each almost larger than one of my hands — were slapped down on the counter. I felt like I was

---

35 As an interesting aside, I found out years later that the Standard Bank techs had been pushed so hard to keep the ATMs running that they quit. They formed their own company and started charging top dollar to fix the ATMs. This little bit of entrepreneurial spirit had a decidedly negative impact on the speed of repairs. The bank would now haggle with them before requesting assistance. There's a moral in there somewhere, maybe more than one.

on a TV show, some kind of Vegas high-roller crime drama; all I needed was a briefcase to slap the bundles into. I picked one up, studying it like some new, exotic artefact. "Uh, do you have a bag?" They didn't. My hands couldn't manage it all, so I pulled the bundles off the counter and hugged them against my chest. As I was leaving, an Englishman sitting near the door pulled himself out of his chair and made his way toward the counter. We didn't make eye contact, but as we passed he said, "Don't worry, you'll get used to it."

A taxis driver I would become friendly with would one day tell me that, "the colour of money was white-man." That was the conventional wisdom, and it posed a problem since I hadn't left D.C. in funds. I had a good job in D.C., but I did my best to live up to the "work hard, play hard," image of a young D.C. professional. My friends and I thought nothing of spending over $200 each on a meal or drinks, an event we'd repeat a couple of times a week. My rent in D.C. had been ridiculous, and I'd blown a lot of pay cheque servicing my student loan and Visa card. Other than the traveller's cheques, I had barely enough in my account to cover the interest on my student loan. As interns, we were being paid peanuts. Nevertheless, people saw me as someone with cash. One night Robel and I were out with Janet and Madeleine. On our way into a patio to see a djembe band, I was stopped and asked for money. I told the guy to go to hell. I'd noticed him watching us as we piled out of Madeleine's car. Madeleine had driven us there and got out of the driver's side; dressed to the nines, she clearly owned the car. I'd been at the end of the line on our way in and he let Janet, Madeleine and Robel go by without saying a word. He waited till I was abreast of him before making his ask. Ironically, his inability to tell the difference between a practicing lawyer and an intern got him into trouble with Madeleine who sent him on his way with a few choice words. I never had a lot of money while I was in the Gambia, and paying my student loans was always a source of stress. Eventually, my stock line with Gambians who wanted money was, "Sorry, I can't. I'm over a million dalasis in debt," which was about right considering my student loan at the time. More often than not, people would back off and actually become sympathetic.

Credit was a curse for everyone. In my case because I'd indulged too much, for the Gambians I'd become friendly with, because they couldn't indulge at all.

I asked a Gambian friend who worked as a driver what his dream was. He told me it was to own his own taxi. With it, he thought he could make enough money to send his kid to a decent school. The problem was he couldn't afford it. I asked him if he'd been to the bank to try for a loan. He had, but they wouldn't loan to Gambians, only foreigners. Was he upset? No, he understood. He wouldn't loan to a Gambian either. One of his own friends got a loan and just blew the money. When it was time to pay it back, he was in terrible trouble. Gambians, he said, just didn't understand money. They didn't understand that loans have to be paid back. Some of the guys I'd eventually work with echoed the same sentiment. We were talking about why a lot of Gambians who make it into the U.K. end up coming back; "money problems" was the unanimous opinion. "They go, get shit jobs, then blow it all on parties and clothes, when the rent time comes...."

A place without real credit institutions just won't make it. BRAC,[36] one of the most successful NGOs in the world, started out as a micro-loan project for rural farmers. In its simplest form, microcredit is simply giving small loans to poor people. There's a lot of wisdom in it. I remember one sunny afternoon a couple of years in the future, driving around with my future boss, Peter. We were scouting out the competition. Peter's business was providing Internet access via a wide-area wireless network. In other

---

36 BRAC (Bangladesh Rural Advancement Committee, formerly the Bangladesh Rehabilitation Assistance Committee) is the world's largest NGO and considered one of the best and most successful.

words, he'd put an antenna on the roof of your house and pointed it back to the 45-metre mast standing in front of our office, where you'd be connected to the Internet. The World Bank had approached Peter with the offer of a one million dollar loan as part of a plan to help build IT infrastructure in the Gambia, but Peter, to my shock, turned them down. The World Bank had moved on to the competition, and so here we were scouting their telecom towers; Peter smiling gleefully at the sight of each clearly-imported-all-the-way-from-the-U.K. specimen. From Peter's point of view, a loan that size was the same as indentured servitude. He couldn't believe anyone working in a market as small as the Gambia's — someone who'd have to pay the loan back in dalasi — would take the loan. To him, it was simply madness; a plan to keep you in debt forever.

The next day, as planned, Muhammad took me to the house to make the payment. I stuffed my backpack with the cash. Before leaving my room I debated backpack-carrying styles. Slung over both shoulders would make it harder to snatch. Holding it in one hand would make it easier to keep an eye on. I finally went with the slung-over-one-shoulder approach because it looked more casual.

The scene at the house was the same as before: *boubous*, sweat and aviator shades. Again, they'd arrived first, and again they were waiting impatiently. There was a new guy this time, older, very thin, wearing traditional Mauritanian clothes. Again, brief introductions before moving into the compound. The landlord handed me a piece of lined, legal-size paper. Slightly askew (the typist hadn't bothered to align the paper), the terms of the lease were listed. The page was only three-quarters full and the type was double-spaced. The user agreement on the back of a bus transfer was longer. Simple, no unnecessary complexities, just who, where, how long and how much. It didn't even say I was responsible for keeping the place clean. I signed both copies.

With the legalities sorted, it was time to count the cash. Reaching into my pack, I pulled out the money, placing the stacks neatly on the veranda banister. Watched intently by serious guys wearing aviator shades, one drawing slowly on a cigarette, I felt like a teenager pulling drug money out of his backpack after being busted by the local narcs. I stepped back and the Mauritanian stepped over to the ledge, picked up the first stack and started flipping the notes back at rocket speed. He finished, put it down, then picked up another. We waited for him to run through all the stacks. It felt like a solemn occasion, no one spoke. The landlord watched the Mauritanian closely; the other man quietly smoked his cigarette, his eyes never leaving the human counter either. Muhammad kicked at stones in the yard, studying the fall of each as if part of some important experiment. When the last stack had been processed, the Mauritanian glanced over to the landlord, nodded and said something. The landlord gave me the keys and shook my hand, so did his friend. Everyone was smiling and happy. Me too. I had a roof over my head, the best one since I was 18. Muhammad drove me back to the hotel. As soon as we arrived, I emailed Robel and told him to pack.

We moved in the next day because neither one of us had to work. The centre had taken the week off to recover from the exertions of the workshop, and Robel had been granted a few days to settle in. The first order of business was to decide who got which room. The one with the bathroom was "for the ladies," insisted our Rwandan friend. As majority shareholder of the new digs, I took the second largest room. A nice big space, almost bigger than my entire apartment back in D.C. Once we dropped our stuff, we leaned over the banister smoking cigarettes, telling stupid jokes, patting ourselves on the back and carrying on like we'd just survived the Normandy landing. We had a place to live, the last stresses of the journey were over and done with, and we could really start to settle in.

Uwimana, the Rwandan intern, left shortly after moving her stuff in.

She was off with a friend for a short trip to Senegal. It was late afternoon and Robel and I admired the sky, the clouds golden orange, surrounded by a warm, blue sky. Surreal Hollywood-movie colours. I'd never seen anything like it before: dusk without the industrial sector. It was stunning. After a long pause in the talk, I asked Robel if he was hungry.

"Yeah, I haven't eaten all day."

"Where do you want to eat?"

"Dunno. Where *can* we eat?" We both stared thoughtfully over the wall, out across the empty street and into the large flat field of green shrub sitting opposite our compound. "Well, when we drove up, I saw a building up the road that didn't look like a house. Maybe we should try there," offered Robel. Off we went, Robel in the lead.

We arrived at our destination. It was a two-story building, painted mustard yellow and shaped like a long shoebox. A small, hand-painted sign on the front read *Jasmine's Restaurant*. In we went. The door was a proper glass door, the kind you see on buildings in North America. The half-dozen four-tops were plastic garden furniture, each with a yellow tablecloth. The room ended in a staircase climbing steeply upstairs and crammed beneath it stood a bar, about the size of a closet. A small strip of glass suspended from the wall by angle-iron brackets held three dusty bottles of booze. A convenience store refrigerator sat beside the bar, filled with bottles of Fanta and JulBrew. We sat down at a table and looked around timidly.

The whole place looked deserted. We started to wonder if the restaurant was even open when a woman, East Indian and dressed in a sari, came out from the back. During our meal of chicken and rice, she told us her story. She was not, in fact, Jasmine; Jasmine was a Nigerian friend of hers and they'd opened the restaurant and attached hotel together. Jasmine had passed away a few years back, leaving her in charge. She'd come to West Africa years before, a popular move for a lot of Indians, according to her. I wanted to know why. Was she running from an even poorer place? Was she like the German and came here to live the good life? It was strange to imagine the Gambia as someone's better option financially, and the instant I thought it, it hit me how naïve I really was. Anyway, she sensed my curiosity and backed away from it. Not seeing any good reason to annoy the only neighbour we knew (and our only food source), I let it drop. We never did get a grasp on her name and would simply refer to her as Jasmine for the remainder of our time in the house.

As I paid the bill, Robel gave me a tap on the shoulder. When I turned around, he gave me a big, knowing grin and held up a large, yellow Tetra Pak that he'd pulled from the convenience store fridge. The label, written with a flourishing red Gothic font, said *Don Garcia*. The rest was in a foreign tongue, but the contents were obvious. We added it to the bill.

Back at the house, we each chose a spot on the banister, which was wide enough to make a comfortable seat, and jumped up, facing each other across the *L* shape of the banister. We tore open our litre "drink'n box" of red wine, and not having any cups, we just passed the box around as we smoked, talked and laughed, often clinking the box against the wall of the house and drinking to its health. Robel explained our suburb was called Brusubi. The place was halfway between three other places, Brufut, Sukuta and Bijilo, and so — for want of a better name — the government had concatenated the first letters of the other more important places. He'd found out from one of the guys he was working with, Saihou. Drunk, we thought it was just hilarious.

Our second box finished,[37] leaving us pretty soggy. We stumbled through the door and somehow I managed to lock it. Turning from the door, I saw Robel stumble out of his room, half dressed, ready for bed. He held a finger in the air and had a quizzical look on his face, as if trying to clarify something he hadn't heard right, "Uh, where exactly do we sleep?" It

---

37 We'd gone for another.

took a second, but it finally struck me: we didn't have beds. We didn't even have anything soft. A few long seconds passed as I mentally plodded through the items in my luggage. "I gotta bag!" I blurted. Not really very funny, but we keeled over laughing with the hysteria of guys coming down off some serious stress. We were safely in our new home, food and shelter sorted. I padded the marble-looking floor with some T-shirts, which improved my comfort level by exactly nothing, but the booze was padding enough. I rolled my empty pack into a pillow, flopped down and was gone in seconds.

Suburbia

The next morning

My arms and legs tensed violently as pure adrenaline pumped into my stomach, followed by a wave of nausea. My eyes shot open: someone was in the room. My ears still hurt from the scream. "*ALLLLLAAAH AKBAR!*" There it was again. My eyes searched the room, too tense to move. Grey light filled the space. "*ALLLLLAAAH AKBAR!*" I couldn't see anyone, but the sound pounded my ears. Someone was shouting straight into my head, the bone in my eardrum throbbed. Slowly, the adrenaline subsided, and my muscles started responding. Pulling myself upright, I looked around. I was alone. "*ALLLLLAAAH AKBAR!*" Through one of my two windows I could see a small green tower — a miniature minaret — only a few metres higher than the surrounding bungalows. A banged-up loudspeaker hung limply off the top, angled straight into my window, which I'd opened before going to bed. It was only a compound away. "*ALLLLLAAAH AKBAR!*" The Islamic wakeup call. The crier was screaming "Allah Akbar," "God is great," summoning the faithful for morning prayers. Very loud, very close, and as it turned out, my empty concrete box of a room had excellent acoustics. I was living inside a bass drum. I closed the window, but it didn't do any good. There was no way I was going to get more sleep.

57

My twisted body hobbled to the door; the three T-shirt bed hadn't softened the tile floor one bit. Opening the door, I met Robel as he emerged from his own room, stooped over in agony. We stopped and looked at each other for a long moment. "Holy shit." I didn't know if Robel meant the noise or the way I looked.

We scrounged up some smokes and shuffled out to the porch, taking our seats. We were in rough shape: Don Garcia wasn't kind to his prisoners. The lack of real beds was definitely a problem that needed a solution, the sooner the better. Beds weren't the only problem. Looking at the sodden T-shirt stuck to my body with sweat, it occurred to me that we had no way of washing our clothes.[38] Robel pointed at my ankles. It looked like I'd gotten chickenpox from the knees down. Despite the mosquito netting on the windows, the little carnivorous bastards had infiltrated the house, and left me — after a thorough count — with approximately 80 welts between my ankles and knees. I couldn't remember seeing a single insect before going to bed.[39]

The problem of the beds was solved quickly by Robel the next day,

---

38 In the end, we discovered you could buy Omo, a common brand of detergent in South Africa and other places, almost anywhere. Combined with a bucket, water from the shower and a clothes line, we learned to wash our own clothing by dunking them in the sudsy water and rubbing them together. It wasn't until later that we discovered we were making a terrible mistake by not ironing the clothes. Ironing was necessary to kill any insect larva that might be laid in the wet clothes while they hung to dry. We were fortunate in not having any incidents.

39 The little bastards were always there. We had mosquito nets but never used them because they were too damn hot. Despite the screens on the windows, they still managed to get in and in great numbers, a regular fifth column working on nature's behalf. Outside of disease, the most annoying thing about them was the incessant buzzing. You'd lay down to sleep listening to the crash of the ocean as it carried in a cool breeze, when suddenly you'd hear the buzz of the first punter. The buzzing sound would build until it was just hovering over your ear. There's no need to go into the number of times I slapped my own face trying to kill a mosquito. Suffice it to say, you could really lose your mind to that buzzing if you didn't train yourself to ignore it.

which was a Friday. He arranged for us to meet Saihou, a guy he worked with, later in the day, and the three of us headed off in a taxi to Serekunda market. We told Saihou we needed beds; he bobbed his head shyly, spoke to the driver and off we went. It was half an hour from our house to the place Saihou had in mind. Serekunda wasn't farther away than Banjul but it was slow going.

Serekunda is the largest urban centre in the Gambia and includes the largest market. All told, it wasn't much different than Banjul market, just more condensed and busier. We crept into the centre of Serekunda on the ruin of a paved road. The pavement was so old and poorly done that the two lanes had eroded into a single bumpy causeway over the mud. Each side of the road looked like a badly torn piece of paper. Peddlers, welders[40] and furniture sellers lined each side. Beyond them, dirt lanes led into blocks of residential dwellings. Most cities I visited in West Africa had residential blocks that were made up of compounds like ours but much smaller and pushed right together, sharing courtyard walls. It gave the impression of a sprawling, single-floor apartment building without a roof, except for one or two rooms in each unit.

We spent most of the trip rocking back and forth in the rear seat of the taxi as it rolled through the streets. We didn't speak but watched the passing tableau through wisps of dust rolling through the windows. People

---

40 Anything in the Gambia that wasn't made out of concrete tended to be made out of welded iron and steel. Workable wood was hard to come by in the Gambia. I asked around to find out why and the explanations usually had to do with one or two basic themes. The major palm tree in the Gambia was the oil palm, so named because of the cooking oil it produced. The value of the crop was so high, no one wanted to cut down a tree until it was dead. Another explanation was that palm wood was very hard to work with hand tools. Another explanation was the harvesting of palm wine, which made the trees too valuable to cut down. There was some wood furniture, but most of it was imported or made of rattan.

squeezed past other people as well as livestock in the streets; sometimes passersby would use our taxi to steady themselves as we slowly penetrated the living mass. It wasn't hard for them to use us as a support since we were barely moving. Occasionally, a torso or back would lean against the window in order to dodge something in the street, leaving a sweat stain on the taxi or my forearm if I didn't move quickly. Our taxi was in terrible shape, but I felt like a British aristocrat driving through the streets of Cairo or Delhi at the turn of the 20th century, a speck of foreign matter moving through somebody else's bloodstream. Some of the looks I was getting told me I wasn't the only one who thought so too.

The taxi stopped at one of the many concrete stalls lining the street, a large concrete room topped with sheet metal: Bed, Bath & Beyond. It opened onto the street and inside were stacks of yellow foam rectangles, each cut to the approximate size of a mattress: there were doubles, singles, kings and queens to choose from. Each piece of foam was about a foot thick and finished with a floral-print cover. We chose three queen-size specimens from the middle of a pile so they wouldn't have as much dust, strapped them to the roof and headed home.

Friday night we slept in comfort, soothed to sleep by another couple litres of Don Garcia. Despite the Garcia, I remembered to put a towel down on the mattress, and sure enough it was soaked with sweat in the morning. Our wake-up call was right on time and just as loud, but not nearly as shocking. While enjoying our morning cigarettes, looking out at the beautiful, appallingly hot morning, I watched as my arm went from dry to moist, to beading, to having rivers of sweat running across it. In real time. As I considered this, Robel suddenly pronounced: "We should explore the rest of the neighbourhood today."

We headed off to meet the neighbours, having showered but not eaten.[41] Our suburb was surveyed out as a large grid. Looking north, the left-hand border was defined by the long highway that followed the coast south, where the restaurant Jasmin's was situated. Our own street marked the top of the grid and stretched east four or five blocks until the pavement and houses gave way to sand and trees. The five blocks south were similar. We walked around the neatly paved grid, but the suburb itself seemed pretty much deserted. The houses were new and most were still under construction. The lack of any kind of landscaping other than the occasional cinder block in the windswept sand added to the sense of isolation. Other than Jasmine, we'd seen only a half-dozen people since we moved in. We decided to head west, across the highway toward the big houses we'd seen the other night as we'd walked to Jasmine's.

We wandered over the highway, down sandy trails through a ragged citrus orchard and past expensive-looking two-story houses. The deep sand path eventually transformed into one of red soil, and following it, we arrived at the edge of a six-story escarpment. The wind blew so hard we needed to lean into it for balance. The few palm trees near the edge had permanently curved trunks. We could see everything, even the curve of the earth gently arching up the ocean. Shadows from massive white clouds slipped across the twinkling water. A fishing boat — a long, open boat with sharp ends — bobbed crazily half a mile offshore. The cliff was steep but climbable, so we headed down to the beach below, which was wide and in the bright sunlight almost white. We strolled along for a bit, then stopped to take it all in. It was really beautiful, and not in a Club Med way. A real tropical paradise. We could see fishermen casting nets up the beach and people buying fish from them. A small kid on a big bike wobbled by, his take dangling from a string

---

41 We still didn't know where to get food. Jasmine's wasn't open for breakfast, Saihou didn't live in the area and had no idea, and our neighbour Muhammad drove to his mother's each day to eat and have his laundry done.

around the handlebars. Little girls passed, the plastic buckets on their heads filled with fish. We sat on the beach and watched the people go by.

We were trying to decide if these fishermen were the local grocery when suddenly the two of us became the three of us. A guy had come and dropped down beside Robel. He was dressed in a blue Bob Marley T-shirt; his jeans rolled to the knee, and he sported a Rastafarian woolen hat, the kind designed to contain dreads. This white sandy beach, wider than an eight-lane highway and miles long, was practically deserted, and yet he squatted down inches away from Robel and stared out at the ocean without saying a word.

After a moment of silence, we resumed our discussion of the fishermen when suddenly Robel flicked his head around to the new guy. I gave it a polite moment before tapping Robel and asking what he wanted; his voice was low and I couldn't hear a thing. Robel shrugged and leaned into me, whispering, "I don't know. He's speaking another language." He turned away again, summoned by our new friend. I leaned into Robel, listening. The new guy was quietly chatting away in one of the local languages. His voice wasn't more than a mumble, quiet and slurred; occasionally, he'd glance at Robel for agreement. Robel replied by bouncing his head up and down, which apparently was a sufficient answer, or at least encouraging enough for him to continue.

So he did. About five minutes passed with the new guy explaining something slowly, emphatically, and Robel nodding away. Robel tried to explain he wasn't a local; that he was in fact Ethiopian, but for naught, the young guy just kept chatting. The "conversation" came to an end when a young Gambian passing along the beach yelled a greeting: "John!" The new guy's attention snapped to the passing stranger and he responded with a greeting that ended with "Peter!" and got up. After a few words in a language we didn't understand, Peter approached with his hand out, saying, "I'm Ousman, what's the lovely name?" Big, sleepy fisheyes stared out from a narrow, bald head. His slight frame was clothed in a white T-shirt and red capri pants. When Robel's friend tried to introduce himself as John, Ousman cut him off abruptly and told him to use his Muslim name: "Be a proud Muslim, don't be ashamed," and so he introduced himself as Mustafa. Apparently, he did speak English.

Ousman definitely spoke English, and for the next 15 minutes he demonstrated his prowess. "So what's the good name?... We welcome you to the Gambia... Our brothers. The skin is different, but the blood is the same... One heart, one love, not so? So where from?... You come to see the beautiful nature? To see the culture?... Yes, you see the fishermen? Yes, here in the Gambia, we live from the beautiful nature. We eat the food from the nature."

The questions, greetings and declarations went on and on. We answered what we could and listened politely to the rest, but Ousman's aria on the superiority of Gambian life was draining: "In Gambia, we live with the nature — we don't hide from it in the cities — we take care of the nature and it takes care of us, gives us the food. We believe everyone is the same. It's nice to be nice, not so? One heart, one love." His patriotism and Bob Marley quotations were relentless. After nearly an hour of forced attentiveness, bobbing my head at all the right moments (I hoped) and injecting an occasional "really?" I was exhausted. I was barely paying attention by that point, using most of my waking mind to consider other weighty issues like where I'd be in North America if I swam straight across the ocean from the beach. As a result, I was caught off-guard when silence fell, giving a lame "uh?" as my brain struggled to re-engage. I caught the echo of the question in my head: "Will you come to our village and eat with us?"

Frankly, the idea filled me with dread. I didn't trust either one of them. Their name swapping earlier hadn't endear one bit, and the last 45 minutes had been dire. I wanted to consult with Robel, but with them standing right there, it was impossible. Robel and I didn't know each other well; just a couple of days drinking wine together, not enough to have a non-verbal rapport. But even in the short time we'd known each other, without saying a word, we'd both arrived at the first law of all expats everywhere: solidarity. Never leave a fellow marine behind. If Robel wanted to go, I'd go, no question. Looking at him, all I could read was his own strained attempts to read me. We danced around with lots of "wells" and "ums," trying to gauge the other's mind. I don't remember who started first, but after a moment or two, prodded on by politeness and politically correct cultural sensitivity, our heads started bobbing in unison. "Sure, we'd love to see your village. We'd be honoured."

Off we went. Back up the cliff, through the trees, following the coast south. Coming out of the brush, we crossed over the highway, back onto the Brusubi side. We could see Jasmine's a half-mile up the road to our left. We walked along the shoulder for a good 20 minutes, and soon Jasmine's, Brusubi and home were lost in the distance.

"What's the name of your village, Ousman?"

"We live in Brufut."

"Where is it exactly?"

"This way, not far now, down the road below Brusubi." Eventually, we turned down a track that ran deep into the trees a couple of miles south of Brusubi, our suburb. Now and again, we'd pass a segment of brush marked off with a low cinderblock wall, the beginnings of a new compound.

"How close to Brusubi is Brufut?"

"Brusubi used to be a part of Brufut, but the army came and made people leave their compounds so they could make Brusubi for the Dutch and the Englishes who come to live," said Mustafa. Jesus. We were here to support human rights and were living on stolen land. How very North American of the Gambian government. I wondered what right we had to come here and tell these people how to run their country.

64

The palm trees and brush eventually gave way to cornstalks. The approaches to the village revealed various domestic scenes: a stand of corn surrounded by a short fence of palm branches stuck in the sand, their natural curve giving the fence a windswept *Robinson Crusoe* look. Farther on, a girl — maybe 14 years old — stood tamping a heavy bough into a hollow tree trunk at her feet, and with each mighty blow bits of grain flew out, to be stolen by chickens scratching in the yard. Across the lane an older woman fussed with wood below a huge cauldron puffing clouds of steam. Their bandannas, T-shirts and sarongs were dark with sweat. They stopped and stared as we passed. Greetings were exchanged with our guides, eyes dropped whenever I gave a smile. On we went.

In the village now, the path became a hard-packed trail as if carved out by a river. It was broad enough to take a car and at some points was eroded almost two feet below the edges of the compounds lining it. Years later I would find myself one afternoon standing under the cover of a corner store's metal awning, watching terrified chickens get swept down a road in Birkama, followed by a street dog, legs splayed, looking bewildered and desperate. The rain could come in a second. I remember another time driving down the highway coming in from Banjul when my driver tugged my arm and pointed excitedly out the windshield. Following his finger, I could see, about 50 yards ahead, a solid wall of water. I hung up my phone, struck dumb by the surrealism of it all: bone-dry here, torrents within spitting distance. In seconds, we punched through the waterfall, its hard lines dissolving into a gritty mist of water and drummed-up dust. Although not as intense as South Asian or Indian monsoons, the water definitely came down hard.

My first experience with the rain occurred one night when, out of the blue, it just started coming down. Robel and I were still new in-country and didn't know when the rainy season started, and one night it sprang out at us in the dark. It'd been a lovely night, warm and humid, but with a cooling breeze off the ocean. The perfect weather to sit outside and have a box of wine. We went to bed with the windows open, so the soft air would wash over and cool us.

Late in the night, I awoke to a shriek and a smash. A moment before, I'd been comfortably snoring away, now having lurched off my stomach due to the crash, I was on my back, wide awake beside the foam mattress. While lying there in shock, trying to marshal my wits, I noticed water on my back and legs — a lot of water, and I could feel a cold spray coming through the windows, sprinkling my arms and legs. I jumped up to close the windows but couldn't. Opened all the way, the windows lay flush against the outside wall. The shriek and slam that woke me was the wind grabbing them and pinning them there. In the middle of the mosquito screen was a small square, just large enough to stick an arm through. You'd slide open the little wooden door covering the hole to operate the windows. Frantically, I stuck my arm out of the hole, right up to my shoulder, and clawed at the windows. No way. Not even Stretch Armstrong could have reached the handles now.

With the windows immobilized, rain poured through the breach. Robel and I went from unconscious bliss to manning lifeboats in seconds. We grabbed everything we owned and chucked it into the living room to escape the flood pouring through the windows, but the house was sinking fast; soon we were re-shifting everything, looking for high ground on the uneven floor as the water made its way from our bedrooms into the living room. We'd stacked our stuff — clothes, luggage, toiletries and beds in the living room — but now we were deciding what was expendable and what wasn't. In less than five minutes every floor in the house had over an inch of water. Just to reiterate: this wasn't a burst pipe or a flood, this was *rain*. The wind was howling louder than ever, and we had no idea how long would it last. Robel and I knew someone had to go out there and close the windows.

"Well?" I asked.

66

"You've got the biggest room — with the most windows." Settled. Off I went. I can remember opening the front door and seeing water draining out from the living room.

The plan was for me to circle the house, pry the windows away from the wall and swing them shut while Robel locked them via the hole in the mesh. The rain wasn't cold, but the blowing wind and sheets of spray disoriented me. Pulling at the windows, often with a leg against the wall and hauling for all I was worth, was tiring work. Almost as tiring as scrambling out of the way when the wind caught them and slammed them shut. The rain came down off the eave so hard I couldn't catch my breath. It felt like someone pounding on my back in a freakish massage nightmare. I'd take a gasp and run to the next window. At one point, I had to plaster myself against the wall of the house to get out of the pounding water that was coming off the roof. I stood there gasping and exhausted. Eventually, we secured the windows, bailed out the house as best we could, grabbed some cigarettes[42] and sat shivering in the middle of the living room, wondering what Africa would throw our way next. We sat on-guard with our self-confidence hyperventilating, our nerves a little bit shorter.

But that was in the future. Looking at that lane in the village, I couldn't appreciate the drama surrounding its gouged and scarred sides. Everything has a history, even the lines in a dirt track.

People tended to live in a walled-off compound rather than a "house." Unlike a North American house, a compound usually had several buildings and always a wall around it. Some perimeter walls were made of concrete blocks, but most were made of palm branches, weaved thatch or junk such as twisted sections of rusted sheet metal or even old mattresses. The ground inside was typically cleared down to hard, brown, packed earth.[43]

---

42 We made sure the cigarettes were on top of our respective piles.
43 Despite the greenery of the landscape, grass as we know it — Bermuda grass, it was

This was done by women using short brooms, like the business end of witches' brooms, the kind they're always shown riding around on. It had to be done. Leaves or brush in the yard could harbour termites, or worse, snakes.

A low rectangular house sat inside, usually made of cinderblocks, but sometimes mud was used. Corrugate or sometimes thatch covered the roof. Houses were normally situated toward the rear, leaving a large front yard. Invariably, a garden of corn and vegetables grew on one side of the house, running around the back. A tree or two — citrus usually — grew in the front and were clearly the focus of most homes, at least for the men. In the front, younger children played, and groups of men sat on wooden benches, usually under a tree, drinking tea and watching the passers-by in the lane. Traffic in the lane consisted mostly of girls carrying huge bundles balanced on their heads: stacks of firewood, large bowls of food, 20-litre plastic buckets of water. In the back, women did the cooking with their daughters. Sheep, goats and chicken roamed freely. It was quiet. Most of the noise in the street consisted of people greeting each other as they passed. There didn't seem to be much going on. Most of the young men loafed under a tree or by the corner stores, small shacks where you could buy cigarettes or a baguette[44], usually listening to a transistor radio.

We wound through the rough grid of the village, which was quite large, one of the largest and most developed in the Gambia, I'd find out later. My sense of direction was so confounded by our zigzagging I lost track of the highway and finally asked, "So, where *are* we going, Ousman?"

---

called in the Gambia — didn't grow without a lot of work. It was a status symbol, the way SUVs are here. The official residence of the European commissioner had a perfectly groomed patch near the highway where everyone could see it. Just a patch, it would have made a fine parking spot for a couple of cars if it hadn't been covered in grass.

44 The local name for a soft baguette was *tapalapa*, translated as "a long and floppy," much to the hilarity of local teenagers.

"In the Gambia, we have to show the respect to the elders. We are going to see one and introduce you to the village. We are going to show them that you are good people who want to know about the Gambia, about the culture, and that you are our friends."

"We're going to meet the village elder?" Some politically correct part of me felt queasy. Visions of standing around for hours being subjected to endless speeches by a village full of Ousmans made swallowing difficult. At the best of times, my tolerance for small talk was minimal. The thought of having to keep it up for hours made me nervous. Nervous because I didn't want to offend anyone and because I knew I might. The odds increased with every passing minute of small talk. I tend to be serious by nature and enjoy finding out about people, places and things, and flowery talk with little substance bores me, which, in turn, irritates me. It's a waste of time and I hate wasting time. The conversation with Ousman and Mustafa had trailed off awhile back. I'd hoped to form a connection with our new friends, to share some thoughts and experiences, to develop a relationship. But it was clear they weren't interested in the place we'd come from. I'd made several attempts to draw comparisons, to try and connect with them, to show our similarities. My attempts were always met with silence or a new subject, sometimes interrupting me midsentence, and when I tried to take an interest in the locality, to find out more about the things in the village, I was cut off with a proverb or Bob Marley quote. "What kinds of crops do you grow here?"

"All kinds Rowbin. We live by the nature here."

"How many people live in your village?"

"Many people Rowbin. Many people live here."

Eventually, we arrived at a small concrete hut that looked to be an out-building within a larger compound but had its own entrance from the road. There were a few concrete steps leading to the entrance, which was covered by a ratty curtain. Ousman turned and with a solemn whisper

69

announced that we had arrived. He loped up the stairs and disappeared behind the curtain, leaving Robel and I to pass the time with Mustafa, quietly smoking cigarettes. I was honoured to be there, but also anxious. During our training at NetCorps, they never missed a chance to remind us we represented Canada while overseas, and we never missed a chance to make a joke about "Canada's little ambassadors." But this felt serious, standing in silence with Mustafa. What if we screwed up? We were grinding the butts into the ground when Ousman poked his head out and gestured without a word to come in. I followed Mustafa up the steps and ducked through the entrance, Robel right behind me.

I kept my eyes down as a sign of respect — and shyness — in the face of the unknown, but the instant the curtain flapped open I caught a glimpse, in a blink of sunlight, of a ragged piece of yellow foam, grey with age and sweat. The air was rank with body odour and the only light swayed against the opposite wall, ragged as the curtain. I shuffled blindly to the right, where I sensed Mustafa had moved, and my eyes began to adjust to the soft light. Ousman was sitting cross-legged near the mattress. The rest of us stood there like schoolboys: Mustafa holding his Rasta hat tight to his chest with both hands, Robel and I standing shyly, hands clasped together in front. A man lay on the mattress, propped up on one elbow. Describing him as an *elder* was a masterwork of understatement. He looked like the oldest man on Earth. He looked at me and I looked back, my curiosity overcoming bashfulness. His lips were folded in for lack of teeth, but it was an open face, made of leather lined with white cracks and topped by white cotton hair. He gave me a gummy smile and I grinned back. Raising my arm halfway up like a wooden Indian, I lamely offered a quiet "hello." He gave a bigger smile and jerked one arm up, then down, disturbing a fly meandering across his forehead. Robel gave him one of his disarming smiles and he looked happy enough. Ousman spoke to him and turned to announce our welcome in Brufut. Ousman stood and we all filed out behind him, giving our *thank yous* as we left. So ended my first foray into international relations.

Outside, Robel and I immediately lit up, exam over. "Come," ordered Ousman before we could take two puffs. "We have to go and meet the son." Dread returned. After a few turns through the streets, we arrived at another compound and passed through its corrugate gate. Ousman skipped ahead, and again we waited outside with Mustafa, smoking cigarettes in front of a curtained entrance, though one in better repair than the last. "What are we doing here, Mustafa?" Whispering in broken English between drags, Mustafa explained that the old guy wasn't up to welcoming us properly, so we'd come to visit the old man's son, of which he had many because as the elder, people brought orphaned children for him to take care of. The man who owned this compound was one of his sons, whether biologically or not wasn't clear. What exactly "greeting us properly" meant wasn't clear either.

Out bounced Ousman: "Come, it's ready." We followed him through the curtain. The house was as dark as the elder's hut, and I had to touch Ousman's back to follow him. As my eyes adjusted I could tell the single story house was broken into several small rooms, and Ous had led us down a central hallway that ended with access to the backyard. Off this passageway near the exit was a short, narrow corridor. We stopped behind Ousman just before the corner of the passage. The atmosphere was heavy; Ousman was solemn and Mustafa had his hat off again. I assumed the shy schoolboy look, the one I reserved for important occasions — funerals and pleading — and stood, hands clasped respectfully, waiting behind Ousman at the entrance of the corridor. He went first. There was a long, silent pause. Peeking around the corner, I saw him on his knees, one hand held to his heart, staring forward. What the hell was he doing? After a few seconds, he got up slowly, methodically. Coming out of the corridor, he said it was my turn: I should go and show respect. With that, he went into the backyard. I turned the corner.

Looking down the passage, I saw a reed mat. In front of it was a small copper bowl. I walked up to it feeling nervous. What exactly was I supposed to do? Was this serious or an example of Gambian humour? I knelt stiffly in front of the bowl and tried to look pious, hands in my lap. Was Mustafa looking at me? If he was, I didn't want to offend him, especially having seen the Osama bin Laden T-shirt in Banjul market. Clearly, this country took religion seriously. I gave the bowl a stiff Japanese-style bow and held it. After what I judged a respectable amount of time, I straightened up and made the sign of the cross. In hindsight, probably not the best thing to do, especially considering the T-shirt, but at the same time, what were Muslims doing praying to a dented bowl of water? I let a few seconds go by in what I hoped looked like thoughtful reflection and slowly rose to my feet. One more stiff bow to the bowl for good measure, and I went outside to join Ousman.

After Robel and Mustafa finished, some short wooden stools were found and set up in the backyard by a young girl working in the back. We were introduced to the man in charge, a huge guy, as big as a bodybuilder, wearing a very short towel as a miniskirt-sized sarong. Apparently, we'd interrupted him just before his afternoon shower. He gave us a friendly smile, "Welcome, welcome," shook our hands with enthusiasm and expressed how happy he was we'd met his father, then swaggered off to his open-air shower.

Ous was ecstatic. We'd shown respect and seen the elder. He kept going on about how other *toubobs* (white people) just came to sleep with Gambian girls or buy houses on village land and act like jerks. We'd come and shown *respect*, met the elder and taken an interest in their culture.[45] We'd come to meet "the real Gambian people." "It's true, it's true," Mustafa kept

---

45 I don't know how Ousman came to the conclusion we'd taken an interest in the culture; he'd rebuffed every question I'd asked about it.

slurring. They were happy with themselves. They'd overcome daunting odds to get their message across; they'd overcome language and culture to make their point: Gambia was a great place with as much to offer as anywhere. They're enthusiasm won me over while we huddled on small benches drinking *ataya*, the local tea.[46] It was Chinese green tea and came in a small, raisin-sized box labeled "Chinese Green Tea: Super Gunpowder," and the entire contents were dumped into a small steel teapot, small enough to fit in the palm of your hand, along with a heaping handful of sugar and water. Boiled on a small charcoal stove, each helping was poured into a shot glass and then aerated with another. Ousman poured from one glass to the other in long arcs like he was a waiter in a classy hotel showing off his decanting skills. I tried to get more information about the ceremony we'd just participated in while we sipped the frothy green sludge. What was the bowl about? Do the elders run the village or is there a chief? Unfortunately, the answers were always the same platitudes. I asked about the tea: "Before Gambians had access to Chinese green tea, what kinds of local tea did they drink?"

"Yes, yes! We drink the *ataya*."

"But before that, what did Gambians drink?"

"It's good for you!"

"Right." That's how things went for the next two hours. The only real answer I got to anything was when Mustafa took the empty box of *ataya*, along with its plastic wrapper, and threw them into the sprawling field of garbage behind us. Rather than a backyard pool, the compound had a backyard garbage heap about the same size. "You shouldn't throw away the plastic, it's not good for the environment," protested Robel.

---

46 I'm guessing this is a habit developed from the tradition of Moroccan mint tea, which is green tea flavoured with mint and sugar. No mint in the Gambian version, but similar otherwise.

"Yes, yes. We believe in that what comes from the nature should go back to the nature," said Ousman.

"It's true, it's true," chimed Mustafa.

"Ah, but the plastic isn't good for the nature," I added.

"You must give back to the land. Here in the Gambia, we take care of the nature. We're not like the *toubob*. We take care of the nature."

So things went until early evening. Through the same non-verbal process that had gotten us there, Robel and I decided it was time to go. We were tired, and the huge quantities of sugar and pure green tea were turning my stomach. We gave our excuses and were off. They walked us back to the highway and down to our house. Ousman and Mustafa's enthusiasm had long since tapered off and we walked in silence. The walk was long and it was dark by the time we were safely in our compound, but it was good to see our home again. At our front gate, Ous remembered he had a tongue and wouldn't stop going on about how happy he was to have met us. When could we meet again? Mustafa was almost asleep on his feet. At one point he closed his eyes and leaned against the compound wall. We spent a good five minutes tap-dancing around whether or not to invite them in. Finally, we told them we'd be happy to meet them next Saturday around noon, but now we had to go to bed. Happy he'd be seeing his new friends again, Ousman left with Mustafa in tow. We went inside, thanked God our little house in the suburb had a great big wall around it, and collapsed with exhaustion.

Patricians

Monday morning

Monday: first real day on the job. The workshop had finished last week and now we were moving back to the centre's offices in Brusubi — no poolside beers this week. Robel's placement was in Senegambia. Having no idea how public transit worked or even if any existed, he got up at the crack of dawn and walked there. For me, commuting was just a stroll across the street. While the suburb stretched out behind our house, a field of flat green shrub stretched out in front. Across it, about two football fields away, sat a peach-coloured shoebox of a building facing the road to the airport, which I vaguely remembered noticing on my drive in. I couldn't tell how high it was from our gate, but it was the tallest building around for miles, towering over everything the way a village church dwarfs its surroundings. In the distant haze, it had the stateliness of a large ship, its flat sides wobbling in the heat, floating over the green shrubbery.

The boxy ship looked huge in the distance, but it scaled down into a three-story building as we approached. The shoebox was about half a block long, its corners smoothed and rounded. A small gazebo-like structure crowned the flat roof, kind of like a poor man's dome.

I walked along with Uwimana, our Rwandan roommate, who'd returned from Senegal late Sunday night. We arrived at a front gate attended

75

by a young man wearing a blue police-style shirt and black baggy pants. Eighties-style baggy, tight at the top and bottom, loose in between, a sky-blue stripe running down the sides. His shoulder flash announced his employer as Uncle Samba's Security Service. Seeing us, he sprang forward to work the heavy latch on the gate. Greetings were exchanged and we passed through. As I walked toward the building's entrance, he skipped backwards, keeping pace, "So, you workin' here now, boss? That's fine! Fine!" He was about to run up the steps to get the door when Uwimana, annoyed with his obsequiousness, suddenly dismissed him. "Sorry, sorry, sister," he said as he scuttled back to the gate.

A friend of mine would point out in the near future that this was the most famous any of us would ever likely be. You got star treatment everywhere you went; everyone wanted to be your friend. People stared at you. One day I'd arrive at an orphanage in Guinea-Bissau and every kid in the place came out to sing the "Welcome Song," which, I was told, was not *de rigueur*.

Interlocking paving stones surrounded the building, and lush flowers of all colours cascaded down the compound walls. A dozen steps covered with white tile formed a semicircular staircase marching up the front of the building. Columns lined the final landing, and beyond the columns were two sets of double doors made of glass and aluminium. It was the nicest place I'd seen in the whole country, and it would be over a year before I saw better.

The inside surpassed the exterior. The white tile was softly lit by a skylight immediately above the entrance. Two black leather couches, built deep, perfect for slouching, faced each other; newspapers and magazines lay scattered on the coffee table in between. Stepping deeper into the foyer, out of the skylight's shine and into the cool ambient light, there was a sense of calm in the still air. "Great hall" would be more appropriate than foyer; it ran the length of the building and glass doors could be seen at the far end, leading to the grounds in the back. Two massive columns, one directly in front of me and another near the rear of the building, held up the roof, roughly three stories over our heads. Ceiling fans turned slowly, sweeping in step like soldiers marching in silence. They looked tired. Off the hall, to the left and right, were large offices, each big enough to hold two executive desks with room to spare, all clearly visible through the large windows and glass doors fronting each space. Five spaces ran the length of the main hall, three on the left and two on the right. Where the first office would have been on the right stood an open area covered by a standard North American office divider. Straight ahead in the middle of the hall was a spiral staircase, wide enough to take three abreast. It wound up three stories to the roof, and the landing was enclosed by the glass gazebo. A small, bubbly fountain sat at the base of the stairs.

In front of the staircase, a long desk stretched almost the whole width of the hall. It looked like the kind of reception gear you'd get from Ikea. Two people were sitting behind it — faxes, printers, keyboards and cellphones crowded between them. One woman was a local Gambian intern, Bintou, who was about 20 years old. Fatou was Senegalese by birth and the dignified head secretary of the centre. I'd met her, like Bintou and everyone else at the workshop in Senegambia. "Good morning!" I offered eagerly. Bintou smiled broadly and shyly dropped her eyes.

"Robin. *Na'nga def*," she replied, staring at her computer but still smiling.

"Uh, OK?"

"That's how we greet people in the morning: *Na'nga def*." She said it with a teacher's "and now you" tone.

"*Naka def*."

"*Na'nga def?*"

"Yeah, *naka def*." They both laughed. "So where do I sit?" I asked with worker-bee enthusiasm, happy to change the subject.

"You are to sit where the last IT intern sat," said Fatou in a tired

77

way, as if she were sad the conversation had shifted to work issues. Pulling herself out of her chair with a grunt and a sigh, she started leading me to my desk. Fatou was a stately woman, her height and width emphasized by her outfit, a traditional West African dress.[47] On Fatou's frame — broader and taller than mine — the effect was regal. She glided forward, her deliberate gait telegraphed by the sway of her hem. The perfect French aristocrat.

Fatou took me back toward the front doors to the space behind the office divider. I was brought to a large wooden table, decent quality, better than Ikea. Sitting under it was a computer tower, grey with grime. On the desk sat a 17-inch CRT monitor, a standard keyboard and a mouse. I was almost enthusiastic. I powered it up and tried the Internet. It needed some coaxing, but it loaded my email.

Most people wouldn't be so enthusiastic about a computer, especially that piece of junk, but it was like a little piece of home; something familiar, something to help ground the surrealism of the strange peach building in the middle of nowhere.

I checked out the official website. Its aesthetic drew inspiration from the early days of the web: menu buttons like segments of a Jersey Milk bar, pulsating 3-D up-arrows and a mailbox labelled *email* that winged letters flew into. Right then, I knew my internship would be a success.

I spent the next couple of hours sorting the machine to suit myself. Sitting, watching the Norton AntiVirus run through a scan, listening to the hum of the hard drive, I stretched out in my chair with a mighty yawn and stopped to consider the place. It was very quiet, and not a good quiet, but the kind that acts as a carrier wave for feelings of resentment. Most offices have a level of energy fed by conversations, telephones and general bustle.

---

47 Basically a straight, shapeless gown reaching down to the ankles and with poofy shoulders, but with a neckline cut in a deep arc in front and an even deeper one behind, reaching almost to the middle of the woman's back. Sort of a femme fatale's muumuu.

Without them, other sounds you don't normally hear literally echo: sighs as people throw open a folder, the sharp slam when they close it again.

In the dim quiet of the place, details began to whisper. There were a couple of wireless access points and a switch or two providing the connectivity. With no ducting, I could trace the cabling with my eyes, up walls, around columns. I wondered who would set something like this up. I could see the logic of the system, trace the decision-making process in the design of the network, and knew this wasn't the work of an intern. It wasn't the best, but the attention to detail was impressive. You could see the care taken when tacking the cables. Tacking cable is hell. Tacking cable three stories over your head is unbearable hell. Here, someone had taken the time to do it right. Every tack was straight and looked exactly one metre apart. Looking at it through the prism of what I'd seen in Banjul market, it was miraculous. I knew whoever did the wiring must have been pissed about the litter in Banjul too.

I was trying to figure out how to set up a centre email account for myself when a screeching wail ripped the air apart. Someone had opened a door, and because it was tight in its aluminium frame, it opened with a shriek. It was appallingly loud, and my keyboard, which I'd been resting on my legs, clattered to the ground when I jumped. The impact of heels on a hard floor echoed through the building. It felt intrusive, but there was nothing apologetic in the steady drumbeat cadence; it resonated self-confidence.

"Robin!" she threw it out like we were frat brothers meeting in the street. "*Na'nga def!* How are you?" I fumbled for my keyboard, then looked up to see Samantha standing there in a knee-length shift dress made with an orange and gold pattern that complemented her short blond hair and freckles.

"I'm doing well, actually."

"Great. I hear you found a place to live. And not far from here either.

See, you've already started your Gambian adventure. I see you've found your computer too. Great! You've got big shoes to fill. Have you seen the server yet?" I hadn't. No one had volunteered to give me a tour, so I hadn't seen much. Samantha fixed that. Soon, I was trailing in her wake, a very different experience than following the majestic Fatou. Now I was trying to keep up, feeling like a loping Frankenstein monster behind this petite woman with her crisp, no-nonsense stride, bouncing red curls and enthusiastic chatter.

She was an interesting woman: early 30s, a graduate of Harvard Law, and director of her own human rights NGO in Africa who has travelled all over the world doing human rights work,[48] and if that wasn't enough, she was also an architect. An amateur architect, but she did design the building I was standing in, and — exploding doors aside — I was impressed.

Most of the running commentary was about the building: she'd look at a corner or a column or a window and launch into an enthusiastic explanation, sounding both excited by the good design and amazed she'd thought of it. A Harvard lawyer's guided tour of the building she'd built between rounds of defending human rights the world over would normally have left me replaying the major decisions of my life, wondering where I'd gone wrong, but with Samantha it was different. She had the wide-eyed enthusiasm of someone who couldn't believe she'd achieved her own achievements. It was open and honest, like a kid who just finished his Christmas pageant and couldn't believe she hadn't missed even one line. It was charming. She was a real American countess: Type-A personality, overachieving and middle class. She made me feel like I could build a building too.

She'd thought through every detail. Each of the offices was designed to take two desks comfortably and so could be shared. People wouldn't feel isolated, but they'd still feel like they had a proper office, like a proper

---

48   She'd visited over 20 countries in Africa alone.

professional. Each office had its own air conditioner and a huge window facing outside and one facing into the main hall. Employees would feel connected to both the outdoors *and* the inner happenings of the centre.

We stopped at a closet and inside were the biggest batteries I'd ever seen, two of them, sitting on a wooden palette, each about the size of a huge camping cooler. They were deep-cycle batteries imported from Canada and were the core of the centre's unique power system. Samantha explained that half the electrical outlets in the building — all the American ones — were hooked to these batteries, which fed standard 110-volt current. The batteries were simultaneously hooked to solar panels on the roof as well as the mains, which guaranteed power without having to pollute the air or the sound levels with a generator. It was her own design. I would find out later that in her spare time Samantha helped run a charity that installed solar power in villages upcountry.

Next, she took me up the spiral staircase. The gazebo at the top of the landing had glass walls and was hotter than a greenhouse. The glint from the glass hurt my head. "This is our Internet connection," Samantha said, motioning to a small blue box about the size of a day planner hanging from a screw in one of the aluminium window frames. Red and green lights flashed wildly on the front, as if controlled by a panicky Morse code operator. Two cables ran out the back. One, a regular network cable, ran downstairs. The other ran through a hole in the aluminium to the outside, where it plugged into a flat, white plastic panel. About the size and thickness of a large coffee table book, it dangled off the frame of the gazebo. The panel pointed off into the distance, out across the flat sea of green, dotted with islands of trees and the occasional house. Samantha walked over to a glass door, and without even trying the handle, threw her tiny body against it. Like the doors downstairs, the aluminium frame screamed and tore itself open.

It was a relief to feel the ocean breeze. I walked around the roof, squinting against the reflection of the sun. You could see everything: the ocean, the neighbourhood, our house. There wasn't a person in sight in any direction. I noticed column stubs sticking out through the roof and Samantha explained that if another floor needed to be added, the supports were already in place, greatly facilitating the construction. This woman thought of everything. At the front of the roof, a solar array, about the size of a pool table, angled up to the sun on a locally made iron frame. They had to be cleaned regularly with distilled water: a thin layer of dust, even the film left from regular water drying on it could reduce their efficiency by 25 percent. Distilled water wasn't easy to come by, but it could be found if you knew where to look. Samantha knew where to look.

After taking in the view for a few more minutes, I walked back to the white panel on the wall. I stood under it and turned to see exactly where it was pointed. Miles off, almost invisible in the heat shimmers on the horizon, stood a couple of telecom masts. I'd never worked with wireless, but I knew the theory well enough, and none of the masts seemed to be anywhere close to where they needed to be for the flat-panel antenna to hit it.

The tour ended back downstairs. Glass doors led into the conference room, a large round room at the end of the building. At the very back of the conference room, under the rear windows, an ailing machine sat on a small computer stand. I desperately hoped she wouldn't point to it and say this was the server because it was just like mine, including the grime. "That's our server. I'm sure you've wanted to see it." I felt like a hot young sales rep who'd just been given keys to the company car only to find out it was a Plymouth Reliant. Shaking the mouse, the monitor yawned to life with a tired pins-and-needles sound. The image came up slowly as if the computer was rubbing the sleep out of its eyes, and it was taking forever to sharpen up. "Don't be shy." prompted Samantha.

I was shocked. A massive building, wireless Internet, batteries the size of sea chests, SUVs in the parking lot, but the gateway to the Internet —the storage for all of their work, their key communications lynchpin — was a broken-down toaster of a computer. It was like a restaurant owner dumping all of his money into the look of the place and then relying on an old home range for cooking meals. After some basic clicking around, I stood up and gave Samantha a hopeful smile. "I'll leave it in your hands, then," Samantha said, and off she went.

It was about 10:30 a.m., and barring the tour with Samantha, it had been a pretty slow morning. Especially since I had no idea what I was supposed to be doing. Other than the broad notion of "technical support," I was floating. While toying with the idea of writing my own job description, came to my desk and asked if I was going for break. "Break? What's that?"

"Free breakfast. Our only benefit."

"Uh, OK. Guess I am. You going now?"

"I am." Off we went. We headed out back, where I got my first view of the centre's backyard. The compound wall defined a sizable space, almost as long as the building itself. The grass was overgrown and knee high, and an old man was on his knees with a short gardening tool. He'd made a dent in the undergrowth, and his brown back was glazed with sweat. Up a short stone path stood a gazebo with a plastic table and chairs inside, open to the air and with a thatch roof. Bananas, mangos, baguettes and avocados were cut into convenient mouth-sized bites in little wicker baskets spread out on a colourful tablecloth. Butter, jam and marmalade were also available, as well as tea, Nescafé and juice. It was more food than I'd seen in a long time, which I hoped wasn't too obvious to the rest of the table, including the other interns and Fatou. The conversation ended as I took my seat.

I gave everyone a smiling "good morning," which was received with polite smiles, and then I turned my attention to the food. I didn't want to make it obvious Robel and I still didn't really have a way to cook, but looking at the torn pieces of baguette, my stomach felt cavernous. Nevertheless, I decided to wait and see what everyone else did rather than grabbing for the closest basket and rummaging through it for the biggest pieces. "So, do you guys eat like this every day?"

"Eat like this? You mean break? Yes. It's Samantha's idea. She thinks it's helpful if the staff take their morning break together," explained Fatou with a touch of regret in her voice.

"Good for discussion, I guess." No one addressed the comment. I pressed on; after all, the conversation ended on my arrival and I felt responsible for reviving it. I asked the table questions I thought would guarantee discussion: *How long have you been in Gambia? What projects are you working on? How are they coming along?* Work questions, true, but if you're not interested in your work, why hold the job? Muhammad, who'd joined us along with Janet, smiled and shook his head slowly, eyes on the bread he was buttering: "My friend. You do ask questions. It seems to me you should have gone into journalism." This brought a round of chuckles.

"It's a Canadian thing. I guess we're kinda pushy."

"That's very interesting," he raised his head back as if trying to recall something from long ago. "I can't remember James being so." He refocused on his bread, then glanced at me. He was smiling politely, but he'd made eye contact for the first time and it felt like a challenge.

"That's because James was a wet kid, straight outta school with no experience in the world. Furthermore, based on the quality of his work, the centre might have done better to have filled the IT slot with a used douchebag." In D.C., under the right circumstances, I would have gotten away with saying that. Naturally, I was a bit more circumspect in my new position here and didn't actually say it. James was young, you could tell by the way he'd maintained his computer, but there wasn't any point in making

84

an issue out of it.[49]

"So, you're going to keep our Internet up and running, eh? Well, I wish you luck. James certainly had his hands full with it." Muhammad added.

"Do you prefer coffee or tea?" asked Fatou, peering at me over her teacup. I broke eye contact with Muhammad and turned to Fatou.

"Coffee, actually. If that's possible."

"Of course. Is there any hot water?" she asked, glancing over the table. Finding none, she lowered her teacup with a sigh, raised her head and boomed out, "*Fatou!*" Being in the line of fire, I shuddered at the sharpness of the blast. Her chest expanded for another go. I clenched my teeth, ready for impact, when a haggard-looking woman appeared from an outbuilding at the rear of the compound.

She was in her 50s, wearing a sarong, a tank top and a bandanna. She slumped her way toward us, dragging her feet heavily, almost theatrically. Her shoulders were rounded and stooped to such a degree, one of the straps to her top dangled around her elbow. She kept pushing it up her arm and it kept falling down. "Fatou!" shrieked the Fatou sitting beside me to this new Fatou, followed by something in Wolof.[50] The new Fatou kept nodding her head, murmuring occasionally.

---

49 Computers reflect personalities, just like your house, your car or the clothes you wear. Looking over the website source code, I could tell he was a skilled programmer. It was just HTML, but he'd carefully spaced and indented it the way you would a proper programming language , unlike the jumbled, auto-generated mess created by commonly used programs. He'd taken his time and done it by hand. Still, the site was amateurish, lots of silly embellishments that computer guys are taught to destroy on sight — letters with wings — pure end-user stuff. Clearly, he'd lost the fight with management. No one with experience would allow himself to be pushed into such nonsense when the core functionality of the site was in such a sorry state. As an information delivery tool, the whole thing was a mess. Making things useful is always job number one. Bells and whistles come later.

50 Fatou was the traditional name often given to the firstborn girl. Bintou the name for the second-born girl. Lamin was for the first-born male.

It was uncomfortable watching this 50-year-old woman — sweat dripping down her face and bags under her eyes thick enough to be seen in profile — being lectured by a woman 20 years her junior. "Uh, it's all right," I tried to interject, but Fatou's sharp voice steamrolled my polite Canadian one. The new Fatou shuffled quickly off to the outbuilding. I put extra effort into establishing eye contact when she came back with a pot of hot water, which she started pouring into my cup without my asking. Apparently, the new Fatou had been kicked while she was down on my behalf. I looked up at her and gave a big smile that tried to say, "I respect you as a person, and I'm sorry that you have to run and fetch on my behalf." Her eyes flicked nervously down at me and then refocused on pouring the water. *God, you make me feel uncomfortable*, seemed to be the reply. I felt like a tourist.

I wanted to protest more strongly, but then again, what about cultural sensitivity? Aren't you supposed to respect other people's culture? Doesn't that include the rules and regulations?[51] Based on the completely nonchalant attitude of the others, Fatou was completely within her rights to bully this other woman. Fatou was a grande dame with every right to speak to the cleaning lady any way she wanted. Based on my North-American-liberal-empirical-post-French-revolutionary perspective, who was I to judge? This wasn't my country, after all.

On the other hand, wasn't this a human rights institution? And weren't "human rights" in the modern legal sense sort of the point — at least superficially — of the French and American revolutions, the English Civil War and all those other events my history teachers insisted were part of my heritage as a Canadian? Didn't my North-American-liberal-empirical-post-French-revolutionary education and cultural bias make me the authority here on human rights? This is what flashed through my head, but

---

51 Isn't culture just a set of rules and regulations? Rules about what makes for appropriate conduct or decent music?

I didn't say anything. I knew it wouldn't sound right.

Feeling embarrassed, I lost myself in the food. I kept my mouth stuffed with bread, butter and avocado. Talk around the table was still minimal and lacked energy, mostly concerning whose tailor did the best work. It didn't take long for the food to revive me, and I decided to make another go, this time using a different tactic. "So, how do you say it? *Naga dep*?" I asked the table during a pause in the conversation.

"No, Robin. *Na'nga def*," teased Bintou with mock agitation. I'd deliberately mangled it.

"Don't worry, you'll get it in time," chuckled Muhammad.

"I've lived here for two years and I still haven't got it," mused Janet.

"It seems you're not talented with languages, are you?" asked Fatou.

"Not one bit. I've taken French since I was in kindergarten and I still can't manage a sentence."[52] I kept asking about Wolof terms: How do you say "my name is Robin?" How do you say "good afternoon?" I'd dutifully listen and then repeat, deliberately butchering it. They liked my interest but really liked my screw-ups. When in doubt, just play "the stupid white guy." Stupid-white-guy sells, no matter where you are in the world.

For some people, help's a right — an entitlement even — but for others, it's just condescending. The fact that time and effort had been spent getting someone from "the developed world" implied no one in the Gambia, or Africa, could do the job. Why not get a Nigerian or a South African? The whole situation had a negative connotation. Asking for help always does, I guess. To some degree, you're admitting you're helpless. One way or another, help can be hard to swallow, but if the guy offering it also needs your help because he can't manage something as simple as a greeting, it's a lot easier to suffer through. Stupid-white-guy can break a lot of ice.

After giving a convincing and entertaining demonstration of my

---

52 Which is completely true.

incompetence with French and complimenting them on their language skills,[53] relations warmed up. After the last chuckles, we broke up and went back to our respective desks. Samantha and Idrissa never made it out, but as I turned to enter my workspace, I saw them heading out to the gazebo. It was about 11 a.m. and I had no idea what I was supposed to do for the rest of the day.

By noon the place was deserted, and I was falling asleep at my machine. Falling asleep at my desk on the first day was certainly a new experience. Usually first-day stress was enough to keep me going. The deathly quiet and dim light in my corner reminded me of university and studying in the library, with its inevitable cycle of quiet, yawning, face plant. Everyone left for lunch, and Samantha had left earlier. The parking lot was empty. I hadn't received an invitation or directions on where I could get something to eat, but at least I didn't feel my efforts over the break were wasted. I didn't feel I'd been ignored, more like I'd been forgotten. People had filed out quickly, as if lunch was the big meeting of the day, on their minds the moment they showed up in the morning.

I needed to figure out what to do with myself. No one had given me the slightest hint of an expectation other than "IT support," which is really a euphemism for, "I don't want to deal with this. You do it." Sitting in front of my computer and waiting for work assignments would be setting myself up for an internship of "other duties as assigned," and I'd been working long enough to know it. For kicks, I wrote my own job position to establish my responsibility for the computers, network and the services contained therein, "other duties as assigned" expunged. I emailed it to Idrissa and waited to hear back.

---

53 Justly, too. All of them spoke at least three languages: English, French and a local language. Muhammad and Bintou were both studying Arabic.

By 2 p.m., most of the staff had returned from lunch. Idrissa responded to my job description with one line: *Looks fine*. Soon after 2 p.m., the printer hummed to life and started clacking out paper. People were pulling themselves heavily out of their chairs, grabbing blocks of notepaper, pens and collecting their printouts. Muhammad, whose office was beside mine, poked his head into my space: "Robin, are you coming to the staff meeting?" I was. Being in the meeting would be another way to ensure I didn't get assigned any silliness. I could intercept any "maybe Robin should be responsible for cleaning our keyboards" stupidity at the discussion phase. It was also something to do. "Normally it's on Tuesdays, but we're having one today because we haven't met in awhile due to the workshop." I found some documentation I'd been issued by the Canadian government commanding me to register with foreign affairs the instant I arrived, and decided the back would be a fine scratch pad. I joined the slow progression to the conference room.

People slumped down into their chairs and waited. Janet sat with her arms tightly crossed; Muhammad tapped the table with his pen impatiently. Fatou looked resigned and Bintou sat on her hands, staring down at her printout. Mamadou came in, working his imposing body around the room between the bookshelves and the edge of the table. He gave the room a tight smile and asked about everyone's lunch. A muffled "fine, fine" and a few half-smiles replied, as if respecting his bravery for trying to lighten the mood. With a series of wheezes and grunts that made me wonder if he needed an oxygen tank, Mamadou settled himself, straightened his tie, opened his fat green folder and started playing with the papers inside, placing some around the table in front of him.

The seat nearest the doors was still empty. After some time, long enough for people's fidgeting to blossom into open agitation, Idrissa came in. He had a folder under one arm and was carrying a coffee cup in the other hand. He greeted everyone with a smile that seemed sincere and took his seat. Still smiling, he made a few comments in Wolof, which based on the way he waved his coffee cup around, I took as a joke about his coffee. No one laughed except him.

Idrissa brought the meeting to order and everyone seemed to tense with his opening comments: "Fatou, the date on the last minutes doesn't seem right to me." He paused for a moment: "It should be the second, not the fourth. It's important to get these things right. What would happen if I needed to know when something was discussed?" Idrissa sharpened his voice as he spoke, much too sharp for the triviality of the issue. His deep baritone sounded barely under control, like a father about to let loose on a frustrating child. "Mamadou!" Idrissa practically spit. "The alarm system is still not working!"

"Yes, Idrissa. I am still working on it."

"Yes, I know! But what is the problem? It's been—"

"You know, Idrissa." replied Mamadou, pre-emptively forceful. "It isn't so simple with such things. There are complexities."

"Fatou, how long has this item been on the agenda?"

"Well, Idrissa, I'm not precisely sure. A couple of months, I believe." She said it in a whisper. The muscles in Idrissa's jaw flexed, his mouth a taut wire. He vented a sharp grunt through his nose.

"Why, then, are we paying you, Fatou, if you don't know these things?" Fatou's mouth worked up and down but nothing came out. Finally, she said lamely, "I can get my file."

"Sit, sit! You should come to meetings *prepared*, Fatou. You are the administrative assistant, Fatou — not so?" Idrissa shuffled through a stack of paper, pausing at each one, as if reading the titles. The alarm system had been on the agenda for almost three months, he announced. Turning back to Mamadou: "Why is it that three months have passed and this issue is still in the agenda? You," he said it like a shove, "are the head of administration. This is your responsibility."

"Yes, yes. I am doing all I can. It's not easy, you know."

"We have paid for this work, not so?"

"Yes, yes."

"Then why is it not done?"

"It *is* very complicated."

"What is so complicated?" Idrissa was practically jumping out of his seat with exasperation. "We paid money for an alarm and it does not work. This is very, very serious. How can we pay but not get anything? This is very serious. These people are taking advantage of us. How can we let this happen? No. We cannot. We can't let people take advantage of us like this. We have *rights*."

"Idrissa, perhaps the intern can do something about it." Right. It's got wires, so the IT guy must know what to do. That's like assuming a race car driver could dock the *Queen Mary* because both cars and ships use wheels to steer.

"I'm not an electrician, but I'd be happy to take a look at it for you." I said it with as much positive enthusiasm as I could muster. What else could I do? It was the first day, which meant I was obliged to overachieve and be helpful. I knew it was an electrical issue, so after scratching my head over a wiring diagram, I could legitimately bow out because I wasn't trained as an electrician. If they insisted I try, I could fall back on safety issues and, finally, my job description. I was suddenly very glad I'd written my job description.

Idrissa went on for another 10 minutes about right and wrong and how people had rights. People couldn't walk on other people. It wasn't right. After he was finished with Mamadou, he turned on Muhammad and Janet. He wasn't pleased with the workshop and wanted answers: "Why do we keep inviting the same people?" It went on and on. Muhammad and Janet were under siege for half an hour. Janet was heaving with every breath, arms crossing tighter and tighter, teeth clenched, spitting out answers that made sense to me: "We discussed the list of attendees before the workshop with

91

you. We met several times."

"It is *your* responsibility to guide and control things," retorted Idrissa. Janet was barely under control. Muhammad, on the other hand, was calm and almost flippant. He answered the questions competently, quietly and professionally, but the sighs he prefaced each answer said, *God, you're an idiot. I can't believe I answer to you.* The rest of us sat with our eyes fixed to our notes, pretending to be making copious notes of the exchange. Idrissa was stooped over his papers like a prizefighter wading into the ring. His outrage with the perceived incompetence of his staff was more than a manager's exasperation, it was filled with moral outrage.

I admit that I misjudged Idrissa then. There would come a time when I would be just as shrill over the simplest things. He was right. The centre *had* paid for an alarm system and the work hadn't been done — for months. How would you feel if you'd contracted someone to build you a deck and months later they hadn't even started? And when you made inquiries, all you heard was, "It's complicated." I'd lose it too. It's about justice. You've traded in good faith and you're being taken advantage of because of it. They say that power corrupts, well, corruption corrupts too. The jackasses responsible for getting the system working couldn't or wouldn't, despite promises to the contrary. Idrissa, frustrated beyond belief, started taking it out on the rest of the staff, venting over incorrect dates and other minutia. His largely blameless staff took it on the chin as long as they could, but the work suffered. No one cared because they knew Idrissa would be all over them no matter what happened.

The noble ship was developing a list. But it wasn't corruption flooding the hold, it was frustration. It would take some time living there, but eventually, I'd learn to fear corruption, not because of anything inherent in corruption, but because it bred frustration. Corruption is an abstract political concept. Frustration is how it plays out in the street. I'd find out a lot about that in the years to come.

Plebs

About three weeks after arrival

And so our working days went, and compared to our social lives, it was positively restful. For all the awkward moments, it was fairly easy to relate to my coworkers. They were professionals; they were educated; we had common points of reference. Occasionally, Robel and I would go dancing with them on a Friday night, but they'd been living there long enough to have lives and had no need to hang with interns. Developing a life outside of work was clearly going to be our own project. But we weren't completely on our own.

Ousman and Mustafa were frequent callers. After our initial meeting, they'd returned to visit every weekend. Thanks to them, we saw things we wouldn't have otherwise. They gave us our first introduction to various craft markets and towns in the region, taught us how to plant and raise corn,[54]

---

54 They planted each seed one by one. They'd take a stick and spin it in the ground to create a small crater in the soil, and then pushed a seed into the middle of the crater. No ploughs, no furrows. We needed to water the plants by hand; we had a borehole in the compound (a pipe descending to the water table with a faucet at the top), but we had no hose ("hose pipe," in Gambian parlance), so we used buckets. One corn plant needed about a bucket of water a day, and don't get me started on watermelons. We'd get up at 5:30 each morning, go for a run, do push-ups and sit-ups, then tend the garden, carrying hundreds of litres of water every week. We planted several rows of

showed us how to use the local public transit and made sure we were welcome at the local disco. The price of admittance to these wonders was simply listening, or at least it was initially.

Saturday, around 11 a.m., they'd come knocking on our gate and generally wouldn't leave until midnight. Ous would talk the whole time. It wasn't the same clichéd banter of our first meeting. As he got to know us, Ousman's loquaciousness awakened. An accomplished local historian and general knower of things, Ousman could explain village names, past tribal wars, social norms and "why nature was good" at agonizing length. Deviations in the topic were not tolerated, and comments about our own culture — compare and contrast — were answered with uncomfortable silence. Listening 12 hours straight to the all-time hardest sell of a country you weren't even sure you liked while straining for the next culturally sensitive question to ask was excruciating.

Nevertheless, one bright Saturday the boys showed up as usual, and we followed them down a sandy track leading into their village, wondering what the day would bring. We joined some of their friends and spent the afternoon hanging out in Brufut, sitting in plastic lawn chairs outside a corner store. At least a dozen young guys slouched in the scattered chairs or lounged on the concrete steps of the store, all dressed like Ice-T. Robel and I assumed our normal positions: a two-man congregation for Ousman's sermons about the importance of nature and how only Gambians still know its true value, and how important it is to be kind, and why integrity is so important, and how important it is to speak from the heart, and why it's nice to be nice, and how only Gambians only really know that. Occasionally, the other boys would chorus in with a worldly "it's true, it's true" or "yes,

---

corn, watermelons, a papaya tree, potatoes, onions, garlic and pot. The garden was our running project and we loved it. Neither of us had gardened before, but between Ous and Musta and my Internet connection at the centre, we figured it out. In the end, we had about 65 ears of corn and some vegetables and fruit to show for our efforts.

Ousman, yes," nodding their heads like sages. Other than that, they smoked their cigarettes without a word. Although Mustafa and Ousman had accepted us as a part of their cohort and "talked" with us, it was clear the rest of the boys weren't so sure. Most treated us with deference, never referring to us as "boy," but rather as "Boss" or "Boss Man" when asking for a cigarette. This was significant.

On the day I went to Banjul market with people from the centre, the Gambian interns decided I needed a real West African shirt. They took me for a stroll, looking over the wares lining Banjul's main road. They ordered me to walk ahead and pick up shirts I might want but to refuse the price and move along. The girls would come up from behind and start bidding on the same shirt, as if buying it for their brother. This would ensure I got a "Gambian price."

Things were going well. We'd successfully acquired one shirt and I was looking over another when one of the interns broke ranks and dragged me back to join them. With no concern for our blown cover, she asked, "You would like that one better, Robin?" Both pointed to a purple tie-dyed job, far up the metal rack leaning against the wall, hanging above the less-than-enthusiastic attendant who sat on the ground bopping to a Discman and looking like an L.A. gang member.

"Well?"

I liked my boring white linen choice better. "Hmm, I don't know if it would fit me. I think it might be too small in the shoulders."

"Boy!" shouted one of my companions. "Boy, boy!" her fingers snapping. During my time in 75 percent black Washington, D.C., the one surest way to get yourself injured or killed was to call a black man "boy." You never — *ever* — called a black man "boy." In some circles, it was considered even worse than another, more notorious term.

The young guy finally realized she wanted service and took the

95

headphones off, head cocked to one side, not happy. "Boy!" she snapped, jabbing her finger at the shirt. He suddenly sprung up and snatched the stick beside him. Oh Jesus. Red alert. I squared up, ready to fight or flee as the situation dictated, and I felt the situation was about to dictate that this guy immediately slam that stick right up my friend's backside. If he noticed my apprehension, he didn't care. He simply turned and hooked the shirt with the stick, bringing it down for my inspection. Despite forlorn glances at his Discman, he was courteous and conscientious, brushing down the sleeves and straightening it on the hanger before presenting it to me. I was amazed.

As we continued down the street, it was explained the term "boy" only meant you weren't married or established. Anyone your age who wasn't married or didn't have a real job was a "boy." Peers — even old, married, wealthy guys — would refer to each other as "boy," using it as a term of endearment, like the British term "mate." Only peers used it affectionately and white men never at all. There wasn't a lot of respect attached to the title. A constant lament while living there would be: "Oh, those boys!" to describe some slight. Nevertheless, it wasn't derogatory and it did carry a little dignity: you were young, on the make, a Gambian Horatio Alger.

Ousman's friends were showing us where we sat in the social spectrum: as far as they were concerned, we were "Boss Men," not "boys." The term "Boss Man" needs little clarification. Those guys would never have accepted us as equals. We were their betters, aristocrats, men from the Big House, whether we liked it or not.

Sometimes the boys would acknowledge Ous's greatness: "Yes, Ousman, yes," but generally when Ous stopped talking, and Robel and I couldn't think of a follow-up question, silence reigned. Lots of silence. When Ous was tired, it could stretch into unnerving 15- to 20-minute chunks.

It was at the naming ceremony for Idrissa's baby where Samantha explained the phenomena of silence to me.[55] I made a comment about how people didn't speak very much. The rich and foreign educated were different, going out of their way to display their small-talk skills. The others, though — the plebs — tended to sit in small groups around small tables, where they'd sit in silence. "So, this is a naming ceremony?"

"Yup."

"Not a chatty bunch," I said with doubt. Maybe I'd missed something.

"Gambians tend to keep talk to a minimum."

"OK," I couldn't think of anything else to say. Weren't people there to be communicated with? That's why you went to a party, wasn't it?

Sensing my thoughts, Samantha added, "People here don't feel the need to constantly talk. It's completely normal for people to just hang around in each other's company — for hours — without talking. Just being together. No need to discuss every little thing. Nothing wrong with that."

I guess she had a point. I know couples who go on about how wonderful it is they can just "be" with their partners, like it's the ultimate attainment of a relationship. Maybe Gambians were just more enlightened.

For as long as I can remember, I've never been able to tolerate small talk. Not just tolerate it, I don't even understand it. Life is short — why talk about the small? What is small talk? Can you define it? Most can't. I know because I've asked. I once asked a girlfriend who was good at it to explain the concept. She replied without hesitation: "It's discussing the impersonal. It's discussing things around you, people's shoes, for instance, or wall hangings, provided you weren't speaking to the owner of the shoes or the

---

55 When Samantha invited me to Idrissa's naming ceremony, she explained it this way: "When a Muslim family has a baby, they wait a few days before giving it a name. Then, on the day they decide to name the baby, they have a big celebration. There's dancing and all kinds of food. All kinds! They're going to slaughter a sheep!"

house." It was a good answer. But what exactly is "impersonal" in a foreign culture? No matter how much cultural sensitivity training you get beforehand, it's impossible to know if footwear is a red-light issue. How about a hole in the ground?

In my last year in Africa, a Nigerian colleague and I went on a two-man road trip across four countries and over 3,000 kilometres of West Africa. We had 10 days to install three satellite dishes and build three networks from scratch.[56] Needless to say, we were pretty exhausted by day eight, slumped over our equipment on the floor of Dakar International Airport[57] in Senegal as we waited for our next flight. My Nigerian friend decided he needed to use the bathroom, leaving me to hold down the fort. Returning a few minutes later, he slumped down beside me looking uncomfortable.

"What?" I asked, barely awake.

"I got some very nasty looks in the toilet."

"Yeah?"

"Very nasty. These locals were giving me *harsh* looks."

"Yeah, what happened?"

"You know those holes in the floor?"

"Yeah."

"What are they for?"

"They're the drains they use for ablutions at prayer time. Why?"

---

56 I'm not talking about those small dishes hanging off the outside wall of your house for your entertainment. These dishes were nearly two metres across and had to be mounted on metal poles that had to be specially levelled and have visual clearance to the horizon in the direction of the satellite we were trying to hit. Due to time constraints, these were usually placed before we arrived, and often they were placed wrong, leaving us to jury-rig something fast. And I do mean fast. At nearly $1,000 a day to keep us in the field, there was no "we'll deal with that tomorrow." Not a chance.

57 Officially the Léopold Sédar Senghor International Airport.

Through the haze of exhaustion, I started to understand. Suddenly I snapped up straight — wide awake — looking around.

"Look!" he shot out defensively, as if I were giving him dirty looks. Hell, maybe I was. "In the rest of Africa, a hole in the ground is for peeing in, not for washing your hands."

With some effort, I got him to lower his voice and eventually he calmed down. The lynch mob I expected never materialised and the whole thing blew over. Nevertheless, the idea of my companion peeing into ablution drains during the war on terror wasn't ideal. I was wide awake and reading hostility in every glance for hours. If a hole in the ground could get controversial, what could a working mouth could do? Maybe Gambians were onto something. Maybe the best way for two cultures to interact was in silence. Maybe less was more. True, silence didn't promote cultural understanding, but it did promote peace and harmony: ask me no questions, I'll tell you no lies.

After sitting around for at least four hours with Ousman, Mustafa and the boys, pretty much doing nothing, we were introduced to the guy who seemed to have some status. Young, he looked like one of the boys, but he made the rounds, shaking hands like a politician on a whistle-stop tour. We were introduced and it was announced his sister was getting married in the morning.

Congratulations." we offered.

"Thank you, my friends. Thank you. A camera? You have?"

"Sure. Two of 'em."

"You are honoured guests! Would you take pictures?"

"Sure, we'd be honoured." We went home to get the cameras, giddy as schoolboys. Finally our patience with Mustafa and Ousman was paying off. A real cultural event where we'd have carte blanche to use our cameras without offence.

Ous could sense our excitement and started to perk up. His solemn wise-old-man was replaced by a happy young guy, thrilled to see others taking an interest in his culture. While hurrying back down the track, he enthusiastically explained about the wedding.

It was a Fula wedding. The Fula was a local tribe, distinguished by their height and thinness. Most of the other tribes in the region — according to Ousman — were shorter and stockier. The Fula were tall and thin, with sharply defined features. The reasons Mustafa sat down with Robel that first day on the beach was because he figured Robel for a local Fula. Robel's Ethiopian (more specifically Oromo[58]) heritage fit the part perfectly. During his time in the Gambia, Robel would often be mistaken for Fula. There were many different ethnic groups living in the Gambia, the most dominant being the Wolof,[59] the Mandinka, the Jola and the Fula. Brufut, being a large village, was home to all four groups. Although they weren't segregated into different quarters, parts of the village were predominantly one or the other. The section closest to our house was essentially Fulatown in the same way Spadina south of Bloor in Toronto, Ontario, is essentially Chinatown.

Unlike Chinatown in Toronto, you'd never know you were in Fulatown as opposed to Jolatown, unless you were with someone like Ous who could tell you the difference. Wolof was the Gambian lingua franca, the Wolof being the largest ethnic group, and everyone spoke it. After some time under Ousman's careful tutelage, it would become easier for us to figure out whom we were dealing with, but nothing was written in stone. Apparently, each group had a traditional line of work and sometimes that could be used to clarify who was who. Cattle herding and trading were the traditional preserve of the Fula. Also musical instruments. The Fula often

---

58 The Oromo are one of the largest ethnic groups in East Africa. They're the majority ethnicity in Ethiopia, Robel's homeland.
59 In French, this is often spelled *Ouolof.*

played a simple stringed instrument with a soundbox made of a hollowed gourd. The instrument was held and bowed like a violin. All this information excited Robel. The physiology, the cattle herding and even the musical instrument were right out of the Oromo handbook. One drunken night, not long after the wedding, we mused that the Fula were probably Oromo who'd migrated with their cattle across the continent millennia ago.

We'd stormed back to the house, but by the time I'd gotten the cameras and whatever film I could find and stuffed them into my bag, the sun was on its way down. Concerned we might miss the action, we double-timed it back to the village. Ousman told me not to worry, that the actual wedding was tomorrow. This was a pre-wedding reception. The bride's family was throwing a party at their compound to celebrate, and they were rich, so a cow would be slaughtered to feed the guests. We'd be eating well that night.

We weaved back through the same sandy pathways we'd come down, ending up back at the same storefront we'd set off from. We were shown to a couple of plastic lawn chairs and the routine went on as it had earlier in the afternoon: smoking, drinking tea, listening to Bob Marley on a cassette player from the '80s and sitting in silence. I must've been visibly frustrated because Ousman explained with an apologetic tone that we had to wait. We were just boys. The cow had been slaughtered and cooked, and the older people got first crack. They were at the bride's house eating. Once they'd had their fill, the food would be brought to us. We'd eat on our own, then join "the grownups" at the compound to enjoy the rest of the evening. Fair enough.

We continued as before and kept our vigil well past sundown. A couple of children joined us, demanding I quiz them on their addition, so I passed the time scratching math problems in the sand. Ous went on about Fula weddings and Fulas in general, but his command of the topic was limited, he and Mustafa being Mandinka. He started to repeat himself for

101

the second time when we heard a voice from up the path, "My friends, my friends!" Our host appeared out of the dark with a group of kids in tow, carrying huge metal bowls of food on their heads. We'd been sitting in small groups and a bowl was put down in the middle of each, filled with about three pounds of cooked rice, some boiled vegetables and a fist-sized piece of boiled meat in the middle. Being honoured guests, our host sat down with us. Everyone started to pull up a sleeve to dig in.

"No spoons, eh?"

Laughter. Ousman held up one of his hands, fingers spread wide, pointing to each as he spelled out *S-P-O-O-N*. Hilarity!

No plates, no utensils, no napkins, but rules and table etiquette were still in play. The bowl was understood to be divided up into wedges like a pie, each diner getting the one closest to him, and it was made clear you didn't poach across wedges. It was up to the host to ensure everyone got a fair share, and so our host picked up large pieces of zucchini, meat and okra from the middle, broke it up with his fingers and threw bits into each of our corners. As honoured guests, he made sure Robel and I got the lion's share, which — as I'm sure you can imagine — was awkward. Privately, Robel and I would later comment on the incredibly small amount of beef. A piece about half the size of a porkchop was expected to feed the six of us around the bowl, and we were honoured guests. I felt bad getting most of it and wanted to say, "No, you take it," but felt it would've been ungracious.

Portion size was an issue for the first couple of months, not in situations like this, but in restaurants. When Robel and I got into the habit of going down to Senegambia on Fridays, we'd always order two entrées. One was never enough. Our Rwandan roommate, Uwimana, once mentioned that while she was at law school in the States, she and two of her African friends would occasionally go to a typical roadhouse for dinner. They'd order a single appetizer and one entrée for the table — more than enough food to feed all three of them. After awhile I got used to the smaller amounts of food, eating even less than what was served. By the time I got back to Canada, I'd lost 30 pounds.

We ate up, quickly mastering the technique of squishing a handful of rice into a sticky ball which was easy to fire into your mouth. Not a word was spoken, but the silence wasn't awkward. The food tasted good. Sitting knee to knee, heads stooped over the bowl, everyone seemed to consider each bite, sighs of satisfaction emanating from each of us as we quietly consumed the meal. We finally had something in common. We were all right there, together, feeling the same things, the same simple satisfactions. The clichés about the importance of food, of sharing a meal with someone: they're all true.

We hadn't eaten all day, but the tomato-infused rice[60] soothed our stomachs and countered the flood of adrenaline from the anticipation of the wedding. It seemed like the best food I'd ever tasted. The kids took the bowls away and we leaned way bay in our chairs, eyes on the sky. More stars than I'd ever seen. We were awaiting orders, waiting to hear if the adults were ready for us. Mustafa explained it was best to wait for the moon to rise high in the sky; its light reflecting off the sand of the footpaths would help us as we navigated around the village. The adults likely wouldn't call us before midnight anyway. To no one in particular I asked, "What star is that?"

---

60 Rice was a staple. In fact, it was slaves who brought the cultivation of rice to North America. The most popular dish was *benachin*, or jollof rice, essentially a rice pilaf cooked in tomato paste and the drippings of a protein, usually fish or chicken. Yassa was one of the most prized dishes: chicken fried with onions and lemon juice. Domoda made up the last of the most common meals and was any protein covered in a peanut butter sauce. I will never forget the day the boys decided to impress us with a home-cooked Gambian meal. After buying a three-foot fish covered in flies from fin to nose in the market, we took it home and they deep-fried it in about an inch of oil. Then they added about four cups of peanut butter and poured it over rice. Noticing the look on Ousman's face as he ate, I asked if the finished product met his expectations. Not really, he said. After all, he explained, they were men. What did they know about cooking?

pointing to an extraordinarily bright one.

"I don't know, but it's beautiful," answered Robel with a touch of awe in his voice.

"Not a star, Robin," murmured Mustafa. "It is a satellite."

"Really? How do you know that?"

"You see, it moves very quickly across the sky. For some time I have been watching it. Too quick for a star. It is a satellite, yes."

So much for my telecommunications knowledge.

We received our invitation; the moon was high above; off we went, occasionally passing a silhouette in the dark without a sound on the sandy track. The moonlight was a godsend, revealing deep potholes in the road. The deep ones could easily jar your knees if you flat-footed into them, leaving you with a limp in no time. Soon the sound of music and unrestrained laughter reached us, and we could see lights and people.

The compound was marked by a fence made of curved palm branches. Close to the gate, a boy sat beside a homemade sound system consisting of a car's CD player connected to a truck battery and a couple of mismatched speakers. The whole assembly was set out on a plank supported by two cinderblocks, blaring traditional music. In the dusty courtyard, a circle had formed around a woman who was bent over, feet stamping, arms out like a bird, spinning around and around at a frantic pace. The circle was clapping, egging her on with hoots and howls. Elsewhere in the courtyard, people were sitting in groups on plastic furniture. The house was near the rear of the compound, and sitting on the front stoop sat the notables: the father and his best friends, the mother and grandmother, village elders and other important people. Introductions were made and thank-yous exchanged, for the invitation on our part and for the pictures on theirs. Then Robel and I went to work. Unfortunately, the flash died early on, and so, amid promises of more pictures tomorrow, we were given honoured seats by the house.

The older folks were clearly uncomfortable with our presence, despite polite assurances to the contrary. As usual, no one spoke. It wasn't clear where we fit in. Mustafa and Ousman stayed with us, enjoying their status as part of the "foreigners' entourage." This was a problem. We were guests, albiet unusual ones, but Ous and Mustafa certainly didn't belong sitting there with the family. They weren't relations; they were just boys from the village. Although we'd eaten with the boys, now we were sitting in the family's compound and we were trying to do our best to fit into the social scene, but our presence was causing ripples. The dancers hadn't taken notice of us, people were having a good time, but the look on Mom and Dad's face said it all. It didn't get any better when we were granted — how, exactly, I don't know — the unheard-of privilege of seeing the bride before the wedding.

Apparently, in a Fula ceremony, no one was allowed to see the bride the day before the wedding except members of her immediate family. As honoured guests, somehow we were invited into the bridal chamber. Escorted by her brother, our host, we were shown onto the house's veranda and lead down to the last entrance on the right, where a curtain covered the threshold. He went inside and we waited, Mom hovered a few feet away, looking concerned. A voice invited us in, so we brushed aside the curtain and entered. Our friend was sitting with his sister, a young woman who was about 20 years old. They sat on a small twin bed that took up half of the concrete room. Heaps of clothes filled the small space and reminded me of my sisters' rooms when they were about that age. The bride sat covered with a shawl that cast most of her face in shadow. The single candle gave a warm orange glow. Apart from the clothes, it was like being in a monk's cell. We sat down quietly in chairs and spoke in whispers, everyone aware of the special privilege with which we'd been honoured. We congratulated her and she thanked us for coming. She was nervous and couldn't wait for it to be over, so she could move in with her husband, who — we were assured —

was a good man. Her brother agreed. I asked if I could take a picture, tried a couple of long exposures and apologized awkwardly when my point-and-shoot unexpectedly let loose with the flash, blinding everyone in the room. We congratulated her again and left.

Outside on the stoop, the older women were still hanging around, eavesdropping. I tried to win them over with a picture, seeing as my flash had suddenly found its nerve. I managed one, and Granny looked happier, but Mom still had doubts. Nevertheless, we were saved by the arrival of the band.

Rushing back to our seats as directed by Ousman and Mustafa, we watched as a couple of musicians and a lady with a booming voice started singing and clapping around the courtyard. They wandered closer to the house, courting the important people sitting in front of the stoop, the rest of the partygoers forming a semicircle around them. Ous bent close and explained we were to give her a little money — no more than five dalasi — and she'd sing a song using our names, which would bring good luck. As an afterthought he mentioned we'd be expected to dance to the song. Maybe we could give the money but decline the dance?

They were working their way through the crowd, coming our way fast. I reached into my pocket and realised I needed to get money out of my wallet, which was a problem because I had hundreds of dalasi and flashing it around wasn't going to score points. Happily, by the time we were on deck, I'd fished a note from my wallet and passed it to the singer all scrunched up in my fist. She pulled it open, held it up to the moonlight and gave a short squeal. The most they'd collected, even from the notables, was a fiver. I'd given her a 50-dalasi note. The musicians stopped playing. She took our hands and asked our names. "Rooobeeel! Roooobiiiiiin!" she wailed while we sat there like idiots wondering if a good or bad thing had just happened. She started jumping and clapping, and the musicians followed her lead with a lively jig, and then she took us by the hands again.

106

Despite our earnest smiles that said, "Oh, thank you, but I couldn't *possibly*," she pulled us out of our chairs, and soon Robel and I were doing our interpretation of their traditional dance. We looked like two chickens with mad cow disease: elbows stuck out like wings, jumping around frantically, maniacally, hoping our élan would heal any cultural wounds our special interpretation of the dance might inflict. Stupid-white-guy to the rescue. Stupid-white-guy rarely failed, and he didn't then. They laughed and laughed. We tried to sit down, but the band felt we should get our money's worth. She'd finish, we'd move to our seats, and then she'd start up again, "Rooobeeeel! Roooobiiiiiin!" and we'd go another round. God only knew what she was saying about us, but judging by the crowd, it must have been funny. We looked like fools, but I was having a pretty good time.

Eventually, the party came to an end, and we were invited to return the next day and photograph the actual wedding. Whether we'd scored points or they just wanted free pictures, I don't know. I like to think the former. Professional photographers were available for hire, and some showed up next day. On the other hand, their old cameras and recycled chemicals couldn't compare with our digital kit. As we stumbled home in the early hours, Ous and Mustafa were both in a great mood, so surely something had gone right. They came by early the next day, Sunday, as promised, and after I purchased batteries for my digital camera, we were off.

The courtyard was packed with people. A bright, beautiful day, an awning had been stretched over the courtyard to make shade. It was as if the party hadn't stopped. Women were dancing in the middle of the courtyard, the musicians were still there, and we were greeted with a loud "Rooobeeeel! Roooobiiiiiin!" People laughed. Robel and I started taking pictures, swapping between my old Nikon and a digital point-and-shoot. Apprehensive at first, people instantly warmed to the photographic experience when they saw their smiling faces on the digital's LCD screen. People began taking an interest: the ladies giggled shyly, the kids were curious and the boys took great pride in being the ones who'd brought us. They scored points and earned some respect, Mustafa told me later.

The boys took to facilitating our photography, Ousman in particular. He'd taken possession of my camera bag, and before the bride was ready, he knew the difference between lenses, films, and the other odds and ends I'd be asking for over the course of the day. He took the job seriously, anticipating my requests, keeping a roll of colour in one hand and a roll of black-and-white in the other for quick deployment.

I discovered, while working on my high-school yearbook, that cameras were really just a licence to go places and do things you couldn't have otherwise. My comrade Stephanie and I covered graduation for senior year. We filled two haversacks with film and hit the scene like five-year-olds who'd eaten their weight in sugar. We were delirious. We went everywhere: creeping around behind the teachers on stage, crawling over parents' knees, popping up among the band to capture embarrassing candids and generally chasing the grads like paparazzi. Nothing was out of bounds and propriety meant nothing. We were *journalists*. We needed to get *the shot*, and God help the civilian who got in the way. We each had about 50 rolls of film and we shot the lot. At one point, desperate to find a new roll, we dumped one of our bags right onto the floor. Our pictures were terrible, but it was a surreal adrenaline rush.

Watching Ous, I could tell he was feeling it. The freedom of the camera. Not just a boy anymore, now he was someone. He'd done right by the community, helping to capture this happy moment for posterity. You could see the excitement in his face as he followed us around, kneeling when I kneeled and moving people around to help compose shots without me having to ask. It was great to watch his enthusiasm. Like with the food, we had something in common, a connection.

The bride was ready. It was midafternoon and the wedding was about to start. Despite asking many times, my understanding of the ceremony was hampered by the general festivities. It was like asking someone to explain the electoral college at a dance club. What follows is what I could make out.

The proceedings started with the bride and groom meeting at a third party's house. This person — an elder chosen by the parents of both families — would act as the arbiter in the event of marital discord. We were waiting now for the bride to make the trip, the crowd chanting, demanding she show herself. Soon, a young woman came out from behind the curtain of the bride's room. The crowd roared its approval. Dressed in white, it looked like she was carrying a huge white cocoon on her back. It must've been heavy because she was stooped and moving with great effort. She descended the stairs and the musicians started playing. She loped through the yard, through the gate and into the street. Confused, I enquired after the bride and was told she was actually *in* the cocoon. She'd been swaddled like a child, wrapped head to toe, even her face covered. She was being carried on the back of her best friend, whose responsibility it was to deliver her safe and sound to the arbiter, just like a baby.

The party moved into the street. More people joined the procession as we wound through the sandy lanes. The magnificent clothes in all colours, happy music and giddy children contrasting sharply with the grey cinderblock walls and rusted sheet-metal fences lining the route. It looked like Mardi Gras. The band played, people banged on plates and pans. Soon, a procession of about 100 danced its way through the streets. At a fever pitch, Robel and I worked the crowd, running up and down, swapping cameras, loading film, changing lenses, aware that this was once in a lifetime. We'd never see something like this again.

Twenty minutes later we piled into a compound with lime-green cement walls: the arbiter's house. The bridle bundle was deposited in the middle of the courtyard, which was finished with tile. The arbiter must've been wealthy. The best friend plopped down beside the bundle, throwing a

109

sweaty arm over it and sat there with the vacant, exhausted look athletes have after a race. The bride's parents went inside to meet the groom, his parents and the arbiter. But the party didn't stop outside: everyone surrounded the bride who still lay on the ground swaddled, only her hennaed feet visible. People danced and sang, using bowls, buckets and serving trays as instruments. The bride's robes were loosened and her face became more visible. The pictures I'd taken of her the night before weren't very good, and I desperately wanted a better shot, but the jostling crowd made it impossible. Soon, her swaddle was loosened enough for her to move around and into the house she went. Outside, the band played on.

A hundred people laughed, danced and joked. About half an hour passed, and with much cheering, the bride reappeared, this time with her mother-in-law. Carrying a large plastic basin filled with water, they put it down in a corner of the yard, away from the group. Next, they pulled out a rag, heavy as a beach towel, and started washing it. The crowd parted to give them some space. Wow, the Fula don't waste time with housework, I thought. Soon, some of the people in the crowd started creeping toward the two women doing laundry. I still hadn't gotten a decent headshot of the bride, so I walked slowly toward them as well, peering through the viewfinder of my Nikon and trying to focus. What happened next took only a second, and all I can say for myself is that I was able to hang onto the camera.

I have absolutely no understanding of the Fula language, but in hindsight, the rhythm of the crowd made it obvious they were calling out in cadence something like "one, two, three." We were within a few feet of the women, and I was right up front, determined to get the shot if only she'd hold still for a second. Suddenly, there was a shriek. The bride sprang up in a flurry of water. Everyone bolted. I pulled the camera from my eye just as it hit. I stumbled and tumbled across the yard, skidding to a halt on my chest. After a few seconds the merry-go-round I was on slowed down, and I knew

I'd be able to keep the nausea down. The whole compound had fallen silent.

Then the compound was in a commotion. Hands tugged, pulling me to my feet. I could tell Robel was right there. Smudges of colour poked around the bushes a few metres away. One smudge straightened and came closer, passing me my glasses. Now I could see the look on people's faces; they'd gathered around and were looking concerned.

In the West, the bride throws the bouquet. In the land of the Fula, she throws — or rather whips — the wet towel. According to tradition, the bride and her mother-in-law wash a rag, and young single people move closer and closer. At a certain moment, everyone scatters, and the bride jumps up and swings the wet rag around in a circle with all her might. If any water from the rag lands on you, it means you'll never get married. Taken by surprise, I didn't run, and so I'd been KOed by the heavy wet towel. Travelling at a good speed, it wrapped around my head and sent me flying. I studied jujitsu for eight years and boxed for two, and yet I'd never been hit in the head that hard before. I was soaked and still dizzy from the impact. Slowly, the crowd came back to its senses, and people came over to comfort me: "It's just an old tradition. Nothing will come of it. You're not from here."

"Now, you will never be married, but you will have *lots* of girlfriends!"

"Don't worry, the magic doesn't work on *toubobs*."

I didn't believe a word of it. Their faces betrayed them. I was cursed and they knew it. The bride's family was mortified: they'd damned the wedding photographer. They wanted good pictures of their daughter's wedding and this might ruin it all. I wasn't bothered by it: my glasses survived the impact, and dizziness aside, I wasn't feeling too bad. Most important, I had somehow managed to keep my camera out of harm's way while cartwheeling towards the ground. I laughed and waved to the crowd, "I'm OK!" like Gerald Ford reassuring everyone after stumbling down a gangway. The party resumed and would carry on well into the night just like the day before. We had to work the next day, and so took our leave after giving promises of prints for everyone. Before leaving, our host thanked us for coming, gushing with happiness or perhaps relief. Although we'd created a scene and I'd inadvertently got myself cursed, they thanked us for coming and clarified where we should bring the pictures when they were developed. Robel and I rushed home, grabbed some Garcia on the way, and babbled like idiots about the last two days. What a difference from work. It was still early when we left, but we were both feeling the strain of the day. Our non-verbal communication had increased dramatically since that first day on the beach with Ousman and Mustafa. I could look at Robel now and know when it was time to exit stage right.

We felt as if we'd connected with our neighbours in a profound way, but hanging out with them was exhausting. It was difficult to know where we fit. On one hand, you ate with the boys; on the other, you were invited to take pictures of the bride. None of the local photographers had won such honour. Being a loose cannon in the social world had advantages: you weren't pigeonholed; you weren't in a clique. You were a free agent and you had access where others didn't. It was liberating, in a frightening way. I could almost understand the obnoxious German I'd seen that night in Senegambia. You could be whomever you wanted there. A year later when a friend of mine needed a job, she simply walked up to UN House, the local branch of the United Nations,[61] and asked for one. Back home, that would've been impossible. You needed an Ivy League degree and rich friends to get the kind of job she ended up with. Being a social misfit never felt so good.

---

61 Being one of the only English speaking countries in West Africa, a lot of NGO and humanitarian organisations maintained regional offices in the Gambia.

Law and Order: Banjul Edition

11 p.m., Senegambia highway, two months after arrival

If you've ever driven down a desert highway on a clear night, you know the tranquillity of a landscape lit by a bright moon in an inky-blue sky. Your arm dangles out the window while the warm night air breezes over it. Even if you have a place to go on a night like this, you're just cruising, in no particular hurry, gliding down the hardtop.

On the night in question, I was in the back of Madeleine's car, enjoying the wind in my face as I mulled over the evening. Robel and I had been out in Senegambia with Madeleine and Uwimana. We'd had a good time: food, drinks and music. It was the first time we'd gotten together as a group and it was a success. The others were ready for bed by 11 p.m., but I knew Robel and I would be up late discussing the experience. Boxes of Garcia awaited our arrival at home, and we had plenty of cigs to grease the debrief. We'd be home soon, the roundabout leading to Brusubi just ahead.

Despite my boozy haze, I became aware that my arm was feeling quite hot, the cool breeze dropping away. I could hear crunching gravel as well. We were pulling over, and because I was crowded in the backseat, I couldn't see why. Once stopped, everyone started getting out of the car without a word. I did too.

"Stand there! Stand there!" snapped a silhouette pointing to the side of the road.

The car lights cut the shadow in half, starkly revealing black leather boots and olive-drab pants. Without a word, my companions did as they were told. Robel and I followed and lined up, shoulder to shoulder, with everyone else. Educated lawyers — patricians every one — lined up like schoolchildren.

"Who is the driver? Open the boot!"

Madeleine lit up in the headlights as she rounded the car to comply. Watching her, I sighed a little too loudly. I was drunk, impatient and feeling my North American sense of entitlement: who were these clowns to hold us up? I suddenly became aware of a shadow approaching me from the right. Stopping in front of me, all I could really make out were the whites of his eyes: bloodshot, tiny black orbs in the middle, glaring with hostility, shifting around, sizing up my face, the colour of my skin.

He stepped up to me slowly, still studying my face and eyes. His hand squeezed and twisted around the grip of his AK-47. My eyes dropped to the gun. He came closer, forcing me to raise my head to prevent bumping his. I couldn't see the rifle anymore, so I blinked back into his glare. My face flushed red. I could smell his clothes — Sergeant Slaughter was stoned.

"Your name?"

"Robin, sir."

He considered it for a second, then baulked, "You are very rude, Mr. Robin!"

"No, no! Pardon? I'm sorry? I didn't mean any offence."

He still didn't look very happy.

"You are very rude! I have asked you your name. Do you not want to know mine? This is very rude!" he complained in a shrill staccato, a droplet of spit hitting my glasses. "In my country, it is very rude to not ask for a name. You meet people and you greet them. You ask them for their name. It is good to be polite. Not so?" He was upset and swayed with the effort of his rebuke.

"Absolutely! We believe the same in my country. We're faultlessly polite. We're known for it, actually. I'm sorry, what's your name?" His eyes went glassy as he reflected. He seemed calmer, drowsy. I sensed him wavering a bit on his feet, but his eyes never left mine.

"I am Gaston." It was a serious moment, the point you start trying to talk your way out of the mess, saying things like, "It's wonderful to meet you, Gaston. Where is your family from? Do you enjoy being a soldier?" It was time to build relationships. Unfortunately, I was pretty green and didn't understand the finer points of these kinds of negotiations. Worse still, all my sodden mind could focus on was that I was being held at gunpoint by the loudmouth bully from *Beauty and the Beast*.[62] Thinking about the ridiculousness of the whole situation — a drunk guy being called to task by a pothead — I almost laughed.

"What are you doing here in the Gambia?" Gaston asked with sincere interest.

I flushed again, a grin starting to pull across my face. I hoped speaking would hide it. "Well… I work… over there!" I almost giggled as I pointed at the centre, which was across the roundabout.

"What is it you do there?"

"Human rights work. I'm here to promote human rights in the Gambia!" I announced with glee, happy with the new direction our relationship was taking. Only after saying it did my soggy mind stop to wonder if the guy with the rifle was as enthusiastic about it as I was.

Gaston gave me a considered look, shifting a foot backwards to keep balance and said: "Human rights… they are good." I couldn't tell if he was joking. Over the next few minutes he went on about how it's good for everyone to be free, and how it was nice to be nice and how great it was that

---

62   Also named Gaston.

someone from Canada would come all the way to Africa to help with Gambian human rights. The inspection of Madeleine's car long finished,[63] I bid goodnight to the rest of the checkpoint squad; Gaston and I parted on pretty good terms.

We drove the last couple of blocks home. Robel jumped out of the car, storming into our compound. I told Madeleine to call when she got home, because she'd have to pass back through the roadblock, and then I locked the gate. Robel was pacing on the stoop with a packet of cigarettes. He pulled one out and slapped the packet to the ground. "I've seen these people before. I've seen these people before," he kept muttering, more to himself than to me. His family had been activists in Ethiopia and were chased out when he was a kid. He'd lived in a refugee camp in Kenya, and his mom had finally been allowed into Canada when he was 12. As far as Robel was concerned, there was so such thing as a good guy with a gun.

Robel told me about being afraid. Not "will I get into a good university?" angst, but about *being afraid*. Not because of fate, disease or an earthquake, but because some guy felt like pulling your wings out. For Robel, the tension of what *might* have happened outweighed any amusement in what *had* happened. Robel had no doubt if we'd shown up five minutes earlier or later, or if he'd been doing a different drug, or if a different person had overheard me, things would have been terribly different.

My next serious interaction with local security forces came a few months later. It was a typical Friday, which meant it was a half-day. Plans were made to go to Senegambia and grab a few drinks after work, and I went home around 11 a.m. to get some money in preparation. I unlocked the door and charged into my room looking for the bag I kept my money in. There was

---

63   They were looking for drugs. It was a routine shakedown. Sort of the Gambian version of the RIDE program.

no easy access to money of any kind there, and so to pay for lunch, wine, cigarettes and other necessities, I had a stash of cash in my room. My room was a bit of a mess, and I made it messier throwing clothes, backpacks and camera bags around looking for the money sack. I found it, but it was empty. I must've transferred the wad to a pocket. I searched the pants lying around my room. Nothing. I stopped to think. My camera bag had felt lighter than normal. It was empty. I called Lisa, the new Canadian intern at the centre, who, for the last month, had lived with us. "Have you been in the house since we left this morning?" She hadn't. I stopped and thought: the front door had unlocked with a single turn of the key, unusual since Gambian locks were of the double-turn variety. I moved through the house. In the front room we had a desk, borrowed from the centre, and we kept it pushed against the wall under the stoop window. The window was open, which wasn't unusual. We kept windows open to vent the house; steel bars covered them all so no one could get through. Looking closer at the stoop window, though, the corner of the mosquito screen had been subtly pried away from its wooden frame, showing a hole big enough for a hand to punch through. Two quick calls: "Lisa! Do you have the spare keys? Robel! Do you have the spare keys?" No. They were gone. I was willing to bet they'd been left on the corner of that table. Passport! I tore through everything I owned in pure panic. No passport. No camera. No anything: traveller's cheques, alarm clocks, immunization card, driver's licence. "Lisa, you'd better get over here right now!" I called Robel as well.

They were pros. They'd come in broad daylight. The best possible time, when everyone was at work. It was easy to tell when a house in the Gambia was empty because the gates were generally closed with deadbolts, one on the inside and one on the outside. When someone was at home, they would use the inside bolt to close the door. When the last person left for work, the only way to close the door was to use the outside deadbolt and then lock it closed with a padlock. Any house with its outside bolt closed was empty. The solution to this problem was to have someone at home all the time: the watchman, but we didn't have one because we couldn't afford it.

They'd taken small things that were easy to carry, no attempt to struggle down the street with a full suitcase. Robel and Lisa were missing money, alarm clocks and a wristwatch, among other things, but their passports were still there. The thief had found but left them. They didn't take anything they couldn't justify later: explaining away a fat wallet is one thing, but a piece of ID with someone else's picture amounted to a full confession. Unfortunately, they used my backpack as the loot bag, meaning everything I had in it was gone, including my passport. The thief probably didn't even know it was there. The instant they detected it, they'd ditch it in a bush. Practiced scoundrels, they even locked the door behind them when they left.

Damage assessment complete, it started to sink in. We'd been violated. It's a cliché, but it's true: violated was the only way to describe the feeling. We were victims. We had no power in the world.

My Nikon FM was gone. It still took perfect pictures and was more rugged than any modern camera I'd ever seen, which is why I brought it with me. If any camera could survive Africa, this was the one. It had been in the family since my uncle bought it in the mid-'70s, some 30 years ago. The Nikon FM was the camera that made Nikon *Nikon*, the camera of the Vietnam War. I had an original model. I was so furious all I could do was stare into the empty camera bag, gripping it with white knuckles. Lisa, who must have been watching me from the door, asked if she should take it into her room, out of sight, and it stayed there until she left.

Our goodwill toward our host country evaporated in seconds. Things were thrown, furniture kicked and bad words said. Lisa, our very own goodwill fanatic, desperate to make local friends, was ready to kill any Gambian who ventured too close. "We came with good intentions. Why are they treating us this way?!" Despite the outrage, the realization that I now had a massive administrative problem started to settle in. No passport. No ID at all. I was pondering what exactly that meant in the Gambia while Lisa and I went back to the centre. We were going to contact the authorities and see what they had to say, and honestly, I hoped they'd say, "We'll find them and make them sorry they were ever born, sir."

Guys like Gaston are there to be afraid of. They maintained law and order by scaring the hell out of everyone. Now the law had been broken, and I wondered what Gaston and his colleagues were going to do about it. Sure, they were the instrument of repression, but that worked for me because now I wanted some guy repressed. The question now was: were they competent? Could they deliver the thrashing they advertised? Could they deliver the oppressive police-state-style whipping I felt the guy who stole my stuff deserved?

Sympathy and cynicism at the centre; the Gambians hoping we wouldn't blame the whole country; the other Africans implying we should get used to it. The sincerity of the Gambians overpowered the bitterness of the others, and I started to calm down. I didn't really want to see a police-state beating. I didn't want anyone hurt, I just wanted my stuff back.

Calling the embassy in Senegal was the first step. It's at times like these you forgive your own government for all the taxes you've ever had to pay. The ability to pick up a phone and dial an emergency number, easily found on the Internet, brought forgiveness for all the bad things I'd ever said about Canadian bureaucracy, the senate and the Queen. The government's website supplied an emergency number for "Canadians in distress" who were in West Africa. I rang it up and it routed to the Canadian embassy in Senegal, a lady answered, "*Bonjour*, hello?" She sounded tired. "Canadian embassy. Can I help you?"

"Yes, my name is Robin Matthias, I'm a Canadian living in the Gambia and I've just had my passport stolen."

"Well, do you think you can call back on Monday?"

"Ummm, I've actually had my passport stolen."

"Yes, but today is Friday. Today is a half-day. We are going to the mosque on Friday. Can you be calling us back on Monday?"

"Monday?"

"Yes." There was a long pause. I had no idea what to say.

"Who am I speaking with?"

"Anna Diop."

"Are you a Canadian?"

"No."

"Are there any Canadians I can speak with there?"

"No, today is Friday. We are leaving now."

"This is an emergency!"

"You should be calling us back on Monday. If you want, you can call the British consulate in the meantime."[64]

"Thanks."

"Yes. Call on Monday." She hung up. My tax dollars working for me. The centre had the British consulate and American embassy on speed dial.[65] After the typical triage, an Englishman came on the line. He was a junior bureaucrat, very concerned, very chatty and utterly useless. What marked him as an above-average bureaucrat, however, was his self-awareness: he knew he was of no use to me and stopped pretending like he was as soon as I called him on it. He dispensed with the sympathy and cut

---

64 There being no Canadian embassy in the Gambia, Canadians at that time were instructed to use the British consulate for most things. You could get Canadian government documents there, for example. It seemed the two governments didn't coordinate well, though. People I knew later who used the service said most of the staff had no idea which form was which, and when the correct one was found, it was usually out-of-date. About halfway through my time there, we were told to use the American embassy instead.

65 A wise and handy precaution for a human rights organization.

to the chase. "I'm going to have to get a police report?"

"'Fraid so. Your government won't issue you a new passport without one."

"There's nothing else to be done?"

"'Fraid not. Best of luck." He rang off. I turned to Muhammad, who'd found the number for me and repeated what I'd been told. Hand to his face, Muhammad studied the floor, and after a long moment looked me in the eye and said with resolve, "I'll take you."

We'd been getting along better. I felt he'd taken my measure and found me up to size. He'd moved into the house beside ours, actually coming over a couple of times while we kicked around on the veranda, never drinking or smoking but hanging around and listening, with his usual thoughtful look. But with each visit he warmed a little more, the thoughtful look giving way to a bemused expression that eventually gave way to participation. He'd actually joke around, sometimes even taking a place on the veranda.[66]

"So, are you frightened, *toubob*?" mused Muhammad with a wry smile a few minutes after we'd left the centre in search of a police report.

"Hell, yes."

"Good. You will look like a local in front of the police then." We both laughed. I really was afraid. Would I get a police report? Would it be

---

66 I wouldn't say he told us his story, but he said enough to fit some of the puzzle pieces of his personality together. Muhammad was a Sierra Leonean and a member of an influential family. When Sierra Leone fell apart, he left, fast — really fast. The specifics were clouded in euphemism, but he was obliged to leave in such a hurry that he did so in an open fishing canoe. The euphemisms hinted at betrayal, but he never provided the details. People could be deadly instruments; he'd learned the hard way. He'd pointed me toward the house months before because he wanted to know whom his neighbours were. You could never be too careful: one minute you're a man-about-town, the next you're covered in fish bait. It might sound paranoid, but a week on the ocean in an open canoe overloaded with refugees was an experience one takes steps to avoid repeating.

acceptable to the Canadian government? How would I get it to the Canadian government? Not a trivial issue considering I'd no passport and the closest consulate was in another country. These things were on my mind and Muhammad knew it. To make conversation, he encouraged me to replay the call to the embassy in detail, embellished with impersonations and commentary. Soon, we were both laughing like idiots at the silliness of the whole situation: two young guys ditching work, driving too fast on a sunny afternoon. Doing what? Looking for the cops.

If the cops weren't running checkpoints, you had to go look for them. There was no 911 or even a general service number; if you needed a cop, you needed his cell. Not having one, we spent an hour riding around to various police "stations" to figure out which one was right for me. After a few false starts, we were directed to the station out in Abuko, a region between Brusubi and the airport, which apparently had jurisdiction over Brusubi. "I am thinking this brush with the local government will cost you about 90 dalasi," Muhammad said as we closed in on Abuko.

"Is that how much it costs?"

"Yes, you could say that," a hint of mischief in his voice. "If we negotiate well." I really didn't know what that meant and I didn't have time to get clarification. We'd arrived.

We pulled over into a dusty pitch around the back of what looked like a school. Slamming the door with resignation, I surveyed the scene. The only vegetation here was a solitary mango tree growing in front of a small concrete house, separate from the school. Stained up to the windows with mud, it looked like it had risen out of the ground. About the size of a garage in Canada, it had no door covering the entrance. We climbed the steps to the landing and said hello to a man quietly smoking a cigarette and dangling his feet off its other end.

I followed my friend's entry, but I could never follow his entrance. It was Friday, the holy day, and he was wearing his best snow-white gown and pillbox hat. Hands clasped behind him, chin thrust forward, he ambled up to the counter and stood waiting with gravitas.   "We   are   here   to report a house-breaking."

The tall, lanky guy behind the wooden counter looked stunned. He gaped and Muhammad repeated himself. After blinking a couple of times, the guy snapped to attention, grabbed a big tattered ledger, turned it around for us and patted himself down for a pen. No pen. I knew he didn't have one because he was wearing a sweaty wife-beater undershirt and dirty trousers rolled up to his knees. He called out toward the back door in a foreign language. Nothing happened. He sounded off again, louder, edgier, more theatrical, implying something like, "Look, I need a little help serving and protecting here, people!"

Finally, a young guy sauntered in from out back. He was young with slight features and a thin mustache, clean-cut, with a football jersey and clean blue jeans. Seeing us, he immediately leaped into action. He was eager to please, and his first act of "excellent customer service" was to grab the guy helping us. They scuffled, but Football Jersey had the edge, and despite protests, dragged Wife-Beater by the arm, throwing him roughly into a room behind the counter. The room was fronted by a green steel door, and holding it shut with his leg, Football Jersey deftly threaded a short chain through the handle, locking it quickly with a padlock. Adjusting his ball cap, he turned to us with a big, nervous smile that hoped, emphatically, we hadn't seen what we'd just seen.

"We let him out for Friday afternoon. For prayer. He shouldn't be telling people he is a police constable."

He flipped fast through the registry. I swear he was blushing. I didn't ask what the other guy had been locked up for. It seemed rude since he could still hear us through the tiny square hole in the door; his helpful eyes, saddened now, peered out at me. I didn't ask the cop what he'd been doing behind the station either.

123

"Please register here." he said with urgency, pointing to a blank line in the ledger. He handed a pen to Muhammad, who stepped aside without taking his hands from behind his back. It was a formal declaration: "I've done my bit. I'm no longer involved." I took the pen.

First name, last name, phone number, reason for visit. I filled in the hand-ruled ledger. Another man had come in from out back; he was wearing a uniform, like the typical police one: button-down shirt, trousers and beret, but all in shades of brown instead of the usual blue. It would take some time, but the Brown Shirts, as I called them, would become my most feared uniformed officer.[67] Brown meant immigration. I didn't know that at the time and was just happy to see someone wearing a uniform. I gave him my best "I wanna be your friend" smile. "*Na'nga def?*" He looked me over for a second, then turned away, bored. I got back to the ledger.

Football Jersey pulled a form out from behind the counter. "Fill this out please," he still smiled and still seemed nervous. I puffed up with hope. Filling out forms is the beginning of something: action about to be taken. But there was no sense of comfort when I looked at the form in front of me. Clearly, it had been hand typed on a lined legal pad, but it was hard to know for sure, since I'd been given a photocopy of the original. Would the Canadian government accept this? When I was a teaching assistant, I wouldn't have accepted anything like it from one of my students. Seriously.

It was good to write it all down, though. Taking action, any action, was the only antidote for problems in this country. Doing something, anything, right or wrong, would save me more than once in the Gambia, as well as the other African countries I would subsequently visit. I learned at least one thing in my three years: only movement matters. Right and wrong are academic constructs, the province of historians. If you don't know what

---

67 The secret cops were the most feared police, period, but it would be some months before I made their acquaintance.

to do, change the options. It's like driving down the street: if you make enough turns, you'll get to where you're going, even if you pass through some bad neighbourhoods. Every intersection you pass, even if it's in the wrong direction, gives you new options. If you pull over and fret, you won't get there, guaranteed.

Finished, I handed it back to Football Jersey and took my carbon copy. Again, I wasn't sure if the government would accept it. The carbon paper was worn and I could barely read my version. "I need a police report. Is this it?" I asked, holding up my carbon.

"Report?"

"Yeah, I need a report. My government demands it. Without one, I can't get my passport back."

"Police report? Yes, it is possible."

"So how do I get one?"

"Please, I need to be speaking to the station chief. Please, feel free!" He gestured like a good host toward the front stoop, still with a nervous smile.

I happily went outside, chain-smoking for the next half-hour and kicking the dirt while apologizing to Muhammad for the inconvenience, which he assured me, was no trouble. I went out back to see what everyone was doing there. Making tea. I went back inside and slouched down on the station couch, formerly the backseat of a pickup truck. I was outside again smoking when Football Jersey appeared in the doorway, motioning me inside. Action, finally. I jumped for the door but noticed Muhammad's thoughtful pace, hands behind him, eyes studying his feet, and I checked my pace as we filed through the door and then through a curtain off to the left of the front desk.

On the other side, there was a small room filled with two ancient filing cabinets, a desk and a few chairs. Every horizontal surface was covered with folders and papers. A woman in a police uniform reclined on a couch.

She was obese, and propping herself up on pillows looked like an effort, but a necessary one since she was having her hair done. Everyone seemed to be in the office: Muhammad, Football Jersey, Brown Shirt, a couple of other guys whom I surmised were plainclothes cops like Jersey, a couple of kids and the hairstylist.

We were all gathered around the couch. Nobody spoke and the silence felt threatening, like standing in front of a crowd you're about to address and noticing they all have their arms crossed. Muhammad was behind me, and with a few small steps had pushed me, if not into the middle of the room, close enough to it. My academic mind kicked in: how enlightened of the Gambia to have women as peace officers, and not just as secretaries, but as station chiefs. How did that work in a Muslim country? Maybe there was more to Islam than burkas and obedience. How many other Muslim countries had a similar arrangement? I suddenly felt a heightened respect for my Gambian friends: these guys were living the equality dream. Did she make the same wages as a male station chief? Was there a glass ceiling here? If so, how high? It was really interesting to think about African—

"*Uhn*! Report? Not possible. Six month minimum," she wheezed.

"Well, I need a report for my government. I can't get my passport back without one."

"No. It is not being possible." Not the slightest doubt in her voice.

"But there must be a way. How do people who have their passports stolen get new ones?"

"Passports are not stolen here. People are careful. You, my friend, are not careful. My friend, you are careless." I ignored the jab. Growing panic made me focus on the issue.

"I'm supposed to leave Gambia in a couple of months. I can't go home without a passport."

"*Uhn*! So ready to leave the Gambia? You are not liking it here?"

"No, no, not at all! I would just like to go home eventually. I'm not from here."

"I can see this!" I didn't know what to say. I hadn't considered what to do beyond simply asking for the report. There was no plan B. I felt helpless standing in front of her, as helpless as I had been staring into my empty camera bag.

"OK, OK." My voice was almost quivering. "If there is anything you can do for me, I would desperately appreciate it. *Anything* at all." She sighed and waved away the hairstylist at the same time. She looked more comfortable now, like she was going to take a nap. "I would *really* appreciate it."

"There is nothing going to be done. It is taking six months for a police report in the Gambia." Her tone was dismissive but calmer. Everyone, including Muhammad and Football Jersey, were examining their feet. The cops — even Brown Shirt — looked uncomfortable. I took in a deep breath and continued.

"I would *really appreciate* it if you could help me. I'd be *very, very* grateful." The chief grunted under her breath and made herself a bit more comfortable. The hairstylist was twisting her face away to hide her expression. I couldn't tell if she thought I was unfortunate or funny. "Is there *anything* I can do to help the process along?" *Anything* at all? *Anything?*" I was losing my nerve.

"There are procedures. We are having procedures here." She said clearly annoyed. She wanted a nap, not to play pussyfoot with a silly white man.

"I would *really* appreciate any help. I'm willing to" — I almost said *pay* — "play any part necessary to get this done. I don't know what else I can say." I'd passed emphatic and was closing in on pathetic. Maybe that would work?

"Six months."

What more could I say? She hadn't ordered me away. I could feel myself blushing and only wanted to get the hell out of there, passport be damned. I turned to Muhammad, shrugged my shoulders and turned to the door. "Thank you for your time," I said politely. As I turned to go, the look on her face was quizzical. *That's it?* she seemed to be thinking.

"Ibrahim!" she snapped, addressing Football Jersey. "There is a fine? He can pay? Not so?"

"Yes, yes!" Ibrahim answered. His enthusiasm was like a light going on, snuffing out the awkwardness. People started to move. Conversation resumed. After some discussions in Wolof, it was "remembered" the fine was 60 dalasis. Just pay the lady on the couch, no receipt, no hard feelings. She counted it without getting up, scolding me in a relaxed motherly way about rules and procedures in the Gambia, how it was not nice my passport was stolen, but there were still rules to follow. I just wanted my report. I heaped compliments on her, her station, and her crack law-enforcement officers and hairstylist.

Ibrahim brought a typed form that the Chief signed and handed to me. *REQUEST FOR POLICE REPORT* was the title. I wasn't happy. Neither was Muhammad. It was explained, almost apologetically, that *official* reports were actually done in Banjul, at the department of records. All they could do was put in the request. But now the shoe was on the other foot — we were customers. We'd paid 60 dalasis and we wanted 60 dalasis' worth of service. Without saying as much, the sheepish attitude of the police implied they agreed.

"For 60 dalasis[68] we should be getting more service," declared Muhammad.

"Of course, of course!" they chorused.

"Couldn't one of the detectives come with us? Someone who knew

---

68 At that time about $2 U.S.

128

people in records? Someone who could help move things along," asked Muhammad.

"Of course, of course!" Their whole tone had changed. They seemed afraid to lose our business. Maybe they were afraid we'd rat them out to their superiors. Either way, it was great to see them trying to serve, if not protect.

It was deemed appropriate for the detectives to view the scene of the crime, and as most police stations had no police cars (or radios, or handcuffs, or sticks or guns), we'd have to drive them. With much "sorry, sorry" and "no problem, no problem" we managed to get Ibrahim and his partner — another clean-cut-looking guy in his late 20s — into our car and on the road.

Back at the house, they wandered around a while, hands to their faces in a thoughtful way, nodding vigorously at our take on the crime scene.

"They must have pushed the mosquito screen open and then used the key," I mentioned.

"Yes, yes, it must have been." More nodding.

"They must've known when we were gone. Probably one of the construction guys working on the houses near Brufut. They see us leave for work every morning."

"Yes, yes, it must have been." So it went.

Sightseeing over, Ibrahim explained delicately we'd never see our things again. I thought of my camera and was angry. We were all angry and Ibrahim could tell. He did his best to calm us down with the only tool he had: sincerity. He seemed truly embarrassed that travellers would be treated this way by his countrymen. He insisted we leave the house and get to the records office as soon as possible. I didn't want to go to the records office, I wanted answers: "What are you going to do about this?" I kept demanding.

"Come, let's go," he kept repeating.

Muhammad and I left with the two cops for the records office. On arrival, Ibrahim leaped into action, jumping out the door before we stopped and quickly running inside. His partner led us to a spot at the end of a ridiculously long line of tired-looking Gambians and made signs to wait. There was close to 100 people in front of us and it was hot. We didn't wait long, though. Ibrahim came out and dragged us past the line and into the building to an area outside an office, in a much shorter line, only four or five people. He was happy working the system to help us.

It was a large building, single story, a sprawling ranch-style house. The corridors, as wide as a hospital's, were beige, quiet and cool. We stood outside the closed wooden door and waited while Ibrahim charged off again. It was a short line, but there was no energy. The whole place looked empty — no lights, no sounds. A fat fly took its time weaving through the floating dust caught in the light of the window, its buzz filling the air. Likely everyone was at mosque. Now I knew where Ibrahim had gone. He was trying to make me happy, to show me that Gambians still cared, but all I felt was guilt for having jumped the queue in the face of 100 tired locals baking out in the sun. Waiting in front of that door was the first chance I'd had to reflect on what had happened. I'd been pretty diplomatic, but the bile was rising up inside me. I'd never see my camera again? The guys who did this would never get caught? I'd have to pay more money to get the justice I *deserved?* Bullshit.

Such was my inner dialogue as I leaned against the wall, arms crossed, staring at that fat, lazy fly. And in fact, with my Western hubris fuelled by outrage, I spent the next year doing exactly what my mind was threatening. I couldn't pass a camera shop for months without scrutinizing its wares, but it was useless. My camera had been sold in the back of a bar somewhere to a tourist too drunk to care where it came from, or to a merchant in a stall somewhere in the market's baffling maze where vendors only asked "how much?" My camera dissolved like a sugar cube dropped into the teacup of African poverty. The first commandment of my Western liberal education: "You can get *anything* you want if you work hard enough,"

130

fuelled my determination to get the sugar out of the tea, creating an absolute conviction I could recover my goods if I just put the work in. I spent whole weekends wandering through shops and stalls, even tailing people carrying a camera that looked like mine. I put so much time and energy into this that years later, back in Canada, I still looked at people carrying cameras, just out of habit. It became something I did, a defining characteristic, like wearing a flat cap or preferring a bicycle to a car.

I've probably never tried so hard to do any one thing in my life. But it didn't matter. I never found my camera, despite skulking around the markets. Africa won. It usually did. Frustration turns good people bad. I'd seen its effects on Idrissa, and in time, it affected my mind like a fever, turning me into a nut who followed people down the street just because they happened to be holding cameras.

Ibrahim knew all about frustration, just as any Gambian knew more about malaria than the doctor who'd prescribed my antimalarial meds back in Washington. He wasn't stupid. Back at the house, he'd humoured me. White people expected an investigation, so he'd gone through the motions. He knew only luck could recover the camera now and every second spent hanging around "investigating" was just more time wasted, more frustration building. Ibrahim knew about white boys. The useless investigation would yield nothing but more frustration when it inevitably failed. In hindsight, he was just doing his best to get me to move on: frustration was the disease and greasing the wheels with promises, his badge or money was the cure. He was bribing and intimidating with the best of intentions: to show a foreigner that justice — after a fashion — could be had in his country. Not a "you're gonna get what's coming to you" style of justice, but a "no harm, no foul" kind of justice. If I got my police report and got my passport back, wouldn't that erase the crime? Wouldn't that lower my blood pressure? True, I wouldn't get the camera back, but there are other cameras. Move on.

Finally, our turn came. The door opened and we were allowed in. It was a big room and an older man wearing a colonial suit was inside at a small desk, barely big enough to fit the old, black, manual typewriter sitting on it. This was where reports came to be made official. First, we needed official stationary —happily there was some left — but Ibrahim, always thinking ahead, had reappeared long ago with extra sheets, just in case. I couldn't believe we'd come this far for a typewriter and stationary, but at this point, I really didn't care. The old man delicately fed the paper into the typewriter, sat back, contemplated the machine for a moment, then started pounding out the report. He was serious. He was careful. He read each sentence thoroughly before typing it. There was no whiteout. In a movie, we'd have been expected to lose patience with this pedantic gentleman plodding away on his typewriter while the hero needs to catch a plane. But after nearly four hours of running around, I didn't mind at all. His slow doggedness, his sense of perfection, was reassuring. The old guy finished, pulled the paper out, gave it a last look and handed it to Ibrahim. Finished, finally. Unfortunately, Ibrahim explained the report needed to be signed by some bigwig out in Birkama, but that would have to wait for Monday. They'd be closed by now.

Muhammad drove back to our place and we arranged for a taxi to take the detectives back to Abuko. When the car came, I asked how much, gave each cop a big handshake and 50 D,[69] more than they needed for the cab. They hadn't asked for money once. I didn't know if they'd get a cut of the 60 D I'd left behind in Abuko, but either way, Ibrahim deserved something; he'd really tried. Dismay filled his face when I shoved the money into his hand; his mouth gaped, looking for something to say. I didn't want to hear it, though. He'd earned it.

"It's not a bribe. Times are hard and you were kind to me. We good people have to look out for each other."

After a moment's thought, he accepted it with a smile. I paid his

---

69 Dalasi.

partner because I didn't want him to muscle into Ibrahim's action. Watching them drive off happy, I felt like I'd done a good thing. I went inside and got drunk with my friends.

Monday rolled around and Muhammad and I were off to Birkama, which is a good 30-minute drive away from the centre. I mused to myself how long it would take to get a police report if you didn't walk it through like we were doing. You made the request in Abuko, got it filled in Banjul (20 minutes away) and then got it signed in Birkama, 30 minutes in the opposite direction, and the cops didn't even have patrol cars, much less interoffice mail vans. Six months? Maybe the station chief was telling the truth. I felt relieved that things were almost over for me. It was another good day for a drive and the mood was light; Muhammad was filled with all kinds of sarcastic advice concerning my performance during the bribe. I ribbed him about his estimate of the amount. He'd guessed 90 dalasi, but I'd gotten off cheap for only 60.[70] He just smiled and said, "We're not finished yet."

Birkama sat along one of the best stretches of blacktop in the land: the Coastal Road, one of the two paved highways in the country. We blasted along at about 60 clicks, rocket speed in a country where bad roads and green drivers kept the speed down to the 20s.[71] In his 30s, Muhammad had only gotten a driver's licence a few years before, and he was thoroughly enjoying himself.[72]

Entering Birkama, we shot into a cloud of dust floating across the

---

70 I didn't include the 100 I'd given the two detectives. That was my choice.

71 A popular joke concerning the quality of the roads was that you could tell if a driver was drunk in North America because they weaved across the road, and you could tell if a driver was drunk in Africa because they didn't.

72 It was normal in most of the countries I visited for people to get licences in their late-20s. It took means to afford a car, so most families in the tiny middle class didn't have a vehicle for a teenaged Mamadou or Bintou to practise in. Oftentimes, a professional like Muhammad didn't have access to one until he was working and established.

highway kicked up by bicycles, vendors and wheelbarrows working by the side of the road. In Abuko they'd given me a name — no rank, no position — of the guy whose signature I required. In North America we say things like "you need to get this signed by the registrar." In the Gambia they say, "You need to get this signed by Dembo."

"Who's Dembo?"

"You need him to sign the report."

"Yeah, but who is he? What's his rank? His function?"

"He does the signing, he signs the reports. You need him to be signing your report."

Right. Got it.

The large police compound was off the main road and easy to find. Like the records department, it looked like a big ranch house with sheet-metal roofing. The front courtyard was dusty and expansive. A platoon of cops stamped dust in the air as they drilled in two ragged, uncoordinated lines. They didn't look happy about stamping around at eight in the morning either. The paramilitary was there too. They wore dark-blue military fatigues. The blue distinguished them from the army, and the fatigues distinguished them from the regular cops who wore light-blue shirts and trousers. The AK-47s they carried also distinguished them from the regular police. You'd often see these guys hanging around in the markets, just hanging around in groups of a half-dozen or more, lazing on street corners or wherever, guns casually laid across their laps. Some Brown Shirts milled around too.

We parked and started making inquiries. "Where can we find Dembo?" People looked us over, then jabbed a finger in a direction. After enough finger-pointing we found the office. I expected my companion to recreate his Friday afternoon entrance, but instead he rapped politely on the frame of the open door. Although he was dressed in Western-style business casual, his impeccably ironed and creased clothes created a sense of authority. I followed sheepishly behind, dressed in jeans and a T-shirt, feeling like a high-school kid following Dad in to see the principal. Behind the single small desk pushed into one corner of the very large room, we could see a young man in his 30s.

"May we enter?" asked Muhammad conversationally, already across the threshold. The man behind the desk stood up to greet us, uniform impeccable, moustache trimmed. Stiffly, he put his hand out, his face fighting between "please come in" and "what's this all about?" Dembo clearly didn't like surprises. Standing across the desk (there were no chairs), I blurted out, "We need this police report signed." I handed it to Dembo and noticed a strained look on Muhammad's face.

Dembo was pensive. Stacks of overstuffed folders covered his desk. One lay open in front of him. He glanced over the report. "I am not aware of this."

"Aware of what? We were told by the police in Abuko to get your signature on this to make it official." I was being pushy and direct and assertive. Reflecting on Friday's performance, I'd decided that firm was the way to go. Seize the initiative and hang onto it.

Dembo wasn't impressed. He sat down calmly, studying my report as he did. Pondering it so closely, Muhammad and I — mere couriers — ceased to exist. Muhammad had apparently decided to "let me run with it" and stood silent, looking concerned.

"No," Dembo mused, as if to himself. "No. No one has told me of this." My official report landed on a pile of official-looking folders and the officer picked up his pen. "Signed. It needs to be signed, but other things need signing first."

At ease behind his desk, forearms on the table, pen in hand, he looked dangerous, as if he could deal serious blows with that pen: serious, precise blows, like putting us behind bars with one signature. Nevertheless, I persisted.

"I need this signed now. I've got to get back to work." Dembo's jaw clenched and he grabbed the arms of his chair, ready to jump up.

"If I might ask, where is your family from, Dembo?" blurted Muhammad. Dembo stopped and reclined back into his chair. Soon, Dembo and Muhammad were chatting like old friends about Dembo's family, how long he'd been a cop, how much he enjoyed it, his mother's health and the price of rice in Birkama. They chatted for a good half-hour about everything except the report, while I stood there being politely ignored. Often, I'd leave them and wander out into the courtyard to smoke a cigarette, which they didn't seem to notice. Muhammad came out during my third smoke. Apparently, Dembo needed to hear from the detectives to ensure the official report was, in fact, official. This was usually done by correspondence, but Muhammad felt Dembo would be willing to simply call the detectives if we'd pay for the call. I would also need to go inside and "endear" myself. "Maybe you should offer to buy him some tea?"

Tea? Right. I pulled 40 dalasis out of my pocket and marched into the office while Muhammad waited outside. Dembo was sitting behind his desk, working away at something. He looked up with an open, tranquil look when I greeted him. "I understand we only need to make a phone call in order to get this done. That's great!"

"Yes, it can be done. The normal procedure, however, is to receive correspondence from the constables who filed the report."

"Well, I would appreciate any help you can give me. I know you work hard — maybe I can buy you some tea?" I stuck out my arm. He stared at the fold of money jutting out of my hand. Timidly, he pulled the paper from between my fingers and examined it with uncertainly, as if it was covered with strange hieroglyphs. Unfortunately, I'd mistaken Muhammad's suggestion as a euphemism for "bribe him." Over the weekend, I'd discovered from friends that offering to "buy tea" was a euphemism for "bribe." If you found yourself in a mess and no convenient fine presented itself, you could always offer to buy tea.

Well, dear reader, there's a lot of talk about corruption in Africa, but I can assure you there's at least one honest cop in the Gambia. His name is Dembo and he's the guy who signs things in Birkama. The look on his face was wide-eyed disbelief. I'd made a huge mistake. Tea for five people cost five dalasi. Handing over 40 could only mean I figured him for a crook. He looked confused, like he was replaying the interview in his head, trying to figure out when he'd asked for money. My face got warm and I started studying my feet and smiling sheepishly. Fortunately, he was as stunned as I was. We both stared at the other.

"I mean, you can buy tea for everyone here. You're doing so much to help me that I think it's really the least I can do. Honestly!" After a second of silence, I croaked out, "I hope I haven't offended you at all." He was still staring, but his gaping mouth started to tighten up. Happily, it tightened up into a smile. I must've been sweating sincerity; after I jabbered on for a few more minutes like an idiot, Dembo looked almost gleeful. Soon, we were chatting happily, the silliness of the situation appealing to Dembo's sense of humour. Stupid-white-guy to the rescue again.

Dembo understood why I did what I did; he understood how things worked, about bribes and corrupt station chiefs and how foreigners could be treated by the law. But Dembo was young and idealistic; he could change things, he was sure of it. He passionately discussed his dreams to rise in the ranks and stamp out all the corruption he could. The Gambia would be a law-abiding place — a *fair* place — for everyone if he got his way. He reminded me of the young idealists I'd known in Washington. In the end, he made the call, signed the report and walked us out. He took the money. He didn't want to take the money, but I insisted. It didn't really feel like a bribe, just a token of honest appreciation, and that's how it was accepted. We wished each other good luck and he waved as we left the station.

Finally, I had an official police report to send back to Canada. Back at the centre, I called the embassy in Senegal and reached the same customer service superstar I'd dealt with on Friday. With all the necessary details, I downloaded the appropriate forms, got the photos done and couriered the package off to Dakar. Weeks later, hearing nothing, I called the woman at the embassy back. Anna Diop didn't remember me at all. Even mentioning my issue — Canadian citizen trapped in Africa without a passport — didn't ring any bells.[73] Finally, after much pleading, she found my file and got back on the phone. Yes, they had received my documentation. I already knew they had via the courier (DHL) and that they'd received it weeks ago. What was the status? She couldn't possibly comment on that. Could I speak with someone who could? No. I called back a couple of weeks later and we repeated the conversation, almost verbatim.

Eventually, I received an email from Anna. My application had been considered and denied: the passport photos I'd submitted were too big. The Canadian government had changed the standard size of passport photos recently, but that information hadn't percolated into the Gambia yet. The good news was that the rest of the application was OK. It was just the photos, a couple of millimetres too big. I called and asked if Anna could possibly cut the photos with scissors. It was not possible.

After much calling and emailing, I managed to get some people back in Canada to advocate for me and a temporary passport was issued. Valid for only six months, it was long enough to get back to Canada to get a real one. The embassy in Dakar sent it with a stranger, some Canadian expat who made the trip between Banjul and Dakar regularly. He wasn't an employee of the embassy or a courier, just some guy. I waited for him on the appointed day by the side of the road in the middle of nowhere.

With the temporary passport, I returned to Canada for a couple of weeks to enjoy Christmas, nearly a year after the robbery. While there, I went

---

73 I guess they get a lot of those?

to Passport Canada to get a proper passport issued. I shuddered when the guy at the passport wicket, going over my application, pulled out a ruler and measured my pictures. Once again, too damn big. Without a word, he picked up a pair of scissors and cut a strip off one side. I got my passport in three days.

A Spot of Culture, Part I: Do You Know Where You Are?

Five months after arrival

It's important to know where you are. Every place has a different scene, a different set of assumptions. When I lived in Washington, Sunday was always "museum day." My best friend and I would troop down to the Smithsonian and take in the latest exhibit or lecture. The museums tired us out, all that standing and learning without any adrenaline to lighten the load,[74] so inevitably we'd end up outside for a breath of air, sitting under a tree on the National Mall with the Washington monument far off to the right and Congress far off to left. Stretched out on a park bench, treating it as our own private couch, we'd get comfortable and watch the show.

Friday night in the Gambia was always "get pissed night." Of course, this was no big change from every other night, except on Fridays we would go down to the Senegambian strip and sample the nightlife. This development wasn't immediate, but occurred after we'd made some new friends.

It was inevitable we'd eventually part ways with Ousman and Mustafa. We'd

---

74 I love museums, but I've always felt that walking through one was kind of like reading standing up.

started to make new friends among the other interns, people we had things in common with. More and more, we'd spend Friday night up in Senegambia with interns from various organizations, and we'd be too hung over to step out with the boys when they appeared on Saturday morning. We tried to keep things going by inviting our fellow interns along on our Saturday outings. Unfortunately, that was the nail in the coffin. Fresh eyes noticed things we hadn't, and one day one of them turned to me and said quietly, "I think you're being *bumpsted*."[75] Her comment was prompted by shoes.

Ramadan was winding down and the guys invited us to come to mosque for the Eid al-Fitr.[76] We eagerly accepted. Naturally, we'd need proper clothes and they took us through the maze of Serekunda market into a room in an old warehouse where a tailor set us up with decent stuff. We were excited; the boys were happy but strangely subdued. When I asked, it was because they didn't have any new clothes for the big day and so would have to wear old *boubous*, which was considered gauche. Without a second's thought, Robel and I whipped out our wallets and asked how much. They were thrilled. So were we. The day came and went and another memory made: praying in the huge open-air mosque with thousands of people, eating with families in the village. It wasn't until we returned to the compound that my friend — who'd only met Ous and Mustapha a couple of times — turned to me and said she thought we were being ripped off.

---

75 *Bumpsted* meant getting ripped off. This was the primary trade of certain young men called *bumpsters*. See Chapter 3.

76 Ramadan is a Muslim religious observance that involves abstaining from food, drink, smoking and sex during daylight hours. About a month long (the official start and end are determined by the phases of the moon, the crescent moon being one of Islam's most important symbols), the fasting is supposed to remind the practitioner of the unimportance of the physical and refocus them on the spiritual. Eid al-Fitr is the celebration that occurs on the last day of Ramadan. People start the day by going to mosque and then spend the day feasting, visiting and helping others in the community less fortunate than themselves.

She thought so because Ousman and Mustafa had shown up wearing the same old Gambian outfits they usually did when they didn't feel like wearing Western clothes. But they were sporting brand-new Nikes. I'd completely forgotten about giving them money for new outfits. True, shoes were part of their attire, but that's not how they pitched it. It was the outfit that mattered, the robes, the *boubous*. When we stopped and thought about it, there had been all kinds of discrepancies like that over the course of our relationship: money given for one reason or another without seeing much result.

After a discussion, a confrontation and some active avoidance,[77] Ousman and Mustafa stopped calling and I never saw Mustafa again. I actually did see Ous one last time, about a year later. We bumped into each other near Senegambia late one night. It was a very frank and honest meeting: two old friends meeting in the street for a quick catch-up. He was going on about a crazy American guy he'd befriended, and the amount of money he and Mustafa had managed to lift from him. The stories were funny and I found myself giggling, and we had a good long laugh at this guy's expense. It was my best exchange with Ousman: no Bob Marley quotes, no "nice to be nice," just an honest exchange of news. I felt there was a mutual respect. I'd been there long enough to respect his grifting of loud-mouthed tourists, and he respected that we'd caught him out, that we weren't total fools, at one point saying his new target "wasn't as smart as Robel and I were." After a good chuckle, we shook hands, parted ways, and that's the last I've ever heard of Ousman.

---

77 We started pretending we weren't home when they'd come knocking. Once, coming in from a long night, we heard loud wailing in our front yard. Carefully opening the gate, we saw Ous lying in the dirt, spread-eagle, drunk beyond belief, howling to the stars — "You fucked my heart! You fucked my heart!" — while hammering his chest with an empty bottle. God only knows how he got in there, but we got him standing, sobered him up with some Nescafé and sent him on his way.

That last exchange with Ous was bittersweet. In that twenty minutes I saw a great sense of humour and a keen sense of irony. I still wonder what might have been if he wasn't playing the part of a "Nobel Child of Mother Africa,"[78] and I wasn't playing "The Good Canadian." But our new intern friends were good compensation; they were from all over the world and decidedly interesting people.

Friday being a Muslim Holy Day, we'd get off work at 1 p.m. Not being Muslims, Robel and I used the holy time to get a leg up on the evening. We'd start drinking somewhere in Senegambia around two in the afternoon, and by about six or so, we'd head off to Sultan.

Sultan was the name of a local Lebanese-run restaurant featuring a huge front patio. We'd meet there every Friday for drinks and dinner, mostly drinks. We'd stretch out at one of the long tables under the canopy and act like the place was ours. In the end, it pretty much was. The waiters knew us by name; we had "our usual table" and they'd keep it clear for us without a reservation, even turning people away to do so, no small sacrifice considering Sultan was popular and we used up a lot of table space. Robel, Lisa and I represented Brusubi, and the table was filled out by our friends from Kairaba Avenue. Rosaleen and Rachel were Canadian interns in their mid-20s working at another NGO concerned with human rights. Rosaleen, or "Roz," was interning on the legal side of their NGO while Rachel was, like Robel and myself, an IT intern. We met them via Samantha; they were renting rooms in her house up on Kairaba Avenue. The last of the Kairaba crew was Abai. Despite being in his late-20s, Abai was already a legal officer at the same NGO Roz and Rachel worked at and held a prestigious degree in human rights law from South Africa. He was an Ethiopian and had fought

---

78 At more than one point he referred to Gambians as "Nobel Children of Mother Africa."

his way through a broken home and a psychotically abusive father to get to where he was now. You couldn't meet a better guy.

And so this was the crew, the core of my social life in-country for the next years to come. Our Algonquin Round Table, albeit rectangular and made of molded white plastic, sat at the end of the patio. Rachel dubbed these weekly gatherings "Sultan Night," and so it came to pass the six of us would meet there on Friday nights, rain or shine. Many guests — interns, occasional colleagues — came and went, but the six of us were the core.

I don't know who brought it up first, but at one of these gatherings someone suggested we get a little culture, get out of the Kombos region.[79] "Hey, let's go upcountry. Let's go see Kunta Kinteh," someone said between cigarette puffs and over the umpteenth drink. Upcountry. None of us had been.

In my mind, it was like going up the river in *Apocalypse Now*. Down here in the Kombos, we'd mastered life, after a fashion. We were comfortable. Upcountry was the unknown. The idea of going there was intimidating yet enthralling. Travelling is about doing stupid things, right? Want to have an adventure? Then do something stupid. And wasn't adventure the name of the game? Imagine the stories we could tell! We all sat silently for a moment, eyes on the table or in the sky, lost in thought as we dragged on our cigarettes.

The decision didn't come all at once. Being creatures of habit, we'd usually leave Sultan around 11, on the ebb of the dinner hour, and then move to Sanity. The latter was a garden of delights, far enough from the sea to be grassy instead of sandy, but close enough that the roar of the surf could drown conversation when it was worked up. Tall palm trees waved over the place; thick green hedges encircled it and kept the rest of Senegambia out. If you didn't know about it, you'd likely never find it. It was very rare to see

---

79　The Kombos is essentially the coastal touristy area that Senegambia is part of.

strangers there, strangers being tourists. The clientele was almost all expatriates, Peace Corps, NGO staff, wealthy locals or any other 20-something with money. It was a 20-something kind of place. No mouthy tourists complaining about the bedding in their hotel, just young people trying to relax and attract one other. And you felt attractive hanging out at an open-air bar in the middle of a garden, feeling the cool breeze, listening to music, invariably the latest electronica from Europe.

Jamal, the owner and occasional bartender, dressed like a million dollars and had a smile to match. He divided his time between Gambia and Europe, and so had all the latest music, clothes, cellphones, and so on. He knew how to take care of his guests, always the consummate bartender and host. Under his care, you felt pampered in the Western style. Westerners are very schizophrenic about service. Or at least we expect service to be schizophrenic. On one hand, it's almost a right to be waited on quickly and efficiently: movers and shakers don't stand behind anyone. On the other hand, we expect the person serving us to accept his place right behind us, passing the phone or a glass of wine when we demand it: and we expect him to be *happy* about it. Service with a smile in the land of empowerment and self-determination! A contradiction that could only be accommodated by a society that's vilified politics while preaching the sanctity of democracy to the rest of the world. When it comes to irony, Westerners are tone deaf. It's essential to our standard of living.[80]

The Gambia, being a more direct and less "sophisticated" society, simply referred to people who served others as "servants." That hurt Western ears and Jamal knew it. Instead, he provided "customer service" and the *toubobs* responded well to its homey ring. It was easy to relax there

---

80 I think the fact that you can build an entire subculture around pointing out irony illustrates the degree to which contradiction is a factor of Western life. I am, of course, speaking of the ubiquitous "hipsters."

in the moonlight, watching the tanned young Peace Corps ladies in their tank tops and sarongs, cigarettes drooping out of their mouths, lounging at the bar, sipping mojitos. Their whole attitude said, "Yeah. I've seen the 'Nam."

There was always something to do at Sanity: talking with friends, flirting with the new crop of interns, playing pool in the house off the garden, lazing in one of the shadowy hammocks strung discreetly around the yard, perhaps with a new friend. These were the usual delights. For me, another was the ability to escape the group dynamic. Living, working, drinking and interacting with the same people almost all the time can drive a person a little nuts. I loved my friends, but I've always found building one-on-one relationships more interesting than group affairs. Drinking at Sanity was also a time for me to take a close look at my Fellow Travellers, to sit back and watch the show. My Fellows were a mixed bag.

If you travel alone and for some time, you inevitably find yourself arm-in-arm and ready to take on the world with a group of people you wouldn't have given a toss for back home. Nothing enhances tolerance like limited options. I guess this is one of the most interesting parts of travelling, one way it opens up your mind and horizons. For me, these strangers, these people I'd have ignored at any other time of my life became — and still are — some of my best friends. Of course, my experience isn't unique, and on Friday nights, our little ad hoc Company of Adventurers would slowly assemble at Sanity.

There were the agricultural interns from upcountry, hippies one and all. They prided themselves on being "one" with the locals and the trees: scientists who liked to spend the evenings sitting on logs, smoking joints and banging on drums. You know the type. Not my thing at all, but I'm still very good friends with the ringleader of the upcountry crowd, Shelby. Their stories of life in the savanna were unsurpassed. We listened to every word, arms crossed, sipping our drinks and feeling inadequate as Tom told us about defending a village against a swarm of locusts,[81] which hit the Gambia badly about my second year there. He told us about seeing a red cloud approach from the distance and land on a lush tree. A few minutes later the red poured back into the sky, leaving a dead stick behind.

Another tight group were the Africell guys. Africell was a Lebanese-based cell-phone provider, the only one allowed to operate in the country other than the government's Gamcel. They seemed to be staffed, almost exclusively, by young 20-something engineers, all of Lebanese extraction. Extraction, because most were from the large Lebanese community living in West Africa. One, Labib, was actually a Liberian who had left for the same reason Muhammad had. He used to joke that he could relate to African Americans: he was a second-class citizen in his own country because of his skin colour. Young, rich, with stylish *GQ*-like clothes and a massive villa paid for by Africell — complete with imported leather furniture and 52-inch flat screen — these guys found the pickings easy among the young ladies of the West. They weren't regulars at Sanity, but invariably one of the group would be there with his latest girlfriend.

Other groups put in appearances. The professional NGO crowd, for example. They were young and ambitious 20-somethings, generally from the U.K., who'd chosen to give up fast-track lives in the private sector to come and do development work. There were flocks of tour guides from England and Spain. They'd spend the day shuttling their charges around from resort to resort, then spend the evening at the Sanity to get away from them.

We were the townies. When people think of African adventures, they tend to think of being out in the countryside, back to nature, mud huts and such. On my return, I disappointed a lot of people by saying I'd spent most of my time in an urban environment, but at Sanity we were, honoured guests

---

81 You try to defend your village by setting smoky fires among the crops when the locusts are first spotted heading your way. You light the fires and pray.

at most tables because of what we knew, particularly later on when I worked for a computer company that counted as clients most of the NGOs in the land. We had juice. We knew what was going on long before anyone else did. We knew when the "riots" reported in newspapers were actually attempted coups,[82] who'd been arrested and why, as well as being able to explain why a certain foreign warship had showed up in the harbour.

These were the cliques that made up my social world. It's hard to link their motivations together with a common thread, but as Rosaleen pointed out more than once, "People who leave everything they're raised with for a totally new place; they're kinda weird." Rosaleen herself was a case in point. Looking at her, you'd see a typical hipster chick from B.C., but over the years and the beer,[83] we got to know each other in an honest way. One comment in all of those conversations really stood out above the others. One night at Sanity, or one of the other bars we'd occasionally hit, I asked her why she'd gone to school in Toronto and not B.C. Coming a bit closer to me, she whispered in a conspirator's tone: "I had to get the hell out of there!"

"How come?"

"Vancouver is just so damn dull. I just couldn't take it."

"Dull?"

"People go out there and meet for *coffee*." She almost spit the word *coffee*. "In the evenings! Can you imagine? No one meets for a drink, no one goes to the pub. The place has <u>no</u>... <u>edge</u>... <u>at</u>... <u>all</u>."

An innocuous comment, except it makes Rosaleen a person like no

---

82 More on this later.

83 And there was an awful amount of alcohol. One night, Rosaleen — who's about five feet tall and might weigh 100 lbs — and I downed over 50 beer. We'd spent so much money that the little Lebanese restaurant we were drinking at (usually referred to simply as "the pizza joint") actually gave us a bottle of wine to take home, free of charge.

other I've met. I've never met a single person — tourists or natives alike — who, when put to the question, failed to endorse B.C. as anything less than the land of milk and honey. Except Rosaleen. It's practically a cliché: the West is the best. When I've asked people *why* they think the West Coast is better than the other parts of the Dominion, I never really get much of an answer. "The mountains" is the usual refrain, and there is a lot to be said for tall rocks. I like the mountains too, but is that enough? Another common answer: "It's so laid back out there." I suspect it's more of the latter than the majesty of the former.[84] For me, the interesting thing is the consistency: I know *a lot* of people who've been out there and only Rosaleen has ever described it in the negative. I guess one person's "laid back" is another person's "dull as hell."

I remember one time back in D.C., it was a hot summer night, and a friend and I took a stroll through Adams Morgan, the District's party strip. A typical Saturday night: music thumping in the air, crowds lining the sidewalks, people eating massive slices of pizza, dropping their litter in the street. Young girls talking with impossible speed about whatever just happened in whatever bar they just got out of, occasionally stopping to wiggle their hemlines down. Chris and I strolled along, taking in the air and absorbing the energy when a milk crate rocketed from an alley, passing us at chest level. It clattered into the middle of the street, narrowly missing some of the crowd who'd spilled over into the street to eat their pizza.

A black man followed the crate. Shoved hard by an assailant, he lurched across the sidewalk. His attacker followed, leading with a right hook. The punch flew wide and turned into a headlock. Breaking free, the first guy retreated, while the assailant — chest out — gave a two-step pursuit to

---

84 I've never been myself, but it's on my list of things to do. My West Coast experience is confined to Portland, Oregon, and some time wandering in San Francisco, California, and its bedroom communities.

establish his win. Now he turned and eyed the two of us as we stood dumbfounded. Wild eyes glared as he closed in, full eye contact, no fear. But he returned to the alley, kicking a few milk crates as he went.

Chris and I resumed our stroll without saying a word. "Life in the big city," Chris joked after a few minutes. Life in the big city indeed. We were thrilled. We had a story to tell. This was why people moved to the city: it's where the action was. Anything could happen in the metropolis.

People who lived in suburbs didn't want things to happen, we concluded by the end of our walk. Suburbs are designed for maximum convenience. You're close enough to the city to have easy access to facilities, doctors and such, but you're far enough away you don't have to worry about milk crates and alleyways. You have space, but you're not risking real isolation, like you would in the countryside. The houses are big enough for you to play your music as loud as you want, no worry about people banging on the walls. The yard is big enough for the dog. When you leave, it's by car, and so your interactions with people in the street are heavily regulated with lines, signs and streetlights. Even if someone did fire a milk crate your way, it likely wouldn't break the safety glass. Everyone has just enough space, so they don't bump into each other. People do live together in suburbs — in my experience, they just don't make eye contact.[85]

Sitting around those drunken evenings, hearing stories, particularly of the upcountry crowd, it slowly dawned on me that the Kombos region, where we'd been exclusively since we arrived, was starting to feel like suburbia. It was feeling worn-in, comfortable, *known*. There were no mysteries here. We knew our way around and that was boring. There were

---

85 Sure, sometimes people fight in the suburbs, but not often. That it gets reported whenever someone does a search-and-destroy on their neighbour's yard or even on their actual neighbour, proves the rule: people don't get eyeball-to-eyeball in suburbia. Suburbia always reminds me of the Talking Heads song "Heaven," where the chorus goes: *Heaven / Heaven is a place / A place where nothing / Nothing ever happens.*

no more stories to tell. We all knew it was time to take another trip.

The plan was to head upcountry to Jufureh. On a map, it sits close to Banjul, not much more than 30 km away, but that was a good reason to use it as our upcountry coming-out party. We wouldn't be that far away, so we'd simply take a bush taxi there. Rachel or Rosaleen had found a lodge we could stay at. So the plan was to head out the next Saturday morning, check out Jufureh, spend the night at the lodge and then come back on Sunday.

Jufureh (pronounced roughly as *Ju-free*) was the town in Gambia where — according to Alex Haley's *Roots* — Kunta Kinte came from. As it happens, there are a lot of question marks beside *Roots*, and the character of Kunta Kinte, played so deftly in the 1977 miniseries by a young LeVar Burton, is probably just that: a character.

Whatever the case, the trip would be worth it. Jufureh was right near James Island: the last glimpse of home for uncounted kidnapped Africans and — I hope — the first of perdition for the white men who loaded the ships. It was a UNESCO landmark, and the thought of going hearkened back to D.C. and Smithsonian Sundays. It wasn't a museum; we were going to go see the real thing: an actual piece of history, in situ.

As you can imagine, I was pretty interested in seeing what was happening out Jufureh way, but before leaving, there were some issues to consider. Whether leaving your country or just one region for another, you've got to wonder if you'll get on with the locals. It's probably the biggest question on your mind. As it happened, our interactions with the upcountry folk went wrong — spectacularly wrong. This was due to a few cultural missteps, but in hindsight, there wasn't a damn thing we could have done about it.

Back in Canada we got almost two whole weeks of training before

151

the Corp[86] shipped us off to wherever. Training provided by experienced sargeants major, people who'd been to all kinds of places. Nevertheless, it was pretty forgettable stuff. All I remember was one exercise where we divided into groups and were given a card outlining a fake "culture" in about a paragraph. A card might say, *Your culture is extremely non-verbal. It's considered rude to look people in the eye. Women always stand to the left of a man if they're married, and to the right if not.* Your group would have to do a little skit for the rest of the kids. Afterward, they had to try and decipher your "culture" based on what they'd seen in the skit. It wasn't a bad exercise. The idea was to give your powers of observation a workout, which hit the mark, because at the end of the day, perceptiveness was your second most important asset overseas. Your first was a big, dopey smile.

Being sensitive is almost impossible to teach. It's the difference between talking and listening. Anyone stupid enough to skip around the pool with their tatas hanging out in a Muslim country, or guzzle beers in the middle of Ramadan — and they are legion — is beyond the help of the typical two-day or two-week cultural sensitivity training workshop.[87]

The study of history was my first serious encounter with cultural sensitivity or "cultural relativity" as it was called in the classroom. Academic orthodoxy insisted people living in the past were so unlike us, they could and should be considered as coming from a completely different culture. In fact, one of the texts we read was called *The Past is a Foreign Country* — no kidding. Although people in history are separated from us by time, not space,

---

86 NetCorps, the Canadian government program that got Robel and I to the Gambia in the first place.

87 Nevertheless, the two-day workshop is a trendy and attractive sacred cow that lopes across the landscape of Western enlightenment. Got a sexist bastard in your office? A racist? No problem! Sign them up for the appropriate two-day, half-day or week-long workshop and watch as the office bigot — struck by the power of *education* — makes a *complete* turnaround. Hell, he'll be handing out copies of *Roots* at the next Klan meeting.

the gist was the same: never take anything for granted, and remember your understanding of things is tainted by your biases. Not bad advice. Basically, pay attention and remember where (or when) you are.

But this kind of education had side effects. Culture — it was drilled into us — was about *difference*. The people of the past were *different*. Culture was defined as a series of differences between groups of people. There's a lot of truth in that, and it's not necessarily a bad thing. For me, those differences were good because they made people interesting. But there's a darkside. It's possible to focus on the differences themselves, even to obsess over them. I watched during my undergraduate as perfectly sane people started to abuse each other during tutorials in the name of those things that made them unique — different — from others. Naturally, neither students nor faculty used the word *different* in their deliberations, preferring the word *culture*. *Culture* had a shiny, upbeat feel to it. *Differences* on the other hand had a dark side and tended to be avoided. I once was reprimanded in class for saying "cultural differences." The prof insisted I say "alternate cultural distinctions," instead. One look at the definition for *differences* in *The Oxford English Dictionary* shows why:

> *Having characters or qualities which diverge from one another; having unlike or distinguishing attributes; not of the same kind; not alike; of other nature, form, or quality.*

> *A diversity or disagreement of opinion, sentiment or purpose; hence, a dispute or quarrel caused by such disagreement: used in various shades of intensity from a simple estrangement or dispute to open hostility.*

> *In a weaker sense, used as a synonym for other, as denying identity, but without any implication of dissimilarity; not the same, not identical, distinct.*

Not a lot of happy going on there. The last one's chilling: "a synonym for other, as denying identity." But we see it all the time. Whenever someone lets off a bomb in someone else's temple, they're denying the identity of the people they kill on the basis of cultural (religious) differences. If the victims had real identities — if the killer understood them as *people*, "punishing the infidel" would sound more like "murder."

For me, playing with culture is like juggling with knives. When it works out, it's fascinating: the smooth spin of the blades orbiting around the juggler is mesmerizing. All those knives spinning in rhythm, it seems impossible people can do that without machines. It's sort of amazing. And amazing is how I felt seeing a Fula wedding, or being invited to worship during Ramadan.

But they are knives. If there's a mistake — one false move — accidents can happen. I remember once in D.C., I'd stopped by a branch just before closing. I was waiting for my friend Hannah; we had dinner plans. It was right after school and her hands were full with the kids who'd come from the principally black high-school up the street; they usually stopped in to get a little unsupervised Internet time before heading home. I was staying out of her hair, reading magazines, when my head snapped up. It was the involuntary reaction you give when you hear the unusual. One of the girls had just violently slapped a paperback down on a table. She was bigger than Hannah in every direction, and I could see her eyes and nostrils flair as she took a menacing step toward her. The reading room was tiny, so her accusation boomed out like a taiko drum: "You're a racist!"

The kid really looked like she might throw a punch, but Hannah stood her ground. The girl was shrieking at Hannah and almost every second word was *racist*. I was halfway across the room in a heartbeat. The optics of two white librarians strong-arming a black high-school kid out of a public library in a predominantly black neighbourhood were bad, but solidarity mattered more than optics.

I clenched my jaw for what was no doubt going to be a bad moment when we were saved. Salvation came in the form of a little old lady flipping through a novel at one of the reading room tables. Her grey hair was curled in the elaborate style of the 1950s or '60s and she wore a pillbox hat cocked to one side. Her dress, shoes and coat all said *prim*.

"Excuse me, young lady!" She had to repeat it a couple of times to get heard, but once she had the floor, she gave this kid a lashing. I was too stunned to remember the details, but basically she'd marched with Dr. King, she was there after the assassination, she watched D.C. burn in '68, and the whole time she'd never stopped fighting for the rights of African Americans. The word racist *meant something*. It was important. It was serious. You didn't sling it around because you didn't get a turn on a computer.[88]

Well, that pretty much ended things. This kid had nowhere to go but out the door. Her fellow African Americans hadn't risen in righteous outrage but quite the opposite. I don't know if the old lady's words hit home and caused waves of self-doubt and introspection, Hollywood style, but it certainly left her confused. You could see it on her face. *She didn't know where she was*, if you get my meaning. Based on her clothes and style, I'm guessing she thought she was in a gritty, inner-city high-school, somewhere in "the hood," when really she was in a quiet, black, middle-class neighbourhood. Suddenly finding herself in a public library she shared with elderly civil rights activists, among others, she and her posse left amid much grumbling. She was the last one out and couldn't help one last kick at the can: "Ya'll just a bunch of racists! *Racists!*" Culture can be pointy.

In light of that story, I guess fearing other people's way of life makes sense. For me, curiosity has always trumped the anxiety of possibly doing

---

88 It turned out that the whole dispute concerned access to the public computers. She wanted to use them, but Hannah had shut them down 15 minutes prior to closing, as per DCPL procedure.

something wrong. I know folks who go blasting down highways on motorcycles at over 120 km/h, but the thought of going to a place like Africa makes them gulp air. It's not just going to Africa. A friend told me how his mother-in-law came to visit from her small town and needed to have the door of his west-end Toronto townhouse locked at all times. She was sure the neighbourhood organic farmers' market was a hotbed for the *Reefer Madness*.

I've found the cultures I've floated through to be inscrutable, and I'm guessing that's because awareness itself is such a mystery.[89] I mean, what muscle do you flex to make it go? How do you know if you're doing it right? It doesn't help that here in the West we're taught to value action over observation. The expression is "Just Do It!" Not "Stop. Observe. Think about what you just saw... now... Just Do it!"[90] We advise the youth to get their voice heard, to *make a statement*. We encourage enthusiasm, not consideration. In the grand sweep of a person's life, I guess these are useful lessons, but just once I'd like to see a T-shirt that said, "Just Pay Attention!"

Do you know where you are? When things go wrong, that's the first thing through my mind. I was at a UN-sponsored clinic that was doing research on a disease afflicting cattle. Foreign scientists, mostly from Holland and Germany, were always coming and going from the place. One day I was troubleshooting a computer when a new guy — a German — started smashing the holy hell out of his landline telephone. He had the handset and was pounding it into the base of the phone for all he was worth. I sat there stunned as he swore about the poor quality of the service and how *nothing* worked in this "goddamned country!" He may have been new, but he should have known better. Landlines were practically useless. No one tried to hide the fact, and he'd been there long enough to know it — if he'd

---

89 Or I'm thick.
90 I guess that's too long to fit on a T-shirt.

been paying attention. "Buddy, do you know where you are? It's not Bonn or Hamburg. Settle down." A bit cavalier on my part considering he was a client, but honestly, didn't he know where he was working? Fortunately, he got the point instantly, and his shame kept him from reporting me to my boss.

I saw it all the time in DC. I watched a guy lose their cool in a magnificent way because they thought there was too much mustard on their Big Mac; they'd ordered "just a dab." I felt like yelling at him: It's a fast-food joint, for Christ's sake, not Le Bernardin! As a librarian, I see it all the time. Every time you *shush* people, you're really just reminding them where they are, and that it's not their living room.

I got pretty good at paying attention while I was in D.C., knowing where I was. At least I thought so. After almost three years there I was feeling pretty comfortable with the whole scene, and it was going back to Canada that felt strange. The fact going home seemed strange shouldn't have surprised me. It's possible to morph into 'other.' In the nineteenth century, at the height of colonialism, the British even thought of a name for it: "going native." One of the most interesting things we learned in our NetCorps training was to expect a cool reception on our return. After six months away we'd return with all kinds of stories, and we'd want to tell everyone we met all about them, but no one back in Canada would want to hear about it. They warned we'd get depressed. They even set up a listserv for the returned, so we could stay in touch with each other, so we would have people willing to talk to. In short, they warned us we'd be *different* when we returned and the locals wouldn't appreciate it. When I went through the training I'd already been living in the United States for five years and felt the strangeness of being back in Canada whenever I returned for a holiday.

Despite feeling more comfortable with American culture, I still had blind spots. The biggest one being my growing conceit that I actually knew what Americana was all about. As a Canadian, I'd been raised on American culture: TV, radio (I still listen to NPR), movies, music, books. I'd been over the border many times as a kid. I'd studied U.S. history academically; I spoke the language, and I'd been living there for years. In terms of cultural understanding, I was definitely in the top percentile of foreigners. I thought.

One night I'd been invited to a poetry slam. I'd never been to one before and I was curious. I'd been asked to come along by the children's librarian from a branch library. Jamie was pretty much what you imagine when you think of a children's librarian: passionate about reading, liked to knit, wore Birkenstocks, believed education could save lives. She'd become a children's librarian to promote the "culture of literacy" in the heart of the inner city. Her boyfriend came too. He was a software engineer who wore his hair down to the waist, complemented by flip-flops and capri pants. I was a bit nervous about accepting the invitation because I already had plans to grab dinner with a friend of mine, but I managed to talk him into coming along. A colleague from downtown, more archivist than librarian, Matthew was the go-to guy for people interested in D.C. history; he counted journalists, historians and authors among his esteemed acquaintances. For Matthew, the public library was the "common man's university," a place where even the homeless could improve themselves with a copy of Hawthorne. Matthew wore a suit and tie every day, even on his days off. He and Jamie had never met, and having heard a little about their personal styles, perhaps you can understand why I was a bit nervous.

My worry was justified. I don't remember the actual details, but we hadn't walked a block before Jen knew that Matthew was a lifelong supporter of the GOP. Great, five minutes and the party flags were already waving. Never a good sign. Fortunately, the bar wasn't far from the subway station. The spectacle of a live performance filled me with relief.

My relief evaporated as we walked in. I looked around the dark space and saw a good 50 or 60 black faces staring back. The joint was packed, and no white-bread in sight. Silence didn't fall like it does in the movies, but I registered the scanning eyes, lingering glances, people gesturing to their friends, pointing us out with their chins. It was a sea of dreadlocks and we'd come wading into it wearing suits and ties and sensible shoes. I was at the rear and pushed my companions on until we reached the bar at the back wall, where we managed to carve out a niche at the end of the countertop. We ordered a round and Jen made conversation with her boyfriend, using the pounding wall of reggae to divide themselves from us. I didn't blame her. I figured Jen knew some of the people there. This neighbourhood was her patch, after all, and Matthew didn't just vote Republican, he *looked* like he voted Republican. Even the barkeep made a point of serving Matthew his drink in a polite yet decidedly distant way, a marked contrast to the smile he gave Jamie on receipt of her order, which she whispered in his ear. The poetry started soon after, and I thanked God for the distraction.

The spoken-word artists had talent. The first couple were impressive arias; I can still remember the intensity. I can also remember the applause. After one particularly impassioned set, I remember hearing the applause die down, except for someone who was out of sync with the rest of us. A friend of the current poet? No such luck. I scanned the room and zeroed in on the enthusiasts: Jamie and her boyfriend. The look on the poet's face said he had no idea who these two white people were. Nevertheless, Jamie and partner were clapping like they were being paid to. The bar noticed too. How could they fail to? There was no music being played, nor poetry being read. With a great sense of relief, the next poet started, moved the house and ended. She was good and the crowd acknowledged as much with hoots and applause. Unfortunately, one couple hooted a lot louder than the rest. When I looked, they were far from the bar and deep in the crowd; Jen was up on a chair near the stage. She and her boyfriend were waving their arms over their heads in a circle and shouting, "*Woot, woot, woot!*" I slugged back my drink and looked for the bartender, and in doing so, I noticed Matthew for the first time since we'd come in. I guess I'd subconsciously cut him loose, putting distance between me and his uptight Republicanism. I was such an idiot. There he was, jacket off and slung over a stool. He had his shirtsleeves rolled up and was leaning against the bar on his elbows, the very essence of cool.

Over the next few hours, Jamie and her boyfriend got worse, and in equal proportions, Matthew got better. He was paying attention to the poems and taking them seriously. By the time we left, he and the bartender were chatting comfortably; he blended in. The other two were clearly a running joke, and I could see people giggling in their direction. It was an interesting night. Matthew had caught me up. He didn't intend to, but he showed me how bad my judgment of cultural cues could be. Despite my pedigree, I clearly had no idea where I was.

Debriefing after the fact, it was clear Matthew had grasped what I couldn't, being too enthralled with my education and its preference for difference. For Matthew, if there was difference, there must also be similarity, and he'd chosen to emphasis the latter over the former. He admitted he was in a completely different environment than what he was used to, but he reasoned that the night was about poetry, and as someone who respected culture, he could respect that. True, he was used to a totally different type of art, but he chose to engage the bartender and some of the poets from the stance of "we both have poetry in common," rather than, "you're poetry is not at all like mine." Our conversation reminded me of a moment in my undergraduate when, in a fit of rebellion, I told one of my profs that yes, Shakespeare's sense of humour was damn different than my own, but he and I both shared the ability to appreciate humour, despite the years separating us.[91] Humour. Laughter. Unifying principles. Not to mention of course a big dopy smile.

---

91 I never got a real answer to that from the prof.

A Spot of Culture, Part 2: "Wow."

A few weeks later.

The weekend came, and we executed the first part of the plan with aplomb. Since this consisted of sleeping over at Rosaleen and Rachel's house, I guess it wasn't really that heroic. Getting out of Brusubi and up to Kariba Avenue in Fajara could be a real problem though. Public transit ran the other direction, east, up into Serekunda and beyond, so getting up to Fajara to visit our friends always took some resourcefulness. After much trial and error,[92] we discovered our best resource for this endeavour was our roommate, Lisa.

The fastest way to Fajara — or Senegambia, for that matter — was to hitchhike, and our success increased enormously whenever we let our blond, curvy friend do the thumb waving. Robel and I would stand at a safe distance or across the road, acting like we wanted to go in the other direction. Lisa would wheel in a driver, then call us over. There was always

---

92 Including an ill-conceived adventure involving some bicycles we bought. It was ill-conceived because the mountain bikes we bought — brand new, imported from China, and looking like the kind of swank machine you'd expect Seamus McGrath to go barreling down an Olympic circuit on — were made of steel. Not stainless steel but plain, old-fashioned, rust-bucket steel. After about a month in the salt air near the sea, every part that hadn't fallen off had fused into a solid block.

much sighing and grimacing when the driver realized "her friends" weren't pretty or even women. Lisa had no problem with any of this as long as one rule was obeyed: she would not under any circumstances sit beside the driver because hands could creep. So shotgun was my normal position. I was also tasked with the job of chatting up the driver and plastering over any hurt feelings.

Hitching was a common form of transport for country folk. In the mornings, our intersection was thronged with middle-school kids, all thumbing lifts to school. Guys on their way to work would stop to pick them up. They'd pull over in a dust cloud, a pack would dash for the car and stuff inside, every seat and lap full. Getting anywhere at that time of day was impossible until the last kid was squared away. Waiting didn't bother me at all; it was great to see strangers going out of their way to get kids to school.

The hitchhike usually got us to Senegambia, halfway to Fajara. From there, we could grab a taxi that would take us to Kairaba Avenue, the main artery in and around Fajara. The process was similar to hitching. People waited around by the side of the road in Senegambia, and eventually a taxi would pull up and people would pile in. It was two dalasi per passenger to make the run. We had the means to hire a private taxi, but the same run would have cost us about 30 dalasis if we hired the car specially. The cost of a hire was negotiable, naturally, and if you showed up looking desperate, God help you.[93]

---

93 The colour of your skin could definitely count against you here. Although I had more money than most, accessing it could be a big problem. When the ATMs went down, you might suddenly have to live on what you had in your pocket. More than once, I had to walk over a mile to get somewhere because the cabbies couldn't believe a white man didn't have 30 dalasi in his pocket. Even in the shared cabs, if the driver didn't have change, you were expected to be the bank. I can still remember one driver looking at me in the rear-view with a sly smile and saying, "Come on, *toubob*, we *know* you have the money." Things got hostile because that day I didn't.

162

We spent that Friday night at Samantha's house where Rosaleen and Rachel were renting rooms. Samantha wasn't there because she travelled a lot. An arrangement had been made with a taxi driver to pick us up in the morning, and so we got up at the crack of dawn and drove the 20 minutes to Banjul in the grey Saturday morning light. The taxi took us straight to the ferry.

Jufureh was on the north bank and that meant crossing the Gambia River. Although Banjul was still stretching and yawning and rubbing the sleep out of its eyes, the ferry was already hopping. We were running a bit late and didn't know how long it would be for the next ferry. With a growing sense of panic, we pushed through the crowd, looking for the ticket booth. Then, with tickets in hand, we saw the queuing fence was empty. Fearing we were too late, we ran as fast as we could, packs flopping as we rounded each corner until finally charging into a dark room.

No one else was in the room, which was about the size of a big garage. A bench ran the length of each wall, another ran down the middle. The far end was capped by a big, wrought-iron gate looking out over the water. We guessed we were in the terminal. Were we early? Were we late? It didn't matter because there was no ferry to be seen. We made our way toward the gate, not just because it seemed the way forward, but because it provided light and fresh air.

The atmosphere was oppressive; the heat was rising and the odour of the last crowd's meal of smoked fish hung in the air like an inky cloud. In the light of the gate, I made out fish heads and skeletons scattered around the sandy floor. You never wore open shoes or sandals due to the state of the ground. This was a general rule, not just a travelling rule. Although the tropics look like a nice place to wear flip-flops, the fact that the street, lane or ferry terminal you happen to be standing on is the default sewer makes it risky business. It's not only fear of snakes or insects. That pristine stretch of beach has no doubt been a toilet for some passing donkey or herd of goats. Your skin could pick up all kinds of weirdness in the sand. I had a rash between my toes for over a year before I'd been enlightened to the state of the ground.[94]

Soon, others arrived and in no time we were trapped against the gate, like being trapped against the door of a subway at rush hour. More fish. Being at the port, smoked fish was in easy supply and turned out to be a popular travelling food. It was a good meal, actually, and once I had a full-time job, I'd eat it for breakfast on the weekends quite regularly. It was a small fish, smoked whole and served in tinfoil. You broke it up with your thumb, ate the good bits and spit out the rest.

The additional bodies — not to mention the livestock — brought the heat and humidity to a boil. A lot of our fellow travellers had live chickens and goats with them. Despite the discomfort, it was fun to watch them. There looked to be regulars. Despite the language divide, you could see the morning commuter familiarity.

I don't know how long we waited, but we were eventually rescued. I was gripping the gate and staring out like Number 6[95] when people started filing by, heading inland. At last the gate was opened and we were off. Busy commuters strutting as fast as they could, just short of a run, a hand steadying a load on their head, the other straining at a tote.

The ferry was a typical double-end affair with space on the main deck for maybe five to seven cars or trucks. We found a place on the upper deck from where we could survey Banjul harbour. It was great to be on the water, out in the fresh air. You could smell the salt. The harbour lined the mouth of the river; the sandy beach filled with fishing boats, nets and tackle. The fishing boats were big, with open decks like giant canoes but with

---

94 A disgusting fact,but a true one. I was having all kinds of problems with my feet until one of the scientists working at the U.K. Medical Research Council (MRC), which has a large complex in the Gambia, clued me in. A friend of mine had such gnarled feet that by the end of her six months she took pictures of them to show her friends.
95 The lead character of *The Prisoner.*

seating for up to 30 or 40 people. Although they had the basic shape of a banana, their cross-section described a *V*, with the keel pointing prominently out from the bow and stern. They were painted all kinds of bright colours, red, yellow and sky blue predominating. Designs, including Islamic motifs, or eyes were painted on their bows.

The trip was short, 10, maybe 15 minutes. We disembarked on the north shore in the town of Barra[96] loping our way down the lane formed by two high brick walls and empting into the street. It was about 8 a.m. and we'd been travelling for about two hours, covering our first 10 km without too much bother. The next steps were a little more complicated.

The plan called for us to find a bush taxi to take us from Barra to Jufureh. We knew from co-workers it could be done: just ask for Jufureh and we'd be pointed in the right direction. But after nosing around for a few minutes and finding the taxi stand, it became clear that locating our ride would be problematic. Imagine the chaos of a large, loud outdoor market, except instead of stalls, it's filled with vans, bumper to bumper. It looked like every taxi on the north bank was there. People were streaming around, looking for the right taxi to take them back to their village with the week's wages in their pockets. The space was as big as a football field but without a trace of grass. Plastic bags and other litter blew around all over. People were yelling to be heard as they negotiated prices. Welcome to Barra.

It was a discouraging sight. The thought of the footwork required to track down the right vehicle left me in a daze. Bush taxis were the basic transit system for most of West Africa. Minivans were the core of the system, typically a Toyota or a Mercedes. Each van was staffed with a driver and an attendant. The attendant was usually a kid, anywhere from 10 to 18 years old, who helped load the luggage, squeezed people in and out, collected

---

96 The city of Banjul sat on the south side of the harbour and the city of Barra on the north side.

the money and generally acted as conductor. The attendant was also responsible for drumming up business. At roadside stops the minivan would roar up and the attendant's head would poke out the window, yelling out their ultimate destination, "Sukuta, Sukuta! Bijilo, Bijilo!" Here, in Barra, a major transit hub, the kids would run around and try to drum up business.

The place could have competed with any major airport for congestion and speed walkers. Everyone was trying to catch a connection. The only real difference — other than some luggage being livestock and the whole thing being in a dirt patch — was the lack of signs. Instead, the hustle and bustle was directed by the taxi attendants who either ran around or stood on top of their vans or hung off the back ladders calling out their destination. They were shouting over each other and the commuters were shouting over them, querying prices and departure times. Some of the attendants tugged at us to come without bothering to ask our destination at all.

The taxis wouldn't go anywhere until they were full. This was a private-sector transit system, after all. The taxis moved when they were full, but if you wanted to leave for Farafenni *now*, then you could walk. Sure, another driver might leave sooner, but most of the taxi stands were regulated. There was always a guy who'd mediate disputes over price or departure time. This kept the prices "stable."

I don't remember who found it or how, but we finally located a bush taxi going to Jufureh. We needed to wait for the seats to fill up, so we killed time. We split up for a while, exploring in different directions, always keeping an eye on the van. It was hot and hectic, so Robel and I passed time sitting on the minivan's floor, feet dangling out the back door, which was open to vent the cabin. We were feeling the early rise and spent the time yawning and making half-hearted conversation with the teenaged attendant who didn't understand a word of English.

"How long till we leave?" Robel asked.

"Yes, we leave. Jufureh."

"Yes, when?"

"Yes. When. Jufureh."

"How much to Jufureh?"

"Jufureh 75!"

"75 dalasi? Wow, that's a lot."

"Yes, wow!"

Well, it kept us awake, and more importantly, out of the way of the action around the car park. We'd spent a good amount of time in Barra, tramping through the dirt and mud, trying to understand and be understood, and sitting in that van was like being in the peaceful eye of the storm.[97]

Suddenly, the limp forms in the van — about 15 or 20, including us — pulled themselves together. Feet swung off empty seats, bags were checked one last time — we were off! Our party was all present and correct, and we climbed aboard. I say suddenly because we'd been waiting for the van to fill up. I didn't do a head count, but I guessed we were light about 10 bodies. But we were moving, and having enjoyed the sights and sounds of Barra for a couple of hours, we were more than ready to roll on.

---

97 I have no talent as a linguist. Despite being raised in one of the earliest French Immersion programs in Canada from Grade 5 through 10, I barely passed Grade 11 French (my final grade started with the number five). It never bothered me, and I've always been dubious about the idea of showing people respect by learning their language. Does it mean I'm allowed to hold all the Ethiopians, Portuguese and Somalis living in my Toronto neighbourhood who can't speak English in contempt? I've never felt like they were showing me disrespect because they didn't speak English. As someone with no linguistic skills, I empathise with them.

The other problem I have with it, being the son of an immigrant myself, is how that kind of pressure can affect people. My family came from Guyana, so English wasn't a problem, but there were other aspects of life, like driving or eating habits, that put a lot of pressure on some members of my family. They felt they had to "fit into Canadian culture," and so learn new habits, but not everyone was able to rise to the occasion and some scares ensued.

It was a nice bush taxi, a tall, narrow Mercedes painted bright colours like the fishing boats in Banjul harbour. The inside was decorated with beads, and the necklaces hanging from the rear view and sun visors swayed like pendulums as we lurched from furrow to furrow in the road. The normal seating had been ripped out and replaced with long rows of steel-framed benches. About as wide as a pew and with straight backs, we looked like a church congregation on a ship: eyes forward, tired heads swaying in time to the roll of the van.

In no time we were in the countryside. Initially, we stuck to the main road, rocking over it like a ship bounding in the rollers. Occasionally, the driver would give a startled "eh, sorry, sorry!" over his shoulder when a wheel dropped suddenly and the bus lurched radically. The crowd answered back with giggles. I could see other vans swaying dangerously as they passed us on the red clay road. The Mercedes minivan is tall and narrow — I can stand up inside one easily — making them practical on narrow European streets and as unwieldy as a Spanish galleon on the dirt roads of the West African outback. A problem dramatically enhanced by the copious amounts of baggage strapped to the top.

Eventually, we turned off the main road, leaving the walls of foliage lining it behind. The savanna stretched out in every direction. Unlike the yellow and brown of the East African savanna, everything here was a shade of green. Long green grass rippled like the sea as wind gust across its surface. You could see isolated thickets of trees, usually palms but sometimes a single massive baobab.[98]

I was admiring one such baobab, fantasizing about baobab juice,

---

98 The quintessential African tree, the baobab is easily distinguished from a distance by its huge trunk, up to 30 feet in diameter. The trunks are so huge, the canopy on top often looks like a bouquet of flowers sticking out of a tall, sturdy vase. The trunk's huge size allows it to hold thousands of litres of water, and the fruit makes a delicious drink which I covet. I'd consider any form of villainy to get a few more swigs.

when I was interrupted: "75 dalasi!" It was the attendant, looking for his money. He wasn't speaking to me, though. He was speaking to Lisa.

"No," she responded, and the edge in her voice snapped me out of my daydream.

"75 dalasi!"

"No, for everyone else it's only 15. We'll pay 15, no more."

"Boss Lady, it is 75, you say!"

"No, we never say. We pay the same as the others. No more!"

It went on like this for a few minutes, hand gestures being used to emphasize amounts, Lisa's diction getting more basic, more emphatic, after each pass.

Lisa was our youngest member, but also our most experienced in terms of travel. She was a modern hippie, the kind who wore bandannas and Birkenstocks and refused to shave her legs. She was studying to be a human rights lawyer and was interning at the centre. Lisa had spent a lot of time in South America on similar internships before coming to Africa. Despite her overseas experience, she'd had a hard time in the Gambia. She wanted to make friends, to meet the locals and hang out with them, learn some of their music. As a traveller, Lisa was looking for a simple human connection. Leaving the place with an email address and pictures of a family she'd befriended — maybe someone she could visit again — would've made the Gambia a happy memory for her.

But when the house was robbed, a corner was turned. During our drunken evenings back at the house in Brusubi, she'd go on about it: "Why was it *so* hard to get on here? Don't they know we respect them? Why don't they respect us? In South America, the locals would come by with their children, they'd play at the intern's house. They *knew* people there. Why was it so hard here?"

The robbery was one thing, but in the end, the petty indignities are what really wear you down. It puts your reason and passion at odds: your understanding of poverty versus your passion for human rights. Safe at home now, writing this with a nice cup of tea, it's easy to be rational about it: to remember the dehumanizing effects of poverty. But if you're the kind of person who takes human rights seriously, who supports Pride, who studies human rights law, who travels around the world to work in a human rights institute, being charged — without any attempt to conceal the double standard — five times the going rate is a slap in the face. You'd be outraged if it happened to anyone else. Sure, on paper we could afford it. Sure, in the grand scheme of the universe we were talking about two and a half dollars, but sitting there tired, hungry and on our way to acknowledge the evils of slavery, our rationale just couldn't compete with our frustration.[99] Idrissa's anger about the alarm system made a lot more sense to me now than it did my first week of work. Frustration rots compassion.

. Lisa was getting shriller by the second. The rest of the passengers — including us — were stunned and silent. The attendant was giving as good as he got, and finally Lisa sprang up and shouted, "Stop, stop, stop! I'm getting off!" She was on her feet, pulling at her backpack. The rest of us were staring at each other, eyes asking the question, *What should we do?* Not that there was any real question about it. Solidarity. That was the watchword for the Brusubi crew. We kept looking at Lisa, the other passengers and back at Lisa. She was screaming to be let off.

---

99 Before leaving for Africa, I had a couple of conversations with a journalist friend who'd spent time in East Africa. Like Lisa, he was a passionate believer in human rights, with strong leanings to the left. He told me how it was the habit of the police to wander the streets and demand "papers" from foreigners, as a subtle and occasionally lucrative harassment. At first, he put up with it: it was their country, after all. But after months of this he finally reached his breaking point. The frustration broke him, and when the next cop asked him for papers, he went nuts. He turned on the cop and started yelling at him: "My papers?! Where the hell are *your* papers, eh? Come on, let's see 'em!" The cop was so taken aback, he actually did pull them out. After that incident, my friend knew it was time to go.

We're really about to get off the bus, I thought. The driver stopped and Lisa jumped out the back. Without an ounce of Lisa's conviction, we all quietly followed. As I write this, I'm looking at a map of the north shore, and I can honestly say I have no idea where we were in the space between Barra and Jufureh. We'd made a lot of turns on a lot of sandy tracks. Even retracing our steps would have been impossible.

Suddenly, the driver was yelling at the attendant. The latter leaned out the back and roughly motioned for us to come back in.

"15!" shouted Lisa.

The attendant just kept waving. "Come!" he pressed. Between the driver yelling, the attendant insisting and Lisa demanding, a kid — maybe 19 — finally spoke up in nervous but passable English.

"Come, the driver won't leave you here. He wants to go. He won't leave you here in the wilderness. Please, come." Somehow the issue of "how much" got put aside, and we climbed back aboard with even less enthusiasm. The driver was clearly angry, the attendant glum, and he left us alone. The other passengers went out of their way to avoid eye contact, but we were moving again and our survivalist skills remained, thankfully, untried.

Something was wrong, though. The murmur in the van seemed to suggest a rising excitement. We'd driven onto smaller and smaller tracks until we were bouncing dangerously down a glorified footpath. Branches whipped the sides and roof of the van until the path ended in a small clearing with huts scattered around. No more cold shoulders, now the passengers were staring at us, giving us thoughtful looks.

The truck stopped and almost on cue the rest of the passengers got out. So did the driver. There was no river. We were surrounded by thick bush. This wasn't Jufureh. We sat there blinking stupidly at each other. Finally, the boy who'd spoken to us in English came around the back and said, "Come, it is time to go. Everyone is waiting. You are going to court." Going to court? We were in the jungle. We sat in that empty bus and let a few quiet seconds go by, each of us pondering "fighting" or "fleeing." We were at the mercy of circumstance. We grabbed our stuff in case the bus took off without us and followed the rest of the passengers.

Everyone had moved into a dirt courtyard, the central feature of which being a short tree, and under its shade, two benches had been set up. They were long and low, like the ones used in public schools for assemblies. The bus driver, the attendant and some of the passengers had already staked one out. No one had to tell us to whom the other belonged. There we were, eyeball-to-eyeball across 20 feet of dust with an angry bush taxi driver and his posse.

Back near the trunk of the tree was a large chair, made of wood, and although not elaborately carved, it was a cut above the usual furniture. It was situated like a throne to survey the courtyard. The space itself was action-packed: villagers and passengers buzzed around with excitement, forming a circle around the benches and chair, ready for the show.

We didn't wait long. Somewhere from stage right a man appeared in a perfectly white and crisply ironed *boubou*, topped off with a snow-white pillbox hat. He made himself comfortable in the wooden chair, and a group of villagers came and gathered around it, while children sat on the ground by its side. He couldn't have been 40 years old. His face was round and lit by a bright toothy smile. His eyes looked happy and friendly. All this gave me hope. As the crowd gathered, one of the little girls kneeling beside the chair tugged at his sleeve, and he came around with a hard slap and a sharp screech. This did not give me hope.

After a moment, he began in decent English: "Welcome, welcome! I am the district chief here. I have been appointed by the president to preside here. I have been asked to arbitrate this dispute. Please prepare yourselves." The silence holding the air while he spoke blew away in a burst of excited chatter around the courtyard. Our opponents huddled.

Prepare ourselves — what did that mean? Fortunately, the kid from the bus came to our aid. The process was simple: we'd give our arguments and he'd make a decision, and that decision was the binding law. He'd give both sides a few minutes to prepare arguments and consult witnesses. We put our heads together and made a few quick decisions. The first was that Lisa would be our official spokesperson. She liked to talk and was interested in the law. We were sure Lisa wouldn't be cowed; her nickname with us was "Boss Lady" after all.[100] The second thing — and this had to be forced on Lisa by the rest of us — was our willingness to pay whatever it took to get out of there and onto a bus. Lisa was still feeling outraged at the double standard that she interpreted as a violation of our human rights, as blatant racism. Rosaleen and I tended more toward wrinkle smoothing than passionate outrage. Furthermore, our blood was up and Lisa could tell. We were mad as hell at the mess she's gotten us into. Rosaleen and I would have paid the 75 dalasi and commiserated later over beer. We didn't want to stand up and pay the 75 now; it would piss everyone off to simply whip out our wallets after delaying everyone's commute. Not to mention the fact that we were all North Americans and deep down just as pissed off as Lisa.

Court reconvened with the chief questioning the bush taxi driver. The driver went on at length, his arms crossed, clearly angry. When he finished, the chief turned to us and interpreted. The driver was angry because he'd left Barra short five passengers. He only did it because we'd agreed to pay for the extra seats, a total of 75 dalasi.

We had a brief huddle and agreed none of us had made such a deal. Lisa stood up at the end of our bench and quietly — choked with respect for the local judiciary — told the august assembly we had no knowledge of a deal, and in fact, none of us had the language skills to have negotiated such an arrangement. The chief translated.

---

100 "Boss Lady" was an address the locals used for white women, or any foreign woman who wasn't afraid to give orders or raise their voice. Lisa took to it instantly.

The driver was almost yelling. He pulled up the attendant. Still sullen, the kid was clearly answering for something. He nodded over at Robel. The chief turned to us and said, "He insists there was an arrangement. The boy, he say he made an arrangement with your friend," indicating Robel with his chin. Enlightenment suddenly dawned.

I replayed parts of the conversation we'd had with the kid while waiting in Barra: "How much to Jufureh?"

"Jufureh 75!"

"75 dalasi? Wow, that's a lot."

"Yes, wow." Dammit. Robel used the word *wow* fairly often. I'm not much of a linguist, but my grasp of Wolof did extend to the basics. *Atcha, atcha!* meant "Go, go!"; *bea* meant "here"; *de det* meant "no"; and unfortunately, *wau* — pronounced *wow* — meant "yes." In the process of making small talk, Robel had inadvertently signed on the dotted line. The driver thought we'd agreed to buy out the remaining seats, now he wanted his agreed compensation. We huddled; I explained, and Lisa addressed the crowd. It was probably safe to agree to pay the 75 dalasi and go by that point, and we did discuss it, but the fear of the unknown had passed. We were getting into the process and the need to defend our point of view goaded us on.

Lisa made the argument that it was an innocent mistake, and we had nothing but respect for the driver, the people of the Gambia, and the esteemed gathering we were now apart of. We would never take advantage of someone in that way. The chief translated. This time, the driver was looking thoughtful, but the attendant didn't look very happy. Most of the talk on their side was between the driver and the attendant. They came back with "a deal is a deal" and "I'm a working man, I have mouths to feed." We stuck to "an honest mistake," and things went back and forth for another 10 minutes. Finally, the chief raised his hands and waved everyone quiet. He pronounced upon us.

174

It was an honest mistake. We were travellers and strangers and it was every Gambian's duty to treat us as they would any guest. However, the driver had to eat, compensation was necessary. Mistake or not, he had a family and he was out of pocket for the seats. However, 75 dalasi from *each* of us was exorbitant. This was not the going rate, and the attendant knew it. The strangers would pay 35 dalasi each: 15 for our seat, 15 for one other seat and 5 to help cover the extra fuel spent on this diversion. Court adjourned.

People seemed happy — except the attendant. The driver was clearly unhappy with him. We paid the driver, gave our thanks and respect to the district chief, piled back into the van and were on our way.

We arrived in Jufureh late in the afternoon. It was a quiet-looking town. The river was off to the right and it freshened the air. By this point, we were tired and stiff, but the ride from court had been pleasant. Our fellow travellers had heard our point of view and understood we weren't just a bunch of white bastards. The mood was lighter and I passed time with an old fisherman in the back chatting, in broken English and Wolof, "How much for the blond?"[101]

We were pretty tired by the time we got there. The first order of business was to find our inn. Fortunately, the kid who'd initially translated for us pointed the place out. It was a typical resort or lodge that consisted of a compound with a half-dozen small circular huts: concrete re-creations

---

101 Blond and blue-eyed, Lisa attracted a lot of unwanted attention the moment she hit the ground. In order to keep the suitors at bay, I married her. At least that's what we told people. Unfortunately, this didn't really help. It seemed a mere inconvenience to most of her adoring fans. Men were always asking me "how much?" Or would their sister do as a replacement? A good number ignored me, despite standing right there. The number of times she was asked "but wouldn't you like to have a brown baby?" was astonishing. We finally figured out the key to crowd control around Lisa: I started introducing myself as her brother. That got a lot more respect.

of a "traditional" African mud hut, usually complete with thatched roof, but with actual doors and windows. At maybe 20 feet in diameter, there wasn't much room for anything other than a bed. Bathroom facilities consisted of a hole or two in an outhouse near the main huts.

These could be good or bad, as circumstances dictated. This being a resort or lodge, and one in a popular tourist spot, the outhouses were higher quality. This one was a spacious room with a clean concrete floor that had a sunken ceramic plate in the middle of it, about the size of a big oval dinner plate and angled slightly downward. At the lower end of the plate's gradient was a hole. You need only drop your pants, squat over the hole and make your deposit. There was even toilet paper (but always a good idea to bring your own just in case). You finished off with the big plastic bucket in the corner filled with water. The size of a garbage can, you cleaned your hands with a smaller plastic jug that floated on top. This was a good john. The floor was clean and flat, and the plate meant you didn't have to aim perfectly, just drop your output and flush via the plastic jug. A few splashes and it would slide easily down the angled plate, through the hole, to be seen no more. The water kept the plate clean, which limited the flies. There was lots of water, and it was clean. As primitive as it sounds, I became a fan of the squat toilet because you never had to sit on a toilet seat. I'm mentioning this in some detail because seeing it was a huge relief. There's nothing worse than being on the road and being concerned about the facilities. Although it could have been otherwise, this was an excellent specimen.

The worst bathroom facility I ever used was at a border checkpoint between the Gambia and Senegal. It was beside the customs station and it was open air. Your privacy was poorly protected by a small fence surrounding the hole, which was made of rusty sheet metal.[102] The hole was

---

102 I could see people through the rust holes and gaps, so I can only imagine that there are Gambians out there who've seen more of me than they were comfortable with.

just a hole in the ground — no plate — so your aim had to be perfect. One look told me a lot of people don't have perfect aim. To keep your feet out of past user bits, the hole was flanked by two cinderblocks you had to balance on. It was hot that day, one I will never forget.

All in all, it was a typical lodge, the typical "hotel" if you're upcountry or just not interested in the more traditional resorts along the coast. Seeing the place was the first good news we'd had since we got up that morning. Rachel had made the arrangement over a cellphone, which for Westerners is a strange experience. Imagine reserving a room at the Hyatt meant calling some guy on his cellphone, and you could tell he's driving down the street in a taxi. How much confidence would you have in that reservation? So it was a relief to see the place. We'd rented two sides of a single hut, a room for the boys and a room for the girls. It was the off-season and so we had the whole lodge to ourselves. It was so off-season, in fact, that the manager Rachel had spoken to over the phone was nowhere to be seen, but with the help of our friend, enquires were made and things started to pick up.

It wasn't just the frantic efforts of the kid, though. I don't know if someone who'd gotten off the bus earlier had called ahead, or if the remaining passengers in the van had spread the word the instant we'd arrived, but within half an hour there was no doubt we had a reputation.[103] While we waited for the manager, our friend introduced us to his cousin,

---

103 The "jungle wire" exists, and in the Gambia, it's made up of a thin line of cellphone towers and call centres spaced the length of the country. Upcountry, making a call could be almost impossible. One of my friends, a member of the "hippie crew," told me how there was one spot in the whole village, just a nondescript "spot" about 20 feet in diameter where — somehow — cellphones could get reception. Nevertheless, the speed at which news could move was shocking. Two future roommates, interns at the centre, went upcountry to take interviews for whatever reason. At one of the stops, their driver was stopped by police when he got out of the van. Apparently, he'd run over a chicken or two over 100 km back up the road and he needed to pay compensation.

who greeted us with, "Ah, yes. You are the ones who went to the court." The word was out. He followed that up with the usual "where from?" When he found out we were Canadians, he replied with the much less usual, "Ah, yes. You have a new prime minister now."

"Who?" I demanded.

"Paul Mart-ain."

Wow, I thought (but didn't say out loud). Seeing our surprise, he just smiled and patted his shortwave radio.

"BBC." It's surreal to be in a place without electricity or running water — a place so profoundly different from your own experience — and be updated about the politics of your land by a guy sitting on a log bench. In my mind, that moment lives beside an experience I had while living in D.C. I was walking through Cleveland Park, up one of the wealthiest streets in the "capital of the free world," when I was stopped by two well-dressed, attractive women. They were part of some church and going door to door, chatting up the "best and the brightest," when they spied me as a target of opportunity. Somehow the fact I was a Canadian came up, and one of them squealed with flirty delight: "Oh, it's *so* wonderful to meet someone from the Republic of Canada."[104] No kidding.

The cousin was a tour guide and he volunteered to take us around. It was the off-season, but he could get things opened for us and get us to our goal. We were close. We could see it. Out in the river, which was wide and flat, you could see a clump of trees growing out of the water about a kilometre away. James Island sits very low in the water, so low, in fact, the various European powers who'd set up shop there had to work hard to keep the island an island. Not much was left now, and in the distance the trees

---

104 Canada is a constitutional monarchy, so it's really "Government of the People, by the People, for Her Majesty Elizabeth the Second, by the Grace of God of the United Kingdom, Canada and Her other Realms and Territories Queen, Head of the Commonwealth, Defender of the Faith."

seemed to just poke out of the water.

In the meantime, he suggested we go and meet Binta Kinte, the great-great-great granddaughter[105] of Kunta Kinte. We headed down to the Kinte learning centre, which was basically an open-air schoolroom with displays and concrete benches lining the perimeter. She was a nice old lady. We sat and walked by her chair, respectfully bowing our heads as we went by. It was an awkward meeting; it was getting late and I got the sense that Binta wasn't impressed with trekking down to the centre for five dusty travellers.

The kid led the way, introduced us to the lady, then vanished. After meeting Binta, we sat on the concrete steps looking at the various posters hanging on the walls. Our friend returned with a large calabash bowl. Clearly, a donation was in order and we all threw in, after which the lad asked, "Would you like a picture of Kunta Kinte?" I admit, I was pretty curious. "Only 10 dalasi."

"Yes, yes! I would like a picture to commemorate Binta Kinte, and as a way to say thanks to the village," pronounced Robel with a big sincere smile. I figured I'd look at Robel's, and if it was worth it, I'd buy a copy too. Robel threw his money in the calabash and the kid produced a piece of paper from a shelf behind him. It was a wrinkly and ratty picture of smil'n Geordi La Forge from *Star Trek: The Next Generation*, except he was shirtless, had an iron collar around his neck and wasn't smiling. It was a printout of Kunta Kinte as portrayed by LeVar Burton in the 1977 miniseries spectacular, *Roots*. Having seen the goods, the rest of us took a pass, with good grace, thanking everyone for the honour of seeing the centre. Our next stop was the lodge, and on the way, Robel muttered under his breath that he wanted his money back.

---

105 Or niece — we never got a straight answer on that. Same thing with her name. We heard both Binta and Bintou.

Although a decent one, the lodge suffered from a one major drawback: no food. This hadn't been mentioned when we planned the trip. It was getting dark now, and our patience was wearing thin. We hadn't eaten since Barra. Enquires were made with the manager (who'd finally shown up to let us into the place), pointing us to a bar down by the beach.

After freshening up, we headed down. The guy running the joint knew we'd been in court that morning and was eager to please. The place was a big concrete balcony with a corrugated iron roof. We ordered food, but it became obvious they'd have to run into the village to find the ingredients. Before our collective eye twitched, he mentioned that he did have beer. They weren't super cold, but their arrival at the table transformed the mood. We were sitting by the water on a cool night with a comfortable breeze, and we had beer and cigarettes. It took a long time to get our food, and then we stumbled back to the lodge, more than a bit tipsy.

Drunk, tired and filthy, we went to bed. There was one bed in the room and it was small, perhaps designed for a couple to get cozy in, and so Robel and I had a pretty awkward night. I didn't ask how it went for the girls in the same bed, and they didn't offer any details. The next morning, feeling the ache of the night layered over the fading but still tangible pain of the bus trip there, we went looking for food. There was no food in the hotel and the bar was closed, so we bought baguettes from the corner store and that was breakfast.

The cousin who was supposed to get us across the river was nowhere in sight, so we decided to check out the area while we waited for him to show. The manager wanted 300 dalasi from each of us and we started to flip out. The girls formed a phalanx and started yelling at him. His first language was French, but Lisa and Rachel were fluent speakers; I didn't understand the details but their fingers were in his face as they advanced on him. He shrugged his shoulders and seemed to be trying to explain himself. Basically, he'd arranged 60 dalasi a night, per person, for a total of 300. Now he was saying the rate was 300 a head and "sorry, sorry!" for the misunderstanding. It didn't matter. We couldn't have paid it even if we'd wanted to. There were no ATMS in Jufureh (that we knew of) and we'd only taken enough cash with us for our projected expenses, plus a bit of padding. We'd found out the hard way that carrying around a wad of cash was stupid.[106] The girls were shouting him down. He couldn't get a word in edgewise. Finally, someone said, "Hey, we've been to court. We know how the law works here."

"Yeah!" I added. "Where's the village chief? We want to go to court *right now.*" My comrades took up the call, and we grabbed our bags, making a show of asking people in the street the way to the chief's house. He caved in. We paid our 300 dalasi and decided to hit the road. We were tired and frustrated. Every move had taken effort: we had to *find* the manager when we got there, we had to find food, we'd been ripped off at the Binta Kinte centre, and to top it all off, our little friend who'd been helping us since the bus incident had decided Rosaleen was the love of his life. He'd been harassing her since last night, a fact I was unaware of until breakfast. It was time to go.

We took the first bus to Barra. The trip itself was generally uneventful, marred only by a dead goat. I was sitting quietly, sandwiched hip to hip between Lisa and Rachel. We were riding along in silence when I felt a drop of water hit my cheek. I unconsciously whipped it away. A moment later, another drop, another wipe. It was getting worse, and looking at my hand, I saw red smears. I scanned around and noticed a deep red splotch on Lisa's naturally blonde, almost white, hair. She too was scanning around. It only took me a second to realize what was happening. A dead animal (a goat, it turned out), freshly slaughtered — no doubt someone's dinner tonight — was strapped to the roof, and through a rust hole a stream of fresh blood

---

106 Both Lisa and I had been robbed by this point. She had her purse snatched and I had been pick pocketed.

was showering Lisa whenever the bus bounced. Lisa was a passionate vegetarian. She blanched and shuttered at the thought of animal blood raining on her head. I thought she might vomit. Rachel and I leaped into action; she had a travel pack of tissues, and for the last 30 minutes to Barra I held a tissue up to the hole, and once saturated, Rachel would hand me another and dispose of the used one. We switched off with the precision of a surgical team.

It was mid-Sunday afternoon when we finally made it back to Rachel's and Rosaleen's place. We stocked up on booze along the way. Because we hadn't had showers in two days, we were covered in dust, sweat and blood (it had dripped all down my arm and under my shirt), so we rotated through the shower, took our sun-downers in the garden and commiserated.

That was the last trip we took together as a whole group. Things were changing. Soon Robel, Lisa and Rachel would be gone, their internships finished. Mine would be done soon too. In fact, I was due to leave at the same time as Robel. But I didn't want to go yet.

You Will Meet a Short, White Man

About six months after arrival.

The end was near. In just a few weeks, my time at the centre would be over. What to do? What to do? It was a familiar feeling; the same one I had at the end of my education. Most of the other interns had a plan. They were there to pad their resumes or use their internship as a kind of short holiday, a little international experience before applying to law school. I didn't have anything to go back to. I'd be 31 soon, there was no job to return to, and at that time I wasn't a huge fan of North America anyway. Sure, the Gambia had its problems, but I was willing to look past all of them, and only because in the Gambia I didn't feel judged. It was amazing what I was willing to put up with to avoid my own lowly status back in the West. I was once at a party trying to chat up a young lady. D.C. being D.C., the conversation inevitably started with "what do you do?" I was trying to impress her with a story about managing the public library's help desk. She listened politely, and when it was her turn, she said, "I manage Ted Kennedy's time," and walked off. Going home felt like going back to prison. A comfortable prison, mind you, with lots of entertainment options and pretty girls, but prison nonetheless. A kind of politically correct Dickensian boarding house policed by soccer moms.

On the other hand, the Gambia was starting to get lonely. Robel and

Lisa had gone, Rachel too. On Lisa's last night, everything she was leaving behind was fed into a massive bonfire in the front yard. We harvested the vegetables from the garden and stuffed our faces, giving away what we couldn't eat. That was our last night on the stoop, and that night in my room I literally curled up in ball and cried — full-scale man sobs — at the thought of losing Lisa, last of the Brusubi crew. I'd like to say it was strong drink that brought on this fit, but it was the fear of having my friends — my security blanket — stripped away. You can get through anything if you have your friends around, and we'd become exceptionally tight friends. We'd been through a lot. But there was more to it than just nostalgia. My friends were my world, literally a microcosm of my universe. They were the only people I knew who understood me and my cultural references, the music I listened to, the news I read, the jokes I told.

It was an intimidating prospect. Only Rosaleen, Abai and I were left of the original crew. Rosaleen and Abai started to date and so naturally were spending more time together. I'm not an extrovert by any means, but the idea of putting down roots in a place where I'd be eating every meal and drinking every drink alone — which was the majority of time — gave me pause. It might sound like I'm exaggerating, but it really worried me. It wasn't a language thing or an intelligence thing, it was a lack-of-things-in-common thing. I knew eventually, as time went by, as I became a local, it would be easier to make friends, but I also knew my whiteness and foreignness would always be something to trip over. I was sure the robbery had been motivated by the fact we were white. Our trip to Jufureh showed just how difficult it was to do simple things like take a day trip. The closest local friends we'd made were Ousman and Mustafa, and we had some good times, but in the end, dealing with them was tiring. Outside the fact they were clearly grifting us, conversation was painfully one-sided: they had no interest in where we came from or even who we were as people. I knew this wasn't everyone, and I knew I would eventually make some new friends, but how long would that take? Could I hold my breath that long?

Another feeling bothered me as well, the feeling of being the last one at the party, of being stuck in neutral when everyone else was moving on. I had worked in restaurants when I was younger, and every place had a waiter in his 40s with a ponytail and an earring who was always trying to hang out with us youngsters. It was pathetic to watch, and now the memory made me wonder how I came across to the interns in the Gambia.

In the end, it came down to a nagging doubt. I still wasn't feeling "finished." I wanted to see more. Luck[107] had gotten me to Africa, and I wanted to see where else it might take me. For me, the Atlantic was the Rubicon, and there was no going back now. I'd gambled on my career, and I couldn't go back with a paltry six months of troubleshooting printers and Internet connections. I needed more to justify my decision.

In my last couple of months at the centre I'd grasped around for options, and eventually opportunity arrived in the form of a small, balding white man with an indeterminate accent. He marched up the stairs of the centre late one afternoon. Short, wearing khakis and a blue button-down, he bounded up the stairs with a cellphone to his ear and strut into the place like it was a public street. A public street he owned, and I guess he did, to a degree. I'd soon discover this was the guy who'd built the centre's network, the one I'd wondered about when I was a wide-eyed intern fresh off the plane. Samantha introduced us and two weeks later I had a new job.

Peter Hanoush was an interesting chap. He was a Gambian, born and raised. Wolof was his first language, but he was, like a large minority of West Africans, of Lebanese extraction, and by extraction I mean he looked whiter than me. His hair (what was left of it) was fair and straight, and his skin was British-style white and looked prone to burning. My olive skin,

---

107 And/or stupidity.

slowly baked over the last six months, looked a lot darker. His family was one of the many Lebanese families that had left the Levant in the mid-19th century.[108] I figured this meant he was a Maronite, although he never mentioned it and I never brought it up. The Maronites were a group of Lebanese Christians who suffered hard under Ottoman rule in the late 19th century. So hard, in fact, that several European powers came to their aid in 1860, and forced the sultan to re-evaluate his preferred mode of governing Christians. Always second-class citizens in the eyes of the Ottomans, a Maronite diaspora began around the turn of the 20th century, and I figured the Lebanese population scattered over a lot of West Africa was a result of that exodus.[109] Every Lebanese I met in the various parts of West Africa I'd eventually visit was a Christian, and the date of their families' arrival suited the timeframe.

Peter was no exception. He told me his family had been living in West Africa since the early 1900s and had done quite well. But when his father died, the family fell into poverty, and it was up to his mother — and a more formidable woman you'd never meet — to pull the family back from the edge. Even among the expats, her hard-nosed, tough-talking, blitzkrieg-bargaining style was legendary. Everyone called her Mama Hanoush. Now in his late-30s, Peter had a degree from a U.K. college, an imported Volkswagen and his own computer business, CompCorp Solutions.

About a week after our first meeting, Peter emailed me, asking if we could talk. He took me for a beer at one of the fancy hotels in Senegambia and told me flat out he saw potential. He needed a project and operations manager who could fill the void left by his business partner who'd taken a job overseas. He needed someone who could really "drive people," who could really "crack a whip." CompCorp was an ISP, an Internet Service

---

108 A lot of the Africell guys had a similar background.
109 A lot of the Maronites went to the United States and Canada as well.

Provider. In other words, they connected people to the Internet. In the same way you'd call Bell or Verizon for Internet access back in North America, in the Gambia you'd call CompCorp. Like all small ISPs, they were reselling bandwidth leased from a national provider. In the Gambia, this was the government-run national teleco,[110] Gamtel. I won't bore you with the details, however, a few comments are in order considering it was CompCorp's primary purpose, and as a result, mine for the next two and a half years.

Connecting to someone's website is pretty much like driving to someone's house. The metaphoric use of highway terminology[111] isn't perfect, but it's not too far off the mark. Imagine you're driving to Cleveland.[112] You get there by navigating through a connecting series of paved roads, each one capable of carrying more traffic than the last. You start at your house. Your driveway connects to a quiet neighbourhood street, which in turn connects to a major city street that handles more and faster traffic. From the city, you'd join the freeway system, which handles millions of cars, all travelling at speed. The freeway system brings you to Cleveland's major streets, connecting you to the smaller and slower neighbourhood roads, and finally into your friend's driveway.

Your computer travels to Cleveland the same way, more or less. It starts by jumping through the air to the wireless device you bought when you "got the Internet," and from there into your telephone line (your driveway). It goes down the same quiet neighbourhood street your car did, albeit in a cable suspended above it on poles or sometimes buried

---

110 *Teleco* is an old term still used by networking people. It was originally an abbreviation for "telephone company," although nowadays it also refers to telecommunications companies as well. (The difference is that telephone companies only provide telephony services, while the latter provides both telephony and data services. Almost all telephone companies have migrated into being telecommunications companies.) Verizon and Bell Canada are both telecos.

111 The "information super highway," for example. "Internet traffic" for another.

112 Who doesn't want to drive to Cleveland?

underground. Those local telecommunications cables eventually meet at a local telephone exchange a couple of kilometres from your house. From there, your computer's traffic is routed through larger and more capable city networks and finally into the Internet backbone (national freeway). The backbone consists of tens of thousands of high-capacity fibre-optic cables that move trillions of electronic messages every minute, connecting major networks, cities and even nations. After flashing down the backbone, your computer gets off at Cleveland and passes through smaller and smaller exchanges until it reaches the cable running into the server from which you're accessing your porn.[113] Again, it's not a perfect metaphor, but it does help illustrate the problems surrounding Internet access in places like the Gambia. To extend the metaphor to the Gambian situation, the problem is that the local roads are awful. There's no easy way to get to the backbone. The backbone is closer to Africa than you might think: submarine cables lie off the West African coast. The biggest is WACS, the West Africa Cable System. WACS was designed to connect South Africa to England, with landing points along the way. A consortium of South African companies put up the money and a French cabling company did the work. The Gambia didn't buy into WACS, but its neighbour Senegal did.

As a result, Gambia's route to the backbone ran through Senegal, so from a communications point of view, the Gambia was landlocked. As long as peace and good cheer reigned, things were fine. You could access the backbone via Senegal. But the connection was tenuous at best. At that time, Peter told me there was about three gigabits of throughput for the entire country to use. In other words, assuming every house had an ADSL modem, the bandwidth we'd use in North America to service about five of six residential streets had to serve the whole nation.[114] Gamtel, the national

---

113 Statistically speaking, our hypothetical user probably is surfing porn.
114 Later, we found out the national gateway to the backbone was actually larger than

telephone provider, managed the connection.

So a connection to the backbone existed, but how did you get to it? The cabling network in the Gambia was about as well maintained as the roads.[115] Trying to get a connection with a dial-up modem could be excruciatingly difficult, and services like ADSL and DSL were nonexistent when I started working there.

Enter CompCorp. Although a full-service computer shop providing hardware repairs, website development and technical support, the core of Peter's business was getting people's computers in touch with the backbone. He did this by flying over the roads. That's right. When you signed on with CompCorp, your computer didn't climb through ratty old cables — no sir! Your computer strapped on a jetpack and flew to CompCorp HQ, and from there it was packed off to the wider Internet. In other words, they used wireless technology. The plan was simple.

CompCorp HQ was only a block away from a major Gamtel exchange, one of the biggest in the country. A cable was strung from the office straight to Gamtel, the short distance improving reliability.[116] The upshot: CompCorp HQ had a fairly good connection to the national gateway. In order to get client traffic to the office, however, a 45-metre mast was set up in the office courtyard. The segments of the mast were imported from the U.K., each painted white or fire-engine red, and from a distance it looked like any telecom mast you've ever seen anywhere.[117] Near the top, several antennas were strapped to it, flat panels, each the size of a large coffee table book. Cables from each antenna ran down the mast and

---

that, and all but 3 GB was reserved for governmental use.

115 Which is to say, they pretty much weren't at all.

116 Every extra foot of cable or extra device on a circuit is something that could go wrong. The shorter and simpler the connection, the fewer problems.

117 Up close, you could see the rusted bolts and notice that the assembled segments weren't even close to straight.

terminated in the office, and from there the traffic they carried was routed to Gamtel. The client had a similar antenna[118] at their home or office, suspended outside on a wall with a cable running to their local computer or computers.[119] If you were a CompCorp client, your computer travelled to Cleveland by running through a cable up to your antenna, which shot it several kilometres through the air to a receiving antenna at HQ, and from there, it went down the mast and into the office where it was routed to the exchange via the leased line running to Gamtel. From there, it was routed around Gamtel's network, eventually ending up in Senegal, where it bounced around its national network and finally into the backbone via the WACS submarine cable, and from there to the U.K. and the rest of the world. Setting up these kinds of long-range Wi-Fi networks and maintaining them was CompCorp's Alpha and Omega. And it was big business.

With families and businesses scattered and transit a mess,[120] information systems and telecom were the glue holding people together:

---

118 The one at the centre was strapped to the roof and you could examine it up close.

119 The router in your house is no doubt also a wireless access point and you use the wireless to connect the machines in your house. We only rarely used wireless routers to set up home or office networks. The frequency Wi-Fi operates at (2.4, 3.5 and 5 GHz) has poor penetrative powers, but in North America, where houses are just wooden frames covered in drywall, it's no problem to put a Wi-Fi router in one room and connect to it wirelessly from another. In the Gambia and most of Africa, buildings are generally made out of cinderblocks. Wi-Fi penetrates cinderblocks about as well as light does, so when we connected a client, we usually had to run Ethernet cabling throughout the house or office in order to connect the machines.

120 It wasn't just the roads either. I came back from a conference in Tanzania only a few months ago, and while waiting for the last attendees to land before going to the hotel, conversation turned to the favourite icebreaker in airports all over Africa: "How long did it take *you* to get here?" I've played this game in every African airport I've ever been in (the Gambia, Ethiopia, Guinea, Uganda, Senegal, Sierra Leone), so it was no surprise to be playing it in Tanzania too. Flying across Africa is almost as nuts as driving. For example, the attendee from Zambia took almost two days to get there, having to fly to Europe first, then turn around and fly to Tanzania, which is the country next door to Zambia. It had taken me less time to come from Canada.

190

travelling workers with their families, businesses with their clients.

CompCorp HQ was in Mama Hanoush's compound, situated just off Kairaba Avenue, the major commercial stretch of the Gambia. In addition to Mama's house, it also contained a massive concrete warehouse used by his brother's grocery business. In the very back pushed up against the back wall of the compound, behind the warehouse, below the low hanging branches of the trees outside the wall, stood a long, narrow building, its single story dwarfed by the three-story warehouse. Only five feet separated the two buildings, and as a result, the smaller one was perpetually cast in shadow. A third of its hundred odd feet was a bachelor apartment. The rest was CompCorp HQ.

The apartment was my new home. It was basically a storeroom, chockablock with chairs and other bits of furniture, everything covered in a thick layer of dust. There were two barred windows filmed with so many cobwebs and grime you could barely see through them. Not that it mattered. The shade from the warehouse and trees blocked any chance of sunlight, but there was a bathroom with a small shower and occasionally hot water.

The door on the other end of the building, the one closer to the courtyard, opened into CompCorp HQ. It was amazingly crowded. The building itself was only about 20 feet wide, which was fine for my apartment but made for some cramped office space. The main corridor was so narrow, two people couldn't pass without pushing flat against the walls. There were three offices off the corridor, and their walls were made of thin plywood painted white. You could see them flex when someone pressed against them in the hallway. The walls didn't go all the way to the ceiling except in the last office, which wasn't an office at all but the server room. Peter occupied the second office and the secretary the last. Both Peter and the secretary had a small, Ikea-looking L-shaped desk with room for one chair opposite. A second visitor would have to stand and lean against the plywood, and a third would be around on Peter's side of the desk or out in the hall. One end of the corridor opened into the workroom where the staff fixed computers on two large tables, and the other end opened into a small kitchenette.

The server room was the core of the operation. It was about as big as a small bathroom in a suburban home in North America. The plywood walls extended to the ceiling to trap the chill from the wall-mounted air conditioner, which kept the machines cool. In the centre of the room was a rack with four blue boxes — each about the size and shape of a pizza box — bolted to it. Cables streamed out their backs, and green and amber lights danced frantically across their front: the servers. There were UPSs in the room as well as a large switch and other networking paraphernalia. This was where the cables running from the antennas on the mast outside met the cable running to Gamtel. The critical importance of the latter was obscured by its appearance, looking pretty much like any other telephone line. Nevertheless, this plywood room was the main communications hub for a lot of people, including most of the NGO sector in the Gambia. This room, with its four pizza boxes and kinked telephone line, routed over half a million emails a month between the Gambia and the rest of the world.

The importance of this little plywood closet to the good works of the NGO sector was staggering. I remember being called on a Saturday by a frantic client because they needed to email a grant application off to the U.K. and the email was down. The value of the grant was nearly a quarter of a million pounds. One of the most important tasks for all NGOs is to maintain financial accountability to their sponsors back home, and accountability meant paperwork: receipts and reports, for instance. All that stuff needed to get to their home office back in Europe or wherever it was. Without email, they wouldn't be able to keep operating. It wasn't sexy work like Médecins Sans Frontières, but we did keep a huge number of NGOs and institutions like the EU connected — tenuously — to the rest of the world. One look at the long, spindly wire stretching from CompCorp to

Gambtel, the bird shit splattering it, the kids whacking at it where it sagged low, and you'd never credit it as the path to the Internet and over half a million NGO emails a month, but it really was the tether to the world for many people. The demand to move financial documents and reports back to Europe or North America would eventually lead CompCorp into conflict with the government, with almost disastrous results.

As a member of the private sector, the bread-and-butter was the nonprofit sector. Whereas in the West the private sector creates the wealth, and the nonprofits and public sector constantly fight for grants and a seat at the foundation fundraiser, in the Gambia wealth was brought in by the NGOs and the private sector tried to chisel a living out of them. Most of CompCorp's business — and that of most other tradesman — came from the NGOs. They were all in the tourist industry. Instead of catering to middle-class families out for a tour, restaurants catered to wealthy World Bank or European Union employees. There were three ISPs in the country worth talking about and they all made the balance of their money providing NGOs with the communications access they needed to get their jobs done. Email access back to the old world, software and hardware support for their offices, as well as networking and Internet access.

I'd be working for peanuts, and to make things worse, Peter was the bank and he'd hold my money. On request, he'd give me what I needed — theoretically. Basically, I'd be an immigrant day labourer, just with more responsibility. There was another snag: I wouldn't have a Canadian sponsor. There'd be no organization back home looking out for me and no one to call if it all went wrong.

I guess the whole venture sounds a little ill-advised in hindsight. On the other hand, it's not my sound decision-making that's made me the man I am today. After all, someone's got to pursue the "not so great" ideas. I signed on the spot. I never really had a paper contract with Peter. My entire time there was governed by verbal agreements and promises, which was the Gambian way.

One of the most important things I learned in my first six months was that personal relationships were everything. You lived and died by your ability to earn people's trust. In the West, we're all about paper. We've got systems in place like the legal system to enforce whatever the paper says. In the Gambia, the courts and police were generally corrupt. The passport fiasco left me with no doubts about that. I reasoned that this might not be the disadvantage it seemed. I'd seen enough of the "official" way of doing things to feel confident I could work the system, and I'd come to feel that "corrupt" was simply a euphemism for "market driven." In other words, if you had money, you could get by. Working in the private sector, I felt I would have real access to the thing that really protected your rights. Certainly it simplified paperwork. Peter just handled it. He knew a cop who handled all the IDs, work permits and general paperwork of the office. I'd give Peter a driver's licence photo and he came back with whatever licences or passes I needed. No questions asked. To be honest, I was more concerned about Peter. If there was trouble and suddenly he didn't "remember" who I was, I'd be in a world of pain.

Office Politics

First weeks on the job.

The atmosphere in the office on my first day was chilly, despite Peter's smiles. I had no relationship with the staff, and they didn't know me or trust me, which they showed with crossed arms and dead stares. Being my first day, I fully expected to be following Peter around in some sort of orientation. Unfortunately, Peter had confidence in my abilities, and so left me in charge after having one cup of coffee.[121] Peter was the younger of two boys. His older brother, Malik, ran a couple of small grocery stores. They'd been opened by Mama Hanoush, and as the senior brother, Malik took over when he was old enough. For whatever reason (I never had the guts to ask), Peter was expected to do the day-to-day management of the grocery stores. His usual habit was to show up at CompCorp for about an hour in the morning, then head off to the grocery store, leaving his partner, which was now me, in charge. After Peter left, things changed.

I was immediately confronted with the angry complaints of the staff. Trust me or not, I was the new manager and everyone wanted to get their complaints registered first thing. The core of the team at that time — the

---

121 Mary made his coffee every morning, or whenever he felt like having one. He'd just bellow at her over the partition.

long-serving Samba and the 19-year-old boy-genius Randy — both swore they'd quit within the week if Mary, the secretary, wasn't brought under control. How Mary became the bane of their existence is a long story that sounds a lot like "for the want of a nail." Basically, the story went as follows.

Wireless installations were the keystone of the business. There were variations, but essentially an install involved us getting a pole — six to 12 metres long depending on the site — strapping our antenna to it, levering it up and then somehow strapping it the client's wall or roof using homemade iron brackets. There were all sorts of variations depending on the locale — we once hired a palm tree tapper to climb up a tall palm and strap an antenna to it — but it usually involved four or five of us balancing on a ladder or second-story ledge trying to sway a pole into a bracket. Fortunately,[122] installs only happened a couple of times a month. Our day-to-day work consisted mostly of doing maintenance on the various installs we'd already set up and their associated networks. Clients would call in and complain about a lack of connectivity or whatever, and we'd send someone out to take a look. Connectivity across the country was so bad that trying to sort these things out remotely via something like Remote Desktop was usually impossible. We had to make house calls. As a result, the technical staff spent the majority of their day on the road visiting clients. After the work was done, the client was invoiced and then the client paid. Straightforward stuff, or at least it should have been. Unfortunately, what it really meant was that the company truck — our only transport — became the number one bone of contention in the office.

The Gambia didn't have much in terms of taxation, and as a result, not much in terms of infrastructure. Now that I'm back in North America, I can only shake my head when I hear conservatives talk about arbitrarily

---

122 Or unfortunately, depending on your point of view. Installs were always an adventure, a welcome break from the   monotony of routine support calls.

cutting taxes. I saw firsthand what happens when the government can't levy taxes, and I think a rational businessman who saw a similar scene would be the first person to pass State House a cheque. Conducting commerce without roads is a ticklish thing.

Later, during my time at CompCorp, I was sent to Guinea-Conakry to install a satellite dish for a client. The client was an orphanage, one of several in the country run by a European NGO. Their sponsors demanded a high level of financial accountability from each orphanage, and so the accountant at this location had to report back to HQ in Conakry once a month to deliver his accounts; a trip of about 600 kilometres. There was no other way to do it. The problem was the cost of moving a couple dozen spreadsheets: the roads were so bad they had to buy a new pickup truck almost every month in order to make the run. Having made the run myself, I could see why. The trucks would just fall apart. Vehicles falling to pieces was a chronic problem everywhere. I saw brand-new trucks — Nissan, Land Rover and Toyota SUVs that were only four or five months old — missing mufflers and other, more important pieces. The installation of the dish made it possible for them to deliver their spreadsheets via email and freed up thousands for the kids. Why was this a problem for CompCorp? In a land without online credit options, how do you get paid? Even an IT company is beholden to paper in that kind of environment, and if the roads were a mess, the postal system was complete bedlam.

The postal system consisted of PO boxes. There was no street delivery because there were no street addresses. We once had a client who ran a security firm and he approached us for help with an office equipment theft problem. He had security guards posted all over the Banjul and Kairaba areas. To keep an eye on them, he equipped his supervisors with motorcycles so they could make the rounds. His problem was that the supervisors were stealing the bikes. The striking thing was how they did it. They'd just drive them home. Since there were no street addresses, the only way to find someone was to simply know where they lived or find someone who could tell you. These supervisors would drive into the thick maze of Serekunda and vanish. With the community's protection, there was no way to find them again. The client wanted us to implant GPS devices on the bikes so he'd have some hope of recovering them.[123]

Checkpoints were another problem with the truck. Their usual purpose was to look for drugs or shake down tourists for money. In my time there, not including the incident with Gaston, I was stopped and detained six times: four times for money, twice for drugs. Unfortunately, in one of the latter cases, a friend of mine did indeed have a sizable quantity of "Gambian tobacco" on his person — unknown to the rest of us — and we were all seized. My friend complicated things by panicking and stupidly agreeing to a ridiculous bribe. Stupidly, because the initial bribe was reasonable, but his hasty agreement and visible relief convinced the officer in question he'd netted a big fish and the price went up to almost $2,000 USD. Instead of holding his ground with the initial offer, he agreed to the new price. When I explained to him that no ATM would spit out that much cash, and that he needed a bank, and that it was Sunday and no banks were open, I could see his eyes get glassy with tears. No doubt he was watching his career go *poof* since he was — as the officer guessed — kind of a big deal in a European consulate. We were saved by another officer. He ranked the first guy and reduced the bribe down to the original amount, of which he took half. As we left, he castigated the other guy for inflating the amount: a good Muslim was a man of his word. If a bribe was struck for a certain sum, you couldn't change it after the fact.

That day was exceptional, it usually wasn't so dramatic. They'd just take your phones and stick you in a shack or lean-to by the side of the road

---

123 We were never able to do it. There was just no place to hide a GPS device where it couldn't be removed. It's easier to hide that kind of thing on a car.

and wait for you to pay the fine. Only once did I sit them out, but it meant both the truck and I were delayed by an hour. Peter was livid because without a phone I'd fallen off the grid for a long time.

The lack of an effective postal system, the difficulty of keeping our only transport running and the constant unknown of travelling around made for a serious conflict in the office: who controlled our precious transportation resource, Mary or me? As the secretary, Mary was also a one-woman accounts receivable, and since there was no postal delivery in the country, she demanded the truck be used as her personal mail carriage. She held a veto over the single driver and truck, and she could even order the technical staff to drive her around collecting payments or delivering invoices if the driver wasn't available. I understood that someone needed to collect the money. The problem was that Mary would leave the office for hours and come back with new clothes and shoes and other personal crap. She was even brazen enough to show off what she'd bought to the IT staff, but never to Peter. Each morning for the first week, as we got into the truck and headed to the first stop of the day, Samba and Randy couldn't stop talking about how often they'd had to wait — sometimes hours — to get a lift to a site. On arrival, they'd be chewed out by the client, and then later by Peter for being late. It might sound trivial, but being screamed at daily — particularly when it's not your fault — can get to the best of us. And in the Gambia, a person's betters could literally lay hands on you if they were annoyed. Getting "chewed out" over there was nothing like the quiet disciplinary meetings you see in North America, where it's considered abusive to raise your voice.

I actually saw bosses grab staff members by the collar and throw them around. Once, at a very swank resort, I watched a white European manager grab a Gambian waiter by the back of his jacket and frog march him to places unknown. It wasn't an unheard-of scene, but that incident stood out in my mind because that kid looked really terrified. In addition to being manhandled, the amount of verbal abuse we endured during work hours would make a seaman quiver. Yelling at people in a way that would precipitate an immediate HR complaint — even possible legal action — in North America was normal in a place where the stick wasn't just preferred over the carrot, but seen as the only option. The guys were terrified of being late anywhere. I'd seen my share of office politics issues in North America, but nothing like this. It seemed as if the office was *designed* to polarize. When I first mentioned this to Peter, he confirmed the suspicion: indeed, he'd designed it to ensure fault lines.

The real problem was that Peter didn't trust anyone. No one I met in the Gambia who made money and handled a lot of cash did. At Malik's grocery stores, they had cameras on the tills at all times. A lot of businesses wouldn't give their waiters or cashiers enough change to break a 20-dalasi note. Cash was kept under lock and key — personal lock and keys. We even had a client, a successful import-exporter who kept all of his cash at home. When he paid invoices, he'd go into a back room filled — literally — to the rafters with currency of all kinds and hand us the required notes.

Peter felt the antagonism would keep the office under control, preventing alliances from forming. When it came to arbitration, Peter always favoured Mary. The bottom line was that he needed someone he could trust to handle the cash. If the guys — the workers who made him that cash — decided to quit, so be it. They were replaceable. It was a hiring market and there was always some poor kid who needed a job. Peter was gambling his family's future on CompCorp, and the guys had a bad history. I'd soon find out that stealing networking equipment was a bit of an office hobby, and their theft, arrogance and grumbling left Peter with a bad taste in his mouth. Despite the risks and travails of the job, they were pretty arrogant. Working in IT was a status job to begin with, and despite the complaining, whenever they overcame a problem, there was a corresponding rise in their own self-image. The guys were always complaining about something, mostly about

Mary. Peter knew it too. At some level he understood the tensions he was introducing into the office by leaving Mary in charge, but in the end it came down to trust.

The trust he had for Mary came down to three reasons. The first was the fact she was a woman. There was a distinct understanding among Lebanese Gambians that women were simply more honest and less aggressive than their male counterparts. The second reason was her religion. Although a "sub-Saharan African,"[124] Mary was a Christian. A small population of Christians existed in the Gambia, centred around but not exclusively on the Christian Lebanese community. Generally, Peter tried to hire Christians, in part because he thought Muslim workers were too sluggish during Ramadan, although I never saw any evidence of that. In fact, Mary got the job because she knew Mama Hanoush from church, which brings me to my final and most important point. Mary had a longstanding relationship with Peter's mother and that counted for everything. Qualifications, merit — none of it meant a damn thing in the face of a personal relationship. Mary's power stemmed from her personal relationship with Peter's mom, and that personal relationship trumped any systematic rules or procedures.

I understood to a certain degree. In a place without certifications, where impoverishment and its entourage of problems ran wild, it made good sense to put faith in your personal history with someone. What other guarantees were there? On the other hand, how well do you know anyone, truly? I was pretty sure Peter didn't know Mary was using the truck for personal errands like clothes shopping, which wore the truck down because of the condition of the roads. Whenever she took it out for a joy ride, I wondered if it would be working tomorrow, or would the guys and I have

---

124 This was the politically correct way in West Africa to refer to "black" Africans, as distinct from North Africans, which meant "Arabic."

to push it back to the office for repairs. The boys complained about this every day, but Peter never did anything about it.

They were so insistent I promised to sort the issue within the week. A pretty stupid thing to say your first week at a new job in a foreign country, but what the hell; I needed to make a splash, and more importantly, win their trust. I needed a reason for them to believe in me as their new boss. I really did need to give them some reason too, because on my first day Randy and I took a call where I immediately screwed up a simple email configuration issue. Like a complete ass, after hearing the problem I jumped right in, assuming this network was arranged the same way as the centre's. After a few minutes and a few nervous laughs, Randy bailed me out. Auspicious beginnings indeed.

In the ensuing battle with Mary, I wasn't completely powerless. Simply put: I was a white foreigner. It took me some time to realize what that meant, but I eventually came to understand how Peter used my foreignness as a marketing tool. CompCorp had a *toubob*. Peter flogged it all over town. "Having a *toubob*" was a competitive edge. I remember one day Robel telling me a story about a guy he knew at work. This guy — a local Gambian — had gotten drunk at a restaurant, failed to pay, became angry and was finally thrown out of the place. On his way out he swore revenge: he had a *toubob*. That's right, he had a white man in his pocket! He was thrown out anyway, but apparently it gave the owner pause. It turned out the reason Peter had hired me in the first place was because a competing ISP had just hired a German. Peter felt like he was being out-gunned in the important "own a white man" race and so came looking for me. True, he needed to replace his partner, but he did it with a mind to finding himself a *toubob*. So I had some influence. He might not trust me, but he needed me, to a degree.

Overall, relations in the office were strictly hierarchical. Peter was the captain, Mary his trusted lieutenant, and I was the lowly sergeant, responsible for kicking the even more lowly technical staff. I didn't really know where Peter found the new recruits, but most seemed to be the sons of our wealthier Gambian clients, generally in their early 20s and educated. The usual arrangement was their parents approaching Peter because the kid had expressed an interest in IT. Some had been educated overseas, either in the U.S. or the U.K. and spoke with the appropriate accent. We had one who'd been in prison in the U.S. and his father had brought him back to the Gambia to keep him from going back. I knew them as well as I could, but my job as their manager combined with my foreignness and my age precluded any real friendship. Most of them treated me the way they would a nerdy teacher.

My biggest concern was my relationship with Peter. He was holding all the cards, right down to my paycheque, and so I moved with as much diplomacy as I possibly could. Nevertheless, we had several friction points, the most basic being our approach to work. I always thought we should sit at the office for a bit, half an hour or so before sending anyone out. After waiting, it would be easier to prioritize the problems. Most problems cropped up in the morning anyway. Peter disagreed. It'd promote laziness. When the phone rang, we scrambled — that was the culture Peter demanded. Keep everyone moving, that was his motto. It reminded me of naval captains from the last century who'd force their crews to dance when there was nothing to do in order to keep them tired and docile. Another point of conflict that flared up in the first months was Peter's approach to planning. He had none. His basic point was that planning didn't prevent risk, so what was the point? I understood his point of view. Humans were fallible. Everything we do ends with a standard deviation. The best you can hope for is plus or minus five percent, and all the planning in the world can't change that. Imagine I told you about a vehicle with a $200 billion dollar design budget and a decade's worth of planning behind it by the top planners in the world. Not only that, but the planners and designers had been working on even more complex vehicles for the previous decade. Twenty years of design and experience by the best in the field with practically an unlimited budget — you'd probably assume it was the safest vehicle ever devised. Now if I told you that very same vehicle could get knocked out of the sky by a piece of foam the size of your backpack, you'd probably think I was crazy. But that's exactly what happened to the Space Shuttle *Columbia*.[125] If the space shuttle could fail, any plan could fail, but did that mean we should not do any planning at all?

I argued that some planning was necessary. The big question was how much, and there was no real answer for that. It came down to experience. I agreed with Peter that planning wasn't a silver bullet, it suffered from the law of diminishing returns: initially one hour of planning yields serious returns, but at a certain point, 10 hours of planning won't yield a speck of value. Essentially, I wanted to take an academic approach to figuring out how much time we should devote to it. My plan was to do anything new with only cursory common sense planning and watch what happened. From there, I'd make notes and apply analytic principles to determine what we needed to do and how to streamline the process. Every time we repeated the task we'd take whatever lessons we'd learned and revisit the procedure in a constant feedback loop. I laid this on him one afternoon, sitting in his chair at his computer with a spreadsheet I'd developed to log our progress. He just stared at me in silence. The look he gave me made me feel like I'd just pulled my glasses off for dramatic effect and announced with a Walter Cronkite gravitas that I was Bippy the Clown. In a whisper

---

125 The space shuttle was designed, prototyped and tested from 1971 to 1982, the year of its first flight. It was designed by many of the people responsible for the Mercury and Apollo programs, which had the even more complicated task of taking humans to the moon. There are differing figures for the total cost of the program, some as low as $190 billion and some as high as $209 billion, so I'm going to split the difference and say $200 billion.

bespeaking simmering rage, he said, "*I* decide what we need to do."

The last major sticking point between us was my approach to the guys. I wanted to create a happy and positive working environment where people felt they could experiment and make mistakes. A true learning environment where we could collaborate on solutions, where everyone would be happy to come to work. Peter was appalled, speechlessly appalled. The first time I mentioned my vision, he made it clear we shouldn't discuss it again. I tried as well as I could within the confines of Peter's dictates to bring my plan about, asking the guy's opinions and generally trying to engage them. I even tried to help them with other aspects of their lives. One time I let one of the older hands drive because he wanted to get a licence but didn't have a car at home to practise with. Within seconds of turning the ignition, he'd taken side mirror clean off while backing the truck out of a client's site. The usual insanity of the day was enhanced by me racing around to fix the mirror between ferrying guys to sites. Peter never found out because I dodged all the usual garages since they were clients and used glue to fix the plastic frame. A local glass merchant replaced the mirror by cutting a piece out of a bathroom mirror.

My insistence on treating the guys like grownups, letting them contribute to the planning (such as it was) and letting them show initiative really stuck in Peter's craw, especially when it went wrong. Which, in Peter's defence, it did often. I remember one time I decided to give one of my best guys, Amat, a little responsibility. One of our biggest clients, an NGO had rigged up a computer lab for training purposes and wanted it on the Internet. There was about a dozen machines, all in good working order, which was an achievement. I knew from my time in D.C. that it was hard enough to keep a computer lab running in North America. Give a kid control of a computer and all kinds of hilarity ensues. When you considered the infrastructure problems of the Gambia, that lab was practically a miracle. A real testament to the determination and commitment of the NGO to train their people.

I'd already looked the site over and had developed a plan: we'd run a cable through the concrete wall of the lab and place an antenna on the outside of the wall. That antenna would connect to the receiver on the main building, some 200 metres away, thereby connecting the lab to the rest of the network. Simple. I figured my guy was up to it, and after explaining the plan I left Amat and a new guy with cables, ladder, antenna and power tools. I told them to call me when they'd finished, figuring it should take them about 30 minutes. Off I went.

Two hours later, my phone calls unanswered, I dropped in to see what was going on. I could feel my jaw clenching as I walked up the drive. Amat was on top of the ladder yelling impatiently in Wolof at the other kid, who was yelling back passionately. They were covered in sweat and white dust. Amat's eyes popped wide when he noticed me and I knew the sweat wasn't all physical exertion. The wall, which should have had a single hole in it about the size of a penny, had been savaged. There were, in fact, several holes, all very large, but only one passed through the cinderblock wall, and that was the size of my head. I could see right though it from 30 feet away. A long and expensive drill bit, which I instantly recognized as not belonging to us, was suspended in the middle of the hole, wedged tightly between two pieces of rebar.[126] Amat was on the ladder hammering desperately with a hammer and chisel. This wasn't the worst part. Before they could open their mouths, I flew into the lab: every monitor, computer, mouse, keyboard, table and chair was covered in a layer of concrete moon dust.

---

126 Rebar, or "reinforcing bar," is the stuff that well-built concrete structures use as a strengthener. If you pass a construction site, like an overpass, you'll see the ends of it sticking out of the structure. They usually bend it into a framework that can be covered with concrete. Using rebar in a small, single-story outbuilding was the sign of people who believed in doing things right, which was part of my panic because it told me that the NGO had really put a lot of effort into the lab.

With calm resignation (read here: *total despair*), I listened to their story as I sucked on a cigarette. They'd figured the drill bits we had weren't long enough, and rather than take a measurement and drill from the other side of the wall to finish the hole, they'd decided to borrow a drill bit from the NGO's maintenance team. I almost cried. One glance said that it was expensive, and that it was destroyed. They'd started the hole, reconsidered a couple of times and finally punched a hole straight between two closely spaced reinforcement bars. When the bit stuck, the drill went wildly out of control, finally burning out — Peter would have my head for that alone — and so they got a hammer and chisel and went to work, trying to salvage the bit, and so increasing the mess they'd already started.

There was no point in being angry when it had been my idea to let them use their initiative. I reprimanded them gently by telling them what they should have done: measured, stayed away from the corners because that's where rebar supports were located in most concrete walls and called me if they still had problems. I slouched off to face the music, figuring I'd just lost my job. Had it been up to Peter, I probably would have too, but the director of the NGO, an Englishman who understood what I'd been trying to do in terms of empowering my staff, intervened.

Peter responded to my attempts at teambuilding by trying to fit me into the Gambian mold. Only he and Mary had offices and desks. My station every morning was literally standing at Peter's side. It showed respect to stand. At some workplaces in the Gambia, it was normal for employees to stand when their boss entered the room. I represented a source of worry to him as well as optimism. He wanted my foreignness, but he didn't trust the crazy Western ideas I was bringing into the office. Naive notions of "teamwork" and "consensus building." Would I be judgmental about the way he ran things? Could I really snap a whip and provide the ram-rod, ass-clenching discipline required to maintain the status quo? I was standing because Peter wanted to show the office that he was still top dog.

Peter was a clever man, though. As his sergeant, he knew he also had to boost me up. When the guys asked him technical questions, he'd always throw them to me first. Fortunately, the questions weren't very difficult. What's the difference between a hub and a switch? Why do motherboards have a battery? How does DSL work? Nonsense like that. It was simple stuff that Peter was confident I'd answer easily but would baffle the guys. He was trying to impress them with my knowledge. It was clever. I looked smart, but he looked smarter. He was the one asking the questions: the sagely teacher to my eager student. I was basically the head prefect.

But in the end Peter was a disciplinarian. There were no kid gloves in his wardrobe, a point he drove home about a month after my start. It was the end of another day riding around with Samba and Randy, troubleshooting email, network connections and collecting computers to bring back to the office for repair. It had been a good day, which was a rarity, and I expected Peter to show up with the energy of a child at Christmas. The last time fate had favoured us, he blew into the office around 4 p.m., slammed the door, clapped his hands and rubbed them together like Scrooge McDuck. "Mary! How much?" he bellowed. How much cash had we collected? How much was in hand? Her answer determined how the rest of the afternoon briefing went. When the news had been good, he called to Mary to make him a coffee. "Coffee, Mary! Straight away, Mary! *Atcha! Atcha!*"[127]

If we did our usual, however, he'd start yelling at her in Wolof, raising his voice to levels that would bring people out of their offices in a North American workplace. He'd storm out of her office and into his own, where I waited to give him my own update on the day's work. He'd waive me out of the way angrily if I happened to be standing between him and the desk (which was unavoidable considering the size of the office), sit down,

---

127 *Atcha* essentially meant "Go, go! Quick as you can."

power up his email and listen over his shoulder to my report. No real work progress meant fist pounding on the desk and more yelling. Once, he hit the desk so hard his pencil holder fell over the side. I'd try to placate, explaining why this job or that was more complicated than it sounded, but he never wanted to hear it. Mitigating circumstances weren't his problem. On the other hand, if it was good news all around, he'd be loud and bluff, making snide comments and visiting the workroom to rib the guys in a good-natured way. He'd never tell them they'd done a good job, but when he mocked your clothes or scoffed at how long it took you to solve a problem, you understood it to be a "job well done."

On that particular afternoon he was different, no bile, no bonhomie. He listened to Mary and me with a distracted pensiveness. Because I lived next door, usually I was the last to leave, and that night, after the others were gone, he asked me quietly if I wanted to go for dinner. It's difficult to say no to the boss, so I didn't. I swallowed hard when I heard we'd be dining next door at his mother's place.

It was a pleasant enough meal. Mama Hanoush was happy, clearly enjoying playing host. We sat down to grilled chicken, vegetables and a rice dish that was one of Mama's special recipes. About halfway through, Peter decided to tell me what was on his mind. It was about work, the way I'd been handling things. He went about it by telling me a story, the story of Hafeez.

Once upon a time there was this kid, Hafeez. He was Peter's best guy, considered a superman because he did wireless installs *by himself*. He was a one-man band. It wasn't just installs, he was capable enough to troubleshoot networking issues alone as well, a nice change from most of our other employees who were either on the phone with me or Peter most of the day, asking for guidance. He was by far Peter's best employee, and like any other super trooper, he eventually demanded a raise, which he needed because he just got his young wife pregnant. And why shouldn't he get one? He was clearly outperforming every other staff member, including the vaunted Mary. Speaking of him over dinner, Peter sounded sincerely awed by his abilities. Later, I would check with the guys and Mary, and sure enough Hafeez wasn't just a CompCorp legend designed to motivate the workforce. Samba and Mary had personally witnessed his feats of IT excellence.

On hearing his demand for more money, which would double his salary, about $20 USD more a month, Peter fired him. The look on my face must have been asking "but why?" and he held my gaze for a second and said: "The most important thing to remember about running something over here, Robin, is that no employee is indispensable. The bosses lead and the workers work. If it starts to go the other way, nothing gets done. It's as simple as that. Robin, you can't let your employees hold you hostage. You just can't."

Taken aback — it was a strange moment — I bobbed my head in. Apparently, that was the right thing to do because both he and Mama suddenly turned up the charm. I found out later he'd spoken with the guys and gotten their feedback. I must have gotten some positive reviews because, in hindsight, this was my "welcome to the family" moment; despite everything, I'd passed muster. We finished dinner and went our separate ways for the night.

A Day in the Life

Six months on the job. A Monday morning.

I tapped the cellphone thoughtfully against my chin. The traffic wasn't bad and my driver Abdu knew his business. He barely spoke English and my Wolof was pretty terrible, but in the six months we'd worked together, we'd developed a system of one-word demands and answers that was primitive but efficient.

"Abdu, Kairaba!

"*Slobin, wau!*"[128]

"*Atcha, atcha!*"

"*Wau, wau!*"

That morning we were on our way north, to Banjul, where some fat-cat importers couldn't get their email to work. I knew I could fix the problem, but the issue on my mind was the situation to the south.

The day had started simply enough. The Banjul problem was the only major issue that morning, so staff assignments were easy. I divided the guys up in the usual way: two stayed in the office to work on the ever-present pile of broken PCs, an old hand and the new kid.[129] That day I'd leashed the

---

128 Abdu had a heavy accent and always pronounced my name as "Slobin."
129 We changed staff the way people change underwear. There was always a new kid.

211

new kid Ediresa — everyone called him Edi — to Pateh to learn the trade.[130] Samba, our most experienced guy, was already on his way to the European Commission, his standard morning gig. The EC was a big client, so they got a man on-site each morning to work out any wrinkles that might have developed overnight.[131] The last guy I left in the office as a reserve, usually Randy.

I deployed my reserves via our new truck. After about five months of slaving, I'd managed to pry a concession or two out of Peter. Tiny things mostly, better tools, bags to carry them in, that sort of thing. But one concession really counted: Peter had bought us a second truck. He revealed it in classic Peter fashion, parking it in the compound the night before so everyone would see it on their way into the office. "Whose truck is that outside?" was everyone's first question when they walked into the office, and their question was met with stony silence or an angry, "What truck? Boy, can't you see I'm busy?" Peter not looking up from his email the whole while. When everyone was there, he marched into the workroom, called everyone to attention and announced that he'd purchased a new truck for the staff, and — in a no-nonsense tone reminiscent of a gruff but lovable dad giving his kid the keys for the first time — he laid out the ground rules about driving it and maintenance, and then turned on his heel and left. The guys cheered him out. Although a pickup truck like the other one, its cab sat four, allowing all the guys to sit inside. This was a big deal. It raised morale tenfold for the staff to be seen sitting inside a big pickup truck, not in the flatbed like common labourers. Sitting inside meant you were a *professional*

---

130 Invariably, I'd start new guys on the ground floor: hardware repair.
131 Problems always seemed to spring up overnight. We didn't have a night shift, although I unofficially played this role due to the fact that I lived on-site. To Peter's annoyance, however, I was usually senseless with liquor by about 8 p.m. most nights. Without anyone at the controls, our network could drift into some very strange waters.

and they were pleased. Samba and Randy had even stopped threatening to leave. Although he presented the truck as his own idea without mentioning me at all, it had been something I'd been bugging him about for weeks. I felt the new truck was my first coup, but I knew Peter was watching me. I saw the truck as his first acknowledgement that I might be onto something, but I also knew that if I didn't get results, the truck would vanish as fast as it had arrived. The tension between us was still running pretty high. Each concession I scored had to be justified every single day.

That morning had started like any other, with the usual deployments, but in 10 minutes storm clouds gathered. Fatou had just called me on my personal cellphone to complain: there was no Internet or email access down at the centre. This wasn't standard procedure. Clients weren't supposed to call me, clients were supposed to call the office, where Mary recorded the call on paper and then passed it on to me via phone. I'd figure out how to weave the new problem into the fabric of the workday based on who was where and what they were good at, how important the client was, how difficult the problem sounded and how many hours were left on the clock. After juggling the variables, I'd call whomever I wanted to handle the problem, then call the person who had the truck closest to him and have the latter collect the former and deposit him at the site. Finally, I'd call the client to let him know that help was on the way. This process was complicated by the state of the phone system.

Mary had three phones in her office and I carried two mobiles. This was due to the fact that there were three telephone providers in the country: Gamtel, the national teleco, which handled landlines; Gamcel, the national cellphone provider; and Africell, another cellphone provider based out of Lebanon that had somehow managed to convince the government to allow it to operate in Gambia. Calling one provider from another was very expensive, so in order to maintain communications, Mary and I had several phones: a cell for Gamcel, one for Africell and a landline via Gamtel for

Mary. Communications were hampered further by the fact that the guys only carried their personal cellphones and wouldn't use them to call my own Gamcel line. I didn't blame them; it was their personal phone and Peter wouldn't compensate them for their use.

Fatou calling me directly wasn't procedure and I'd become utterly paranoid over any deviation from routine. Having experienced the uncertainties of getting a police report or taking a weekend jaunt, not to mention the chaos a misplaced word or the wrong bill coming out of your wallet at the wrong time could cause, changes in routine gave me pause. It always meant something unexpected was going to happen, and once things started to drift off course, it became harder and harder to right them. If I moved to catch the unexpected, would I be able to get things back on track?

I knew why she'd called me directly: she wanted to leverage my personal relationship with the centre in order to jump the cue and get first crack at service. I could have turned the truck around right there, "Abdu, centre!" and we'd have been heading south in seconds. At this point, it was almost an equal distance either way. But I took my reputation seriously. The guys in Banjul were a big deal. Like the EC, they wanted first-class service and were willing to pay for it. They'd signed a contract in good faith and took us seriously. We'd made promises to them, *I'd* made promises to them.

Reputation was everything. As a businessman, my dad hated movies about business. He hated the backstabbing and boardroom cat fighting; he thought it was total nonsense. He used to say, "You get by in business by the number of people willing to shake your hand, not the number of bodies you step over." I'd made promises and I had to come through on them.

Of course, leveraging personal relationships happens everywhere, but it took on a new dimension in the Gambia. The obligation to answer personal favours was so strong I had to warn our guys about handing their numbers out to clients. Often I'd send them somewhere, only to find out they'd left in the middle of the work because another client had made "a personal request."

Whereas in D.C. or Canada, I could — if I had to — weasel out of a personal request by saying I was double-booked or that I'd promised to edit someone's report. In the Gambia, this didn't impress anyone at all.[132] A contract with a client? So what? I'd *eaten* with the centre staff. Once, I'd even eaten dinner at Fatou's *house*. Honoured by being invited into the sanctity of her home, her request for help trumped any mere business arrangement.

"Robin, we have an emergency here." She spoke with clipped formality.

"I understand. I'll send one of my guys over right away."

"You are not coming yourself?" she asked with flat contempt.

"Unfortunately, Fatou, I'm halfway to Banjul. I'm nowhere near you guys."

"Eh, Robin, you act like you don't want to know us anymore!"

"That's not true, Fatou."

"But, Robin, you leave us in this state. No one can work."

"I know, Fatou. I'm sending someone right away."

"But you yourself are not coming?"

"Nope."

"Eh, to be treated so!" And she hung up. I immediately called Mary and had her dispatch the guy I'd left behind, Randy.

So here I was, obsessing over possibilities. Had I made the right decision? What might happen? What could go wrong? Was I using my own problem-solving skills the right way? Should I be heading south, to Brusubi

---

132 This was pretty much true of everywhere I've done any work in Africa. Years later, while working in Toronto, I attended a seminar given by a woman who ran an organization that sent volunteers in the medical field to needy places. The whole theme of her orientation was: "Everything rides on personal relationships. If people don't trust you, they won't even bother with you, no matter what services and supplies you've got. Your fancy medical and academic degrees don't mean a thing." She was right.

and the centre? What could be the matter? My mind flipped through the history of both sites, the one in Banjul and the one in Brusubi. Had we made a recent fix to either that might have created a new problem? Every network's different. They're organic things, adapted to their environments, no two alike. Like any organism, they develop aches and pains, and some are chronic. You get a feel for them, understanding the kinds of problems a particular network is likely to suffer from. I was hoping I could figure it out in the truck. If I could figure out the most likely cause of the problem in Banjul, I could quickly run in, apply the fix and run out. If I could figure out what was wrong — or likely wrong — at the centre, I could telephone Randy with the answer. Could the antennas have gotten out of alignment? Not likely at the centre, but possible with the importers in Banjul. I knew the damn thing was a bird roost. I knew because I'd climbed through inches of guano to install it in the first place. Maybe the network switch was causing problems? Or the proxy server? Could someone have rolled a chair over a cable? It'd happened before. There was another option: could the problems with email in Banjul and Brusubi be related? Something wrong at the office, our connection to Gamtel, for example, or our core router? Should I head straight back to the office and forget Banjul and Brusubi?

I can still remember sitting in the truck pondering these ideas. In the larger sweep of my life, those decisions were the tiniest details, but there I was, literally sweating the details. Health and wellness types always tell you to try and look past the little things, but as an IT professional, details were my whole world. I knew a detail as small as a strip of tape could kill 70 people. Sounds fanciful, but it happened. In 1996, Aeroperú Flight 603 crashed into the sea while flying from Lima, Peru, to Santiago, Chile. Shortly after takeoff, the instruments and flight computer went nuts. They were flying too low, too high, too slow and too fast, according to the warnings firing off in the cockpit. They tried to return to Lima, but flying at night over the water, without visual cues, they flew the plane right into the ocean. The investigation reported that during the cleaning of the plane, pieces of duct tape were put on the plane's static ports to prevent damage. The static ports are small holes in a plane that measure air pressure and feed that data back to the instruments, where it's interpreted as altitude and airspeed. Someone forgot to take the tape off. As a result, the instruments on this $50 million dollar machine stopped working and 70 people died. Because of tape. No matter which decision I made, the results wouldn't be anywhere near that tragic. I understood this intellectually, but emotionally I was fearful of what would happen if I screwed up. My money, the roof over my head, even my legal status in the country depended on the good will of one man, and he was fickle. It didn't help that so far my enlightened ideals of planning, preparation and creating a positive work environment hadn't yielded any results. If I failed that day, would it be the straw that broke the camel's back? Of all the questions running through my mind, that one was always front and centre every morning.

Too much planning? Too little? One way or the other, I'd made my decision. Aces high, jokers wild, off we went — north. In the end, I felt I knew the network at the centre well enough to fix it over the phone. Randy was there, a solid guy. I was sure I could walk him through any problems, so Abdu and I blasted down the highway toward Banjul. Abdu, sensing my pensiveness, was hunched over the wheel, fists tight at the three and nine o'clock positions. I was rolling the importer's network over in my head, readying myself for arrival.

We arrived, and I jumped out of the truck before it stopped. Every second counted. With relief, I diagnosed the problem instantly. The switch wasn't working, probably blown in a power surge. No problem, all I needed was a new switch and I could vacate Banjul and get down to Brusubi. The importers were surly because email had been out for awhile (it was almost 9:30 a.m.) and now I needed to find a part. I told them this wouldn't be a problem; only yesterday we'd been told that one of our hardware vendors had a switch for sale, and it was in their Banjul office! For once, coincidence was working on our side. I ran down the stairs, jumping the last few, and Abdu — who'd been enjoying a cup of tea with the watchman — slammed his glass down on a cinderblock and leaped for the door of the truck, "Abdu, ITS!"[133]

"Kairaba?"

"No, Banjul office. Banjul!"

"*Wau!*"

It was the middle of the morning, and so the five-minute ride took about 25 because of traffic. We pushed along slowly in first and second gear, through the donkey carts and milling pedestrians who seemed to be walking in every direction at once. On our way there, I got a call. It was the guys I just left — the importers — and they wanted to know where I was. The boss, a Dane with a Viking's temper, got on the phone to let me know that he was losing faith: I'd told them only 15 minutes and they'd be back up and running, and that was 20 minutes ago. He might have to talk to my boss, his voice heavy with "you've forced me to do this, kid." I got threats like that a couple of times a week, so it didn't have much impact. He was just panicking, and experience told me that the best way to deal with panic was to solve the problem. I hung up and moments later got another call from the centre. Pateh got on the line, which was weird because I'd left him in the office with the new guy working on hardware.

"Pateh, where's Edi?"

"He's here with me. Don't worry, Robin, I brought him."

"Yeah, but you're supposed to be fixing machines in the office."

"Yes, I know. Don't—"

---

133 Most places had a paid watchman who basically sat in the compound as a low-rent security guard and go-for. Invariably, they'd have a kettle going, and Abdu would usually spend his time drinking *ataya*, the same heavily sweetened green tea we'd drunk with Ousman and Mustapha.

"I told you to stay in the office. What's going on? And if you're there, where the hell is Randy?"

Apparently, they'd decided to switch places because Pateh felt he could sort the problem and was bored. Randy didn't feel like going to the centre and so decided to stay and fix computers. Pateh was good, but he was still pretty new to the networking world. The thing that really bothered me though, was that he'd taken the second truck. Despite investing in a new truck, Peter refused to hire a second driver; instead, the guys took turns driving the new one. I didn't drive for a couple of reasons. To start with, I didn't know where a lot of places were. There were no street signs, so to get somewhere, you had to know where it was. The other reason was that there were rules in the Gambia about foreigners driving cars. Foreigners weren't allowed to drive at all upcountry. The idea was that if you drove yourself, you were putting a Gambian out of a job. This rule was enforced haphazardly, but in the interests of efficiency, I decided it wasn't worth the risk. The final reason was that by having a driver, the truck was independent. I could send Abdu to pick someone up while I was at a site.

Rather than have Randy drive him up there and return with the truck, he'd just taken it. In other words, if another call came in, I'd have no way of getting Randy to the site. Not only that, but Samba would be done at the EC soon and someone would have to get him. The guys were still sensitive about being left somewhere, and now their recriminations were almost worse when it happened. They'd guilt me about it, complaining with a "you promised this would never happen again." Without the truck, 50 percent of my workforce was marooned. The other problem was that neither Pateh nor Edi had a driver's licence. They'd driven through one of the busiest intersections of the country and then about 10 kilometres down the coastal highway to reach the centre. I knew Pateh could do it. I'd let him drive before, but Edi couldn't. He was also too raw to be left alone at a site. Pateh would have to stay with him and now the truck was grounded.

A few minutes after hanging up, Pateh was on the phone again, full of enthusiasm. He wanted to know where to find the antennas for the Wi-Fi network at the centre. "Uh, they're hanging off the pillars. The big boxes." They were in plain sight.

"Yes, Robin, yes. I see them!" He rang off. I might have felt some relief because I suspected he was on the right track, but asking where the antennas were made me feel like he'd volunteered to fix my car and then asked how to pop the hood.

With a rising sense of panic, I arrived at ITS and ran inside to enquire about the switch. The young woman manning the counter was on the phone, and I chewed my lip waiting for her to finish. When she did, in broken Wolof, I asked her about the switch. She had no idea what I was talking about; she didn't even know what a switch was. I pleaded with her to call her boss and she did. We usually dealt with the boss, whose office was in the Kairaba branch, the very branch that only yesterday had mentioned the switch. She called and chatted away happily, clearly friends with the person on the other end of the line. After a friendly laugh and goodbye, she hung up, and said that it was all a big mistake. There was no switch. Sorry.

"Is there anyone else in Banjul who sells computer stuff?" I asked the same question in several variations until I was understood.

"*Wau.* HighTech Computing."

"Great, where's that?"

"Hmmm. I don't know." She gave a flirty smile, and I was out the door. I called Peter to find out where it was.

"It's near the petrol station. Not the one on the main entrance to Banjul, the other one." The other one? I had no idea what he was talking about, but he was the local, so I told Abdu to go "to the other petrol station." Blank stare. I called Peter again, who was irritated by the interruption. He demanded between curses that I hand the phone over to Abdu. "*Wau, wau…*

Yes, *wau*," answered Abdu and then we were off.

More calls: the situation in Brusubi was critical. The guys and the intern there (my successor, a generation or two removed) couldn't seem to make anything go. Now Idrissa, director of the centre, was calling. "Hello, Robin. Tell me, how can this be?" His tone heavy with disappointment. I listened to the accusations and the insinuations with a clenched jaw, and finally said, "Idrissa. I'll be there as soon as I can be." Cold comfort, but there just weren't any pieces left on the board to move. He hung up.

Another call: the importers again, "What's taking so long!" Another berating, which I cut short by telling them what they wanted to hear: "I'll be there in 20 minutes." A real time of arrival. I wasn't lying either; I thought we could make it.

Another call, Samba this time, the guy I'd sent to the EC that morning, but the number on my phone wasn't the EC's. "Robs! I'm at Opportunities Against Poverty." (What the hell was he doing there?) "They're having a problem; they are having a problem with their email." I listened before tearing into him for abandoning one of our biggest, most prestigious contracts before the appointed time. I'm glad I did too, because Samba, being older and more seasoned than the other guys, already knew what I'd say and was ready.[134] He gave me the full rundown. His time at the EC was almost up when Mary rang saying that Opportunities was driving her mad, calling every few minutes to complain. Samba talked to the head of the EC, explained the situation, and since it was nearly time for him to leave anyway, walked over to Opportunities, which was only a couple of blocks away. The problem was simple: a new email account needed to be set up, but the network at Opportunities was configured in a way Samba wasn't familiar with, so he was calling to find out how to get it done. He was a good man, our Samba. I walked him through it over the phone while looking for

---

134 Just like I used to be ready for Peter's standard criticisms.

HighTech Computing and waving away people trying to sell me mangos, water and nuts through the window of the truck. "OK, Samba, you've got to get Mary to make the new email account in the office, and then you've got to link that email account to their account on the proxy. Then, you've got configure their Outlook account with the account on the server. That's the local proxy server, not the one at the office. Got it?"

"Yes, yes! Start with the proxy."

"Start with Mary. Call her and see if she's made an account for this person, and if not, have her make one."

"Right, Robs!"

"Then you create a local account on the proxy server for them, and add the email credentials to it."

"That's the server, not so?"

"Right, the proxy server is running on the domain controller."

"The server?"

"Yes, the server's in the director's office. Do you know what you have — Sorry, sorry! *De det!*[135] No, thank you. I don't want any ground nuts!"

"Robs?"

"Hang on, Samba. *De det!* Abdu! OK, Samba, you know what you have to do?"

"Which account do I link?"

"The one Mary creates in the office. Just call me back from the director's office. Don't force your way in, though. If he's in a meeting, wait for it to finish."

"*Wau!*" Twenty minutes and no sign of a petrol station, much less HighTech Computing. Dammit! More calls. I didn't even answer them except for one from Randy, who'd managed to destroy the battery on a UPS he was "troubleshooting," or at least that's what it sounded like. Twenty

---

135*De det* was Wolof for "no."

minutes to get to ITS and wait for the girl to get off the phone, another 10 wandering the streets of Banjul looking for HighTech meant my 15-minute estimate was off by 100 percent and we were still nowhere. For five minutes I'd had Abdu asking people in the street for directions. No one knew anything. A call from Peter: "Where the *hell* are you! What's taking so long?!" I explained, and after a strained pause, he told me to keep looking for the petrol station and hung up. Bullshit. There was no station. Back to ITS, someone had to know where the place was.

We returned to ITS.[136] I knew the woman behind the counter didn't know enough English for me to explain to her what I wanted. "Where's the manager?" I asked. "Manager? Manager *bea?*" She understood and brought the manager out, and to my delight she greeted me with excellent English, and then, as if reading my mind, she told me she knew the way to HighTech. I didn't understand the instructions, not having spent much time in Banjul (and you needed that local knowledge because there were no street signs or numbers, remember), so I asked her if she could explain to my driver and she was happy to. I charged down to the car and dragged a bewildered Abdu up the stairs. Finally, I had my driver in front of someone who knew the way. He greeted her with "*nakam*," and she stared blankly.

"Oh, I'm Sierra Leonean. I don't speak Wolof." We all stood and stared blankly at each other. Confounded, my brain was slow to absorb my own appalling luck.[137] When it did, I pushed my way behind the counter, much to the shock of the manager and secretary. I knew ITS taught computer training classes, which meant someone had to speak Wolof (and hopefully English too).

I started running down the hallway, banging on doors and

---

136 Easier going this time — only 15 minutes. I always thanked God for small favours. Even really, really small ones.

137 During my whole time there, I only met three Sierra Leoneans in the Gambia, two who worked at the centre and this woman.

interrupting classes, the office manager being too horrified to stop me. "*Nakam!* Does anyone know where HighTech Computing is? Oh, sorry, sorry." More knocking. Finally, yes, an instructor knew the way and with dignified indignation at the rude interruption explained it to Abdu. Tack 10 on the clock, but alas, we had a destination.

HighTech was across from the main (and only) filling station in Banjul. Peter called, "Status?!" I explained. "Oh, yes. The one I was thinking of closed. Keep me informed." Right. Another call. It was Samba calling back.

"Robs! I'm at the server."

"OK, do they have a local account on the proxy?"

"Uh, one moment, Robs." I waited about five seconds, then started talking through the half-dozen clicks he'd have to make because I didn't have time for him to figure it out.[138] I'd memorized the layout and configuration of most of our 100-odd client networks. Even if I didn't know it cold, I could ask whoever was on site to describe a few details to figure it out. After getting Samba through the server, I asked him to finish up on the client's machine. I was pretty sure he could manage that without a problem.

No call from Brusubi. Should I call them? No, it'd just give them another shot at me, and by this point, it didn't matter anyway. There were three balls in the air: Brusubi, Opportunities and this one in Banjul. The busted-up UPS in the office wasn't a priority. If Samba made the catch at Opportunities and I sorted Banjul — which I was only minutes away from doing — the odds would flip back in our favour, two out of three. We'd have the initiative again, and we'd be in a position to respond, not just react. True, the centre was an old and valued customer, but I'd be down before

---

138 Occasions like this drove me mad. This would have been a perfect educational moment. Figuring things out via trial and error is the best way to learn IT. Samba was keen too. But time ruled our lives.

noon, and besides, the "personal favour game" worked both ways. I'd patch it over by appealing to Idrissa on a personal level. "Idrissa, you know how things work here. Do you remember the trouble you had with the alarm system? How long did that take to fix? Months? We were slow today, but we got it fixed before the end of the day. I'd take it as a personal favour if you'd let this one blow over, and you'll be my first stop next time you need us." Something like that.

At the assigned street corner, we strained our necks looking for the place. Nothing. There was a Star Tech computer shop and I asked a passerby if this was the only computer shop in the area,[139] "*Wau*," so in I went.

It was an old colonial building that'd been "renovated" into a shop. It looked like a junkyard had parked itself inside the lobby of a Carnegie library. I introduced myself and explained my need. Great, they had a switch, but I'd have to wait while they searched for it, so they quietly beckoned me deeper into the gloom, offering me a chair in a little room with a single buzzing neon light and no windows. I thanked them and they shut the door. Dead, dissected computers — most older than me — filled the space, stacked four and five deep. Something was wrong. I felt I knew just about everyone in the IT business in the country, more or less, and they definitely knew me.[140] I'd never seen any of these people before. They wouldn't even look me in the eye. Why did they shut the door? I couldn't hear a sound, not the street or them searching. What was taking so long? It wasn't a big place, so after about five minutes I let myself out and headed for the door. They were all over me, jumping up to catch me before I left. With pathetic desperation, they pushed something at me. If it was a switch, it was one

---

139 At least I thought I did.

140 Most white foreigners in the country worked at NGOs, or were interns or freewheeling individuals, enjoying their retirement on the beach. To have a young white guy join the local private sector was newsworthy. Not long after signing with Peter, people I'd never met were greeting me as "Peter's *toubob*."

they'd used to put Sputnik into orbit. It looked like the offspring of a Commodore 64 and an 80s-era VCR. I wasn't that desperate.[141] This couldn't have been the place.

After one more call — a threat from the importer swearing to tear up the support contract in my face — we finally found the place. It was near Star Tech, just around the corner. They had a switch, so I got it to the client, installed it and spoke with the boss. As I suspected, once things were working, there were no hard feelings. The guilt kicked in when I told my story and heroically volunteered to take all blame from Peter. No need, he called Peter and told him how I'd prevailed against the odds.

I was in a great mood. Both Samba and Pateh had used their initiative, with mixed results mind, but there was a time when none of them would have volunteered to put a CD in a drive. It had been chaotic, but fast-moving situations always are, and besides, we kicked our way through the mess with sheer determination. Samba made the catch at Opportunities, I'd sorted Banjul, and within 30 minutes I'd be at the centre. We were two out of three and it wasn't even noon. We were winning. I called Samba and told him I'd swing by and pick him up on my way to the centre. I told him I'd be there in 15 minutes, and sure enough we were.

It felt good to have an ETA that actually turned out as planned. We rocketed up to the centre, and Samba and I strode in. Samba — flushed with his success at Opportunities — was keen to troubleshoot the problem, so I told him to dive in and went to find Fatou and Idrissa. I made my apologies, going through the script I outlined above, and it didn't take long before we were all chatting happily. Choppy waters smoothed, I went to see how the guys were doing. I didn't give them hell for violating my orders, rather I was

---

141 Clearly this was a computer morgue. Basically, the computer equivalent of a chop-shop. Most of the machines in there would have come out of the trash, or, more likely, stolen from tourists.

patient and explained why it caused a problem with the truck. They responded with grins and shrugged shoulders. I had them give me their diagnosis, and I was happy to hear they'd almost figured out the problem. One of the idiosyncrasies of the centre network was their wireless LAN. The typical wireless kit you have in your house is designed for North America, where houses are essentially hollow walls covered with drywall. Unfortunately, like most buildings in the Gambia, the centre was made of cinderblocks, causing the radio signals to bounce all over the room. The result was highly unpredictable Wi-Fi access, and this was a problem because this internal Wi-Fi network was how the computers at the centre talked to each other. There wasn't a lot we could do, and I used the atmosphere of détente I'd established with Idrissa and Fatou to explain. Maybe we could wire the place up, cables would fix the problem, but they would cost money. I spoke and they listened with the excessive politeness of friends who'd just patched over an unpleasant disagreement. We made a show of adjusting antennas and power cycled the access points, which brought things back to life for awhile, and off we went.

Samba drove the other truck with the guys and I was with Abdu. We made a stop before heading back to the office. Mary had called to say a client was having problems reading files off a disk. We found his compound in Bakau and went in. He was irate, cursing us, computers and the world in general. I asked him to demonstrate the problem and I could see the issue straight away. He waved a 3½-inch floppy around, smacking it in the palm of his hand while explaining he needed the files off it *immediately*, but the drive on the stinking computer he'd bought through Peter wasn't working. He pushed a button on the front of the computer, the CD-ROM tray extended, and he slapped the disk onto the tray and pushed the button again. "You see? Nothing!"

Over my shoulder I could hear Samba mutter under his breath, "Ehhhhhh, boy!" I turned and snapped at them to wait in the trucks. The guys were young, and I didn't even have to turn around to know their faces were filled with mirth. They had to go before the first open guffaw. I didn't blame them. I wanted to grab that floppy disk, wave it in the guy's face and say, "This is *small* and *square*, the guides on that platter are *big* and *round*. What the hell is wrong with you?" Peter wouldn't have endorsed that particular comment, so I demurred.

I sorted the problem by taking the disk and telling him I'd copy it to something more appropriate for his machine (a CD) and have it run over. We stopped at another client on the way back to the office and collected a computer for repairs, promising the owner to have it back the next day. By about 1:30 we were back in the office. Randy was there fixing computers, and I gave him hell for not doing what I told him too. He shrugged it off. We grabbed lunch. I had the office specialty, half a baguette filled with sardines. I walked to the end of the dirt lane connecting our office to Kairaba Avenue, bought my bread and fish at the usual corrugated metal shack and ate sitting on a cinderblock nearby. We'd had a good day so far, and if we could make it to 5 p.m., we'd be home free. That was when most people knocked off work, so there would be no more problems reported from our office clients. Residential clients might call, but those would wait until morning.

There were a few more calls, which I dealt with myself while sending the guys out to buy parts for the various computers in the workshop. By about 4 p.m., the staff was back in the office. I was using Peter's computer for email, another concession he'd awarded me. The guys were in the workroom chatting and laughing in Wolof.

I'd just hung up with a client and was calling over the partition to Mary to schedule a visit for tomorrow when the front door crashed open, giving us all a start. Peter jumped in: "Samba!" he yelled at the top of his lungs as he strutted into the workroom.

"*Wau*, Peter!"

"You're driving. Head over to AP Trading and get a waterproof box. Mary will give you some money. Mary!"

"*Wau.*"

"Randy, Pateh, gather the tools! Have we waterproof tape? Find it. If not, Samba!"

"*Wau*, Peter. I'll fetch some as well."

"Robin, come with me. The rest of you be ready in 15 minutes!" A wireless job, at the eleventh hour. Everyone jumped. Peter and I drove to his office at the grocery store just down the street; Peter on his cell the whole way. In his office, out of a locked drawer, he produced a small blue box: the bridge. This was attached to the antenna and allowed us to configure the antenna to speak to our network.[142] Out of a closet came a chrome rod with small nobs along its length, like a two-sided gravel rake a metre long: a Yagi antenna.[143] These things were kept at the grocery store because Peter didn't trust anyone with them, not even Mary. We headed back to the office.

After considerably longer than 15 minutes, time spent rounding up cables, screws, wire cutters and ladders, we were on our way toward the airport. Peter and I rode in his car with the boys following in the pickup. On the way Peter explained: we were about to do a wireless install near the airport.

Everyone was excited; you could feel it. An install was more than maintenance, it was an *event*. As I got to know the guys better, I'd learn working at a place where they "built the Internet" was considered prestigious. Like the rest of the world, Gambians wanted access to the

---

142 Every antenna needed a bridge to work. Just think of them as part of the antenna.

143 Although we generally used a flat panel for the client, we'd sometimes us small parabolic or Yagi antennas. Each antenna type had its ups and downs. Flat panels don't have the range of a parabolic but were easier to align with the mast back at HQ. Yagis had the highest gain and so the longest range; conversely, they were the hardest to align because their beam was so narrow.

Internet. Maybe they wanted it more. Anywhere families had to separate for long periods to make ends meet, the need to talk, to connect, becomes obsessive. The NGO and embassy types I encountered — with a few notable exceptions — never really clued into that. They had typical Western snobbery about the deficiencies of online communications, preferring a warm handshake and the intimacy of "one-on-one contact." Which was fine, but of course their children weren't working as immigrant labour in a foreign land.

On a wireless job, everyone had the same question on their mind: what would the site be like? Would we be climbing a water tower to strap our pole to the side? A high building or roof? Would we have to climb a telecom mast? Would we be on the side of a three-story building, working with one hand while holding on for dear life with the other? The mystery was compounded by Peter's love of theatre. He never let us see the site beforehand. Hell, he never even let us know he was planning a job until the second we were to do it.

As we drove down toward the airport, Peter gave me the skinny. The client was an NGO working in agriculture (providing training or something like that) and Peter had promised them a connection. It was important to them. They needed it for administrative purposes to help run their farm, but they were skeptical that a Wi-Fi shot of over 10 kilometres could work. I was skeptical too.

The farm was out by the airport, and we were greeted by the European staff, all agriculturalists or biologists. Peter was in fine form, working the crowd with smiles and handshakes. When the boys pulled up, they slumped out of the truck, their excitement apparently exhausted during the 20-minute drive, but Peter barked orders and got them going immediately. For my part, I stood close to Peter and tried not to look worried. Looking around, the first thing I noticed were trees, lots of them, all over the place. There were no vantage points, so our tower couldn't be seen from anywhere. Apparently, the solution was a pipe lying in the dust, which was actually made of two 10-metre pipes welded together. Twenty metres long but only about five centimetres wide, small half circles made of rebar were welded to the pipe two-thirds of the way to the top. The plan was to strap the Wi-Fi kit to the top, heave it up somehow and strap it against the small water tower in the compound.[144] Guy-wires were to be run through the half circles to help steady it when it was up.

The next two hours went down like an Inspector Clouseau movie. Naturally, the bridge needed to be protected from the rain, which is why a waterproof box had been procured. It was just a two-dollar white plastic box. Punching holes for the cables wasn't a problem, it had openings covered with rubber grommets for that purpose, but to connect it to the pole was another task entirely. We needed to punch holes in the back of the case. No one brought a drill. One of the guys scrapped two holes in the back with a screwdriver by main force. The Europeans didn't look impressed. Now we needed to bolt it to the pole. We had a "bracket," which was a strip of flat-bar beaten with a hammer to give it some curve, and then finished by drilling a hole in each end. The curve was too slight to fit around the pole, so we'd need bolts three inches long to do the job. We didn't have any. A frantic search was initiated in the truck, even the floor mats were ejected. The Europeans stood around, arms crossed, looking European. Eventually, they produced some bolts for us to use. Now the holes needed to be waterproofed. The waterproof tape we had wouldn't stick to the box, so we tore a metre of tape off for each hole and jammed it into the punctures as best we could. Despite the awesome amount of tape, the odds of it holding seemed slim. Even then, the ends were coming loose and dangling in the

---

144 Most compounds had small water towers, about 30 feet tall and made of angle iron. The top was just a flat platform that held a large plastic water tank, usually about the size of a small compact car. They were needed to provide enough water pressure for the sinks and bathrooms inside the adjoining buildings.

breeze.

And so it went. We needed a cable to run from the box, 20 metres in the air, down to the office. The mostly used box of cable we'd brought was too short. We found several loose pieces in the truck and Peter spliced them together with wire strippers, his teeth and electrical tape, all the while assuring the clients it would work just fine — no problem. Nothing flustered that guy.

The climax of the operation was heaving the pole into position. It needed to be straight, but it wasn't. It looked like we were trying to raise a cooked noodle on its beam ends. Alas, it was too flimsy to hold its own weight. It sagged ridiculously, and when it threatened to break along the weld, the client called a halt. The guys were exhausted; it was an hour and a half past business hours and none of them would make any overtime. Peter had driven them on by saying it would all be done "in just 10 more minutes," a pronouncement he repeated every quarter hour. But the client had lost faith, so we packed it in and headed home. The truck got stuck in deep sand along the track leading to the road. With the help of some barefoot local kids, it took us another half hour to push it out.

The President's Men

Almost a year on the job.

I was happy. It had been another long day juggling calls, but we'd manoeuvred the day's work to checkmate. Quitting time was close, and I was on my way to a meeting that promised to change my life. We'd been working hard to fight our way through the day-to-day grind with varying degrees of success. I have to admit, the grind was getting to me, and it must have been showing because one afternoon Peter decided I should take his place on a trip to Guinea-Bissau. I was completely surprised by the suggestion. Relations between Peter and I were at an all-time low. Only a week ago I'd goaded him into a white fury by insisting we have a staff meeting to air grievances. I didn't know if Peter was afraid I might leave due to the fallout from staff meeting argument, or if he just had bigger fish to fry. Nevertheless, I jumped at the offer.

The client ran orphanages all over the world, and their West African regional office was in the Gambia. They'd hired us to manage their local concerns, and satisfied, they wanted us to look after their regional IT needs. Peter had made a few trips to do routine maintenance and pad their infrastructure, and now it was my turn. My first trip to another West African country.[145]

The only problem was my tardiness. I was running about 15 minutes late for the meeting, but I wasn't too worried; I'd gotten used to explaining away my lateness, and 15 minutes was nothing. We skidded into the parking lot, I jumped out with a stupid smile on my face, and after only two steps toward the entrance, Peter came crashing out the door. He was pissed; it was clear from 20 feet away. "Where have you been?" he yelled, throwing his arms up in frustration. "Get in there now. Now! The deputy director will tell you what you need to know. Get in there! I have to go. I got a call from the compound; there are people from the president's office over there. I have to go, get in there!" He said the last couple of sentences as he marched to his car. The president's office? What the hell was that about?

I'll be honest, I didn't care. The meeting of my life awaited, and in the end, I sold myself well. It was very much an introductory meeting, no details that might have spoiled my buzz. I jumped in the truck half an hour later with plans already running through my head; the orphans of Guinea-Bissau would get everything I had to offer, every skill I had, every spell I knew. It was time to head back to HQ, and I made my call to get the guys heading home. I only needed to make one call because it was only Samba and Randy I needed to worry about. Pateh and Edi had left for school a few months back.

We turned onto Kairaba Avenue. I was flouncing around a self-involved daydream and barely noticed Abdu saying, *"Slobin, Slobin!"* He tugged at my sleeve and pointed. Following his arm, I saw Mama Hanoush in her Rav 4 coming from the other direction, waving frantically. She pointed to the packed dirt strip that made up the parking lot for businesses lining

---

145 Sure, I'd been to Senegal several times, but that went hand in hand with the general feeling of the Gambia being the day-to-day. Going to Senegal was like living in Washington and day-tripping to Virginia Beach.

the street and Abdu turned in. So did she.

"Is everything OK?" I asked.

"No, they've got Peter!"

"What?"

"They've taken him. People from the president's office. They took Mary too, and are looking for anyone who knows about computers!" I called Samba and Randy and told them to meet me at the parking lot, and spent about 10 minutes speaking with Mama Hanoush. Basically, the secret police had raided our office. She didn't have many more details, but she knew Mary had been beaten up. She'd been there, had seen it happen, but they weren't interested in her, only in "computer people." She told me they knew Peter had a foreigner working with him. Under no circumstances should I return to the office.

I had no idea what to do. The guys had seen where we were parked and were pulling up, and I'd have to tell them something. Peter's mother filled everyone in and left, heading to a friend's place. The guys spent the next 20 minutes cursing and slandering the president of their republic, which I encouraged because it gave me some time to think. I needed it because my mind was a complete blank. I'd never even considered a circumstance like this, but I knew I had to do something. The guys were punching the trucks and kicking the dirt like it was the president's prone body, but their anger would blow itself out, and when it did, I'd have to say something. Something useful. Something practical.

Eventually, their energy flagged, and their anger simmered down to hard glares and long looks. We huddled and I gave them my orders: I told Abdu to take one of the trucks to his compound and keep it there. "Don't worry about coming to work, I'll be in touch," and off he went. I didn't actually know why I'd sent him away. At an instinctual level, I knew less was more. Abdu out of the way was one less variable to manage. Before he left, I had Randy and Samba ransack the truck, taking every wire, screw and tool, and putting it all in the other truck. I got them moving with short, sharp commands, projecting (I hoped) confidence, projecting (I hoped) the idea that this was just the first step in some well-conceived plan I'd worked out. Which of course was nonsense. I made sure there wasn't a scrap of paper left in the truck, no invoices, no receipts, nothing that might say Abdu worked for Peter.

The final inventory: half a box of cable, a CD case with two-thirds of the CDs actually working,[146] a bag of tools with a crimper but no hammer or decent screwdriver,[147] about 15 cable heads, 30-odd cable tacks, a roll of waterproof tape, wire cutters, half a role of electrical tape, one PoE adapter,[148] about three U.K.-type electrical plugs, two French-type electrical sockets, two eight-port routers, a small broken UPS, about 25 metres of electrical cable, and one pickup with half a tank of gas.

On the negative side of the ledger: we had no access to any passwords we hadn't memorized and we didn't have access to any of the servers or machinery in the office. We didn't even know if they were still running. If they weren't, I didn't have access to any contacts, phone numbers or email. Even if it was working, I'd only have access to the names and numbers already in my email. Most nagging of all: I didn't have my passport. It was locked in Peter's office desk for safekeeping.[149]

The last point weighed on my mind and inspired my next move. I

---

146 Due to poor connectivity, we kept almost everything on CDs so our staff wouldn't have to download anything across our network.

147 We used crimpers to head cables, to attach those little plastic ends that plug the cable into the back of your computer. Obviously, these were a pretty important bit of kit. What's the point of wiring a place if you can't connect the wires to a computers? I wasn't impressed with the one we had. The hammer was important for tacking cables.

148 Power over Ethernet. It allows you to run power down an Ethernet cable to power a device on the other end. It works by running power down the unused twisted pairs in a standard 10 or 100 MB cat 5 cable.

149 Yeah, I know, can't this kid keep his hands on his damn passport?

got in the cab with Samba and Randy, and told Samba to head back to the office. They were stunned. I told them — summoning all the "fuck this scene" moxie I could muster — that I wasn't cowed by these bastards. No way. The truth of the matter is less heroic: my no-nonsense manner had gone to my head. Carried away with the part I'd been playing the last hour — the career sergeant who always knows what to do — I really started to believe I did. That confidence, combined with a need to see if I could get my passport back, goaded me on. It wasn't all vainglory, though. I hoped my bravado would inspire Samba and Randy, help them keep their chins up, and it did. As we drove, the mood in the truck went from sullen to belligerent and finally to macho. I was angry and — I have to admit — excited. Samba was losing it completely; he'd become a one-man pro-democracy demonstration. He hated the president, he hated the National Intelligence Agency (the secret police),[150] he hated police bullying, and most of all, he hated what they'd done to Peter. Randy was pissed too, scared mostly, but angry as well. Peter was a greedy bastard and we all knew it, but if there's ever been a test of a leader's leadership, this was it, and Peter passed like a superstar. Here we were about to face off with the secret police on his behalf.

In truth, I didn't know what I'd do when we got there. Our arrival at the turnoff sobered us up a bit.[151] A quiet tension settled over the cab as we rolled slowly up the dusty lane, and I could see the gate was open. I told Samba to drive past so we could get a look. Inside, security people were all over the place. Some were carting computer equipment to a waiting truck, some were just standing around. Randy spoke first. "What are they taking apart?"

"The office," I mumbled. Randy looked nervous, in need of

---

150 I wonder where they got the name from?
151 CompCorp was half a block off Kairaba Avenue on an unpaved dirt lane.

reassurance, but I ignored him. I was fixated on Peter. He was there.

I told Samba to pull over after we'd passed the gate and rounded the corner. Piling out, Randy and I had to jump on Samba to restrain him. He was beyond angry. It was like trying to hold someone back in a bar fight. He wanted to go in there and throw punches. How dare those bastards mess with people's lives like this! Wasn't life in the Gambia hard enough? What's the point of the police if they just made it harder? It took a lot of effort to calm things down. When it was over, I announced my intention to go speak to Peter. Randy blanched. Samba's demeanour changed instantly; he was suddenly very calm, and he reminded me what Mama Hanoush had said. I insisted. I wanted my passport back and all my clothes were in there. Randy was quiet and sullen. Samba was resigned, and in I went.

I lit a cigarette and strolled in like I owned the place. Why not? Movies condition you to expect the bad guys to be wearing trenchcoats and fedoras and to speak with heavy Russian accents. You expect to see guys in German army helmets kicking in a door, not wearing polyester overalls and fumbling over a mouse sliding off the computer they're carrying. The scene seemed average enough, and sure enough, no one said a thing. No one really noticed; they were too busy packing the place up. Peter was sitting on the low step of his mother's house, elbows on knees, head in hands. He looked like a school kid having his locker ransacked by the principal. The significance of Randy's question suddenly struck me. What *were* they taking apart? Sure, some computers had been brought out of the office, but in the middle of the compound stood a metal frame and most of the action centred around it. Uniformed Gamtel technicians were taking parts off it, but it only took me a second to realize what it was. *Oh Jesus*, I thought.

While all this washed over me, my attention was abruptly brought back to Peter. He'd noticed me come in and instantly jumped to his feet, startling the two gentlemen standing over him smoking cigarettes. The two men were both wearing traditional *boubous*. The small weasel-looking one

238

wore aviator shades. Peter had been facing the gate and got a good head start, marching over to me with fast, controlled strides. He got right up in my face and said, "Don't tell them who you are. You rent the apartment, that's all." He whispered it fast, before his minders were in earshot.

"Who are you?" The weasel in shades demanded sharply. His partner was a tall, roly-poly type with a round stomach, plump cheeks and an easygoing smile.

"I rent the room in the back," I offered almost apologetically. Peter's quick bit of advice — the panic in which he'd said it, not to mention the metal frame in the compound — knocked the wind out of my esprit de corps.

"What the name?" The weasel snapped.

"Richard," I lied. "I rent the room in the back." Peter started talking to him in Wolof. "I just want to get some clothes from my room," I interrupted.

Peter was kicking up a storm and the trio was ignoring me. I caught roly-poly's eye and pointed toward the back of the building. He didn't say anything, distracted by Peter, so I walked past them. Halfway to our HQ building, I heard the weasel yell something shrill in Wolof, no doubt aimed at me. I played stupid-white-guy and kept walking. Nobody tried to stop me, and I turned into the alleyway between our HQ and the warehouse wall. The door to the office was just ahead, and my heart jumped because I knew no one in the courtyard could see me and the drawer holding my passport was only 20 feet away. I headed to the door but noticed it was ajar. I readjusted my stride and made like I was heading down to the end of the alley to my room. I'm glad I did too, because as I passed the windows to the office I could see guys — some paramilitary, some technicians — all over the office. No one stopped me as I walked to the end of the alley and entered my apartment. *Dammit*, I thought. I'd never get my passport. In addition, I'd have to pass back out through the courtyard. Would I be that lucky again? I gathered some clothes, threw them in a plastic sack with my toiletries and thought about other ways out. I could get on the roof easily enough. From there, I could make it over the compound wall without a problem. But it was a stupid idea. By that point, I'd climbed across enough buildings in West Africa to know that the instant I was up there the guys in the office would hear me tramping across the sheet metal.[152] After a minute or two, I accepted that the way in was the only way out and left. I passed the office door that was swinging wide open and I could see the door to Peter's office was also open. I turned the corner, and Peter and the others were back by Mama Hanoush's house. I walked out without looking back. No one said a word.

Samba and Randy looked at me like I was Theseus just back from Crete. I filled them in on what I saw and we sat in silence; Samba leaning against the side of the truck, head low; Randy sitting on the open tailgate, legs dangling off. I hadn't been completely honest with them. I didn't mention the frame in the courtyard. Randy had spotted it when we rolled by and seemed to have forgotten about it. I hadn't reminded him. I knew what it was, and I was pretty sure it was the reason we'd been raided.

The frame was for a satellite dish, a fairly large one, about six feet across. There were satellite dishes all over the Gambia, just like the rest of Africa. They were used for audiovisual feeds, primarily television. There was no cable network to speak of and so almost all entertainment and news arrived via the Internet or AV satellite. As a result, there were a lot of satellite dishes around the Gambia, so why would government technicians be taking

---

152 I spent a lot of my time at CompCorp walking around and on top of buildings sighting antennas. Some only a single story, some several stories high. We had a couple of close calls, but thankfully none of my guys got killed. Getting on the roof of our office without a ladder would have been child's play, but I knew concrete walls and a lack of insulation turned sheet-metal roofs into soundboards. If someone was walking on a roof, you could easily hear it from the other side of the building. Outside the compound wall was a row of trees, lime and mango mostly, and the sound of a mango falling even from a short height was like a cannon shot.

ours apart?

The thing about it — what Peter and I knew, and what Samba and Randy didn't — was that all satellite dishes weren't made equal. The one sitting in our courtyard — that used to sit quietly out of sight behind Mama's house — was a VSAT: a Very Small Aperture Terminal satellite dish. What exactly that means in a technical sense isn't important to our story, the important thing here is that in addition to receiving data feeds, a VSAT can transmit them too. An AV dish is a one-way ride, receive only. With a VSAT, the operator can transmit information as well as receive it, making VSATs very useful if you were in the ISP business, and also making them completely illegal in the Gambia.

Peter was using it to boost our available bandwidth. He couldn't grow the business with the cut of bandwidth the government had furnished us with. Every customer meant we needed more. Peter and I had come up with all kinds of tweaks to stretch what we had. We'd placed serious cache servers on every local network, we policed the network for unusual or unnecessary activity and squished it immediately,[153] we adjusted traffic priorities,[154] we even throttled bandwidth to favour businesses during the day and home users at night and on the weekends, but in the end, we needed more. So Peter bought the dish and the service that went along with it. Getting it into the country wasn't that big a deal. It looked like any satellite dish unless you knew what to look for. The only real difference was the horn: the bit of kit suspended at the focal point of the dish.

On a parabolic antenna (which is what a satellite dish is), the actual antenna is that tiny thing suspended in front of the dish on the struts. The

---

153 Strange bursts in activity across the network usually meant a machine had a virus and one of my running tasks was to track those machines down and clean them up.

154 We could configure our servers and routers to give a higher priority to certain kinds of traffic. So during business hours we could give email a higher priority than file downloads, for example.

dish itself is simply an amplifier, reflecting signals from another antenna into the focal point of the dish. On a dish that only receives, the horn is small and uncomplicated, usually just a flat disk-like thing. On a dish that can both receive and transmit, the horn's a much more complicated affair. It usually looks like a small metal block about the size of a large book with a funnel sticking out of it, wide end toward the dish.

One look at the dish in our courtyard and anyone in the know could tell it was capable of transmitting out. Why was that a problem? Peter had never given any specifics, but I knew damn well any government that could be described as a "regime" didn't care for free and open communications. Access to a VSAT meant you could access the Internet directly; you didn't need Gamtel's routers or infrastructure to connect to the rest of the world, meaning they couldn't filter or monitor your communications. The upshot: you could talk to people outside the country without them knowing, or knowing what you were saying.

My relationship with Peter had a certain bipolar aspect to it. We'd fight like cat and dog, but then there were moments of great camaraderie, just as ardent as our arguments. It was as if we both wanted those moments of bonhomie to wash away the taste of our more bitter moments. During one of these moments, after a more successful day when everyone else was gone, Peter had shown me the VSAT. He asked me to keep it to myself, and I did. I didn't see any reason to change that now. What would be the point of telling Samba or Randy? If they got in trouble, their ignorance would help them. What was done was done, now it was about living through the whirlwind. To that end, I launched into an outraged, fist-pounding rant. I was going to see Peter through this mess. How dare the government seize Peter? Or beat Mary? Was I the kind of guy to let a fella down when it really mattered? Hell no! Letting the business fail was giving into repression. Peter had staked his whole family's welfare on that company, and I sure as hell wasn't going to let it fold. No goddamn way.

242

Was this a plan? Nope. It wasn't even thoughtful. But whatever it was, it worked. The guys were all over it. I didn't want them to join me and told them so. I was a foreigner with an embassy and not nearly facing the same risk they were. They weren't having it. Samba stood there, eyes wide, slamming a fist into his palm, "*Wau, wau*, Robin! We mustn't let Peter down." Was it my finest hour? Rallying the troops with an inspirational plea? In hindsight, I think it was a way of hitting back at those bastards. And they were bastards. What else can you think about people who scare the hell out of you? But we weren't going to go quietly. No damn way. Whatever we may have thought of Peter or Mary, those assholes turned them into martyrs as far as we were concerned, and we aimed to do right by Saint Peter.

Convinced by Samba that I'd be better off with a couple of locals who spoke the language, and with our revolutionary fervour stoked, I told the guys we'd meet in the morning at the same dirt lot Mama Hanoush had stopped us in. Samba would keep the truck, and he dropped Randy at home and me at the centre. I took the papers from the truck, gave Samba a solid "fight the power" fist bump and watched him off.

After the drive, my head was clearer. I knew they weren't pleased with the service I'd given them recently, but I figured the centre was my only chance, and so I dragged myself up the stairs. Fatou, sitting at the front desk, saw me as I entered, and I could see her shoulders slump. "Robin. These people. I cannot believe these people. Do you know where they have taken Peter?" I'd only found out myself two hours before and couldn't believe she already knew. Fatou was sympathetic. We chatted for a moment about the state of human rights in the Gambia before I asked to see Idrissa.

Idrissa was at his desk, and when I walked in, he threw aside the folder in his hands and faced me, ready for conversation. I slumped down in the chair opposite his desk. "Hey there, Idrissa. I guess you've heard?"

"Yes, Robin. These people... these people." He said the last slowly, as if lost in thought.

"I don't know what to do, Idrissa. They've got my passport."

Dropping his gaze, he sighed. "That is not good, Robin."

He shook his head almost imperceptibly and sighed again. "They cannot do this to people." Leaning back in his chair, he stared out the window, as if thinking back on every wrongdoing he'd ever heard about, feeling exhausted by the effort. He reminisced about why he and Samantha had founded the centre in the first place. We sat there for about an hour as he told the story of their meeting as interns at the African commission; how they'd been appalled at the number of human rights complaints being dismissed due to simple procedural ignorance; how one night, over dinner, their conversation conjured the idea of the centre, a place people could learn how to submit complaints properly; their giddiness as it became real, initially just the two of them in a living room, but eventually, through hard work, to their own building filled with full-time staff.

Listening calmed me down. He wasn't speaking to a template, the usual legalese and sympathies generally reserved for such occasions. Listening to the story, I knew Idrissa saw me differently: not just another white-faced kid here to bang a drum. *You see now why we built this place! Do you see?* That was the message. Yes, I did see. When he was finished, he shook the memories off, leaned across the table and told me what I should do. The plan centred around the passport I'd had stolen when I still worked at the centre.

One of the by-products of that adventure was a small file I'd compiled to keep the paperwork straight in the event of another passport mishap. It included a photocopy of my new, current passport. I'd asked Idrissa to hold the file, and happily, he still had it locked way. The plan was simple: I'd call Idrissa personally every day at 3 p.m. If he didn't hear from me by half past the hour, that meant "they'd got me," and he'd inform the Canadian embassy in Dakar that I'd been detained. Idrissa — being Senegalese — had great contacts in Dakar, including ones at the Canadian

244

embassy.

I didn't write the embassy or foreign affairs even though you're supposed to in an event such as this. To start with, my last interaction with the embassy proved they weren't the "go-to guys" in a problem like this — or any problem, really. Another reason to stay silent was the warnings I'd gotten during the stolen passport fiasco. I'd had another passport stolen when I worked in D.C., and so when I requested a second, the Canadian government arched a doubtful eyebrow. My sister had called Passport Canada, and they implied that having two passports stolen was in bad taste, and I could expect some uncomfortable questions when I got back to Canada.[155] Finally — and perversely — I was afraid my government might actually come through. They might actually get me home before the situation played out, but I wasn't interested in leaving yet.

I was allowed to stay in the centre's intern house. They'd finally bought the house next door to the one Robel, Lisa and I had lived in, and I was allowed to shack up there for the duration. Each night I'd get drunk and each morning Samba would come by in the truck to pick me up.

My plan of action to keep CompCorp going was pretty simple. The three of us would stick together in one truck and touch base with as many clients as possible. I wanted to know where Samba and Randy were at all times. The farthest I'd let them wander was about a block away. If we had two clients on the same street, for example. Generally, things went well. The guys' loyalty to Peter and the business was inspiring. The crisis brought out the best in them, and it became clear I wouldn't have to worry about them violating procedure or generally going off half-cocked. We were a well-galvanized team, and I was proud of that, but I felt even prouder of our network. Clearly, the NIA hadn't ripped out our servers or wireless kit, and everything was running relatively well. Occasionally, I'd log in remotely from

---

155 I guess they figured I was selling them to Al-Qaeda.

a client's place and tinker with things, but basically our network was solid. It was also a lot slower because we no longer had the VSAT, but we'd be good for awhile. For how long I had no idea, and I knew it was only a matter of time before something would bring everything to a halt, but there was nothing I could do about that.

When it came to dealing with the clients, the biggest problem was roadblocks, which weren't frequent but could pop up in the most unlikely places. Part of me doubted information flowed smoothly enough within the local security services for a beat cop or soldier to be able to link Samba, Randy or me to the raids, but why gamble if you don't have to? So we stuck to familiar routes and focused on the majority of customers living in the Kairaba area. Once or twice we ventured out to Bijilo or beyond, more than once careening off the main highway and into some village when we sighted cars stopped by the side of the road. Could have been a taxi stand for all we knew, but better safe than sorry.

The purpose of these visits was to troubleshoot any problems we could, to give them my direct cell number so they could report any new problems, and finally, to explain the situation and ask for patience. This last point was completely unnecessary. Everyone had heard. In fact, we were welcomed into people's houses with sympathy and they often offered us food. Normally, there was a reserve between the rich Lebanese who made up a good number of our clients and us: a white foreigner and his staff of "sub-Saharan" Africans. It was more awkward for the latter than for me, but there was still a certain distance. After the raid, everything changed. People who would've barely acknowledged Samba's presence were putting a hand on his shoulder and asking how he was holding up. One time, on foot and alone and spooked by some paramilitary guys buying bread at a corner stand, I charged into a client's compound without announcing myself. My momentum took me to the front door of the house, which I found unlocked, so I let myself in. I closed the door carefully and turned to offer

246

a hello, only to see the lady of the house staring at me from the kitchen, gobsmacked. The client and his family were Muslims, and thinking she was alone, she'd removed her hijab. A Christian man — a stranger — had seen her in jeans and a T-shirt, but even this astonishing wrong was forgiven under the circumstances. At the end of the day, I had Samba drop me at the intern house where I'd spend the night blind with drink.[156]

About the second or third morning, Samba showed up all excited. Mary was out. I surprised myself with how happy I was to hear it. We didn't get along, but no one deserved to be terrorized. Unfortunately, she didn't know much about Peter, but what she did know didn't inspire hope. Late in the afternoon, three guys from the NIA and about a dozen paramilitary showed up at the compound. They came storming in and demanded Mary get off her phones and move away from her computer. At about that moment, a phone rang, and driven by reflex, she answered. One of the NIA guys yelled at her to put it down, but before she could, there was a struggle. Mary was thrown across her office with enough force to rip some of her hair out. They kept her at NIA headquarters for a couple of days, occasionally questioning her about Peter's clients and Peter himself. Mostly, they intimidated and threaten her for not obeying their orders in the office. After a day or two, they let her go. She was at home now and full of fury.

And so it went. People were adjusting, though. I was getting more calls all the time as the initial impact of the raid faded and business as usual started to reassert itself. About a week and a half after the raid I grabbed my phone to check a text and stopped cold when I saw the name.   Peter.

It was a meeting request. I was to meet him in the morning at a small café called Le Palais du Chocolat.[157] I tried calling his number and got no

---

156 By this point, I could easily down a bottle of whiskey on my own and still appear OK to most people.

157 I have no idea who built Palais, but it was trying its hardest to be a French bakery. They had ice cream fridges like you see at Baskin-Robbins, croissants and a real cup of

answer. I told the guys, and Samba pulled over. We sat there in silence for some time.

"Are you going, Robs?"

"I guess."

"We should come too, Robs."

"Nope. You and Randy need to keep your distance." I could see the protest coming, and I cut it short. "He should stand out if he's there. I'll be careful." It went back and forth for awhile, but I'd made up my mind. That night I discussed it with my fellow interns over half a dozen boxes of Don Garcia. They didn't like the plan one bit.

I had no reason to believe it was Peter. I remembered a little book I had when I was a kid. It was a "spy manual" for children that taught how to code notes by substituting numbers for letters, how to use shop windows to see if you were being followed, and the importance of always carrying bus change in case you needed to make a quick escape. By the standards of that book, written for 10-year-olds, I was an idiot for going. One of the lessons a junior spy had to learn was the danger of a false drop. Always have a code word to identify compatriots. Peter and I didn't have any code words. The text came from his phone, but the fact that I couldn't call back to actually hear his voice was disconcerting. Anybody could have been on the other end of that text. Without question, the NIA took Peter's phone during the arrest. Despite Mama Hanoush's warning, I just couldn't believe the secret police forces were interested in a guy like me. I'm very average, not important or distinct in any way. But during our rounds, a troubling fact had emerged: Peter wasn't the only one who'd been nabbed. It turned out to be a general dragnet that scooped up about two-dozen IT guys in the area, pretty much anyone in the networking game. Strong tonic for any sense of

---

espresso. The prices were beyond anything the locals could afford, except for the wealthier Lebanese. It relied on the expat and NGO crowd to survive.

adventure. But what could I do? I had to go. I didn't really have any other move to make. We couldn't creep around forever in a truck.

The next morning I had Samba drop me a block away. I approached the café from the other side of the street. Both sides along Kairaba were big dirt pitches that acted as parking for businesses and sidewalks for pedestrians. There was enough foot traffic to obscure my approach if I stayed near the middle of the pitch. As I got closer, I could see Peter's car. It was impossible to miss, being the only fire-engine-red Volvo station wagon in the country. As I pulled up opposite the café, I could see one person sitting at a table on the small deck in front of the place, back against the wall.

From across the street it was obvious the guy against the wall was Peter. He had a baseball cap pulled down tight over his head and was facing the street, legs and arms crossed. I crossed the road and was going to walk past him and go inside to get a coffee, all "spy-cool," but I caught his eye just as I was about to open the door and he gave me a "where the hell are you going?" look. I sat down instead.

He didn't look himself. He clearly hadn't shaved for a day or two and was uncharacteristically quiet, hiding behind his hat, but he wore a wry little smile as he sipped his coffee. I didn't really know what to say. He just sat there smiling and sipping.

"What the fuck, Peter?" He laughed, puncturing the strange tension that stretched over the moment. He still wasn't himself exactly and he was speaking under his breath, but he was happy, and soon I was attributing his smile to exhausted relief. We chatted and he told me the story.

When the NIA showed up, Mama Hanoush called Peter, and he left his meeting for the office, bumping into me on the way. When he got there, they'd already carted Mary off and found the VSAT. He argued with them to no avail, and not long afterwards I'd come by. When the VSAT had been dismantled, they took Peter to secret police HQ, a big, secluded compound on the outskirts of Banjul where they interrogated him. He wouldn't go into the details, but it sounded like a heavy dressing down with outraged interrogators, fists slamming on desks and a lot of verbal abuse, threats of imprisonment and the like. They wanted him to admit he was breaking the law, admit his guilt. Guilty of *what?* I wanted to know. Espionage? Online criticism of the government? Broadcasting porn in a devoutly Muslim country? No, none of those things. They wanted him to admit he was making online long-distance phone calls. Long-distance phone calls — that's what the whole thing was about, not freedom of speech, not democratic ideals flooding the land via the hosepipe called "the Internet." The whole damn thing was about phone calls.

To be more precise, it was about Social Security numbers and meaningful street addresses. Even more precisely, it was about a lack of those two things. You see, Peter explained, without any way to uniquely identify an individual, the Gambian government had a problem: how do you raise taxes? Sure, they tried, but in a country with only about two-dozen surnames, they were never as efficient about it as they could be. What does this have to do with telecommunications? Well, the cost of the infrastructure required to tag individuals with a unique number — to create proper Social Security numbers and street addresses — was enormous. But when people bought telephones, they did just that: their phone number *was* a unique identifier. Everyone in the Gambia had at least one phone.[158] True, most of the communications over the Gambian telecom network was text messaging, but it added up. The phone system was a pay-as-you-go service, no contracts. Even the poorest could afford a five-dalasi top-up card, which could get you almost 50 text messages. You simply bought the card,

---

158 There are two areas I knew the average Gambian could put the best educated Westerners to shame: linguistics (almost everyone was multilingual) and cellphone knowledge. They knew more about cellphones than I ever imagined there was to know.

scratched the film off the back, typed in the number and you were ready to communicate. There were higher denominations as well, cards costing 25 or 50 dalasis, but I knew from contacts at Gamtel that the five- and 10-dalasi cards sold best. Small numbers, but it added up. People love to communicate.

All of this meant big money for the government. The telephone system was nationalized and so all proceeds went to State House. In other words, the telecom system was like a surrogate tax system. Instead of a Social Security number, you had a phone number. The sums were paltry, but it had the advantage of breadth: in a country with no street addresses and only a small number of traditional surnames, it was easy for people to avoid paying their taxes. The phone system was a way around that. Although daily cellphone usage represented a huge sum of money for the government, long-distance and overseas telecommunications represented an even bigger income line. So big in fact, that failing to use the national provider or one of its designated proxies got people's attention.[159] The advent of services like Skype hit the Gambian government like a bomb. As far as the government was concerned, free long-distance calls was the biggest tax-fraud conspiracy in history. As a result, the national network dutifully filtered out voiceover IP services such as Skype; however, anyone with a VSAT could still provide those services by beaming the traffic over the national network via satellite. With no real detective branch of the police force, the government's response was to task the secret police to "investigate" potential illicit service providers by cracking heads together.

And so there we were. The government responded to the drop in its revenue by rounding up anyone who might know how to connect a

---

159 The only proxy you could really use was Aficell, a French-owned, Lebanese-operated cellular provider. In order to operate, they had to pay a huge fee to Gamtel, the national provider.

computer to the Internet in such a way as to make a service like Skype viable. They wanted answers. *Did you use Skype? Did you allow it on your network? Did you know anyone who did?* Almost anyone who was anyone in the networking world had been detained, according to Peter. Between interrogations, they were allowed to hang around in the compound's courtyard. Peter felt this was done to encourage conversation; he was sure some of his fellow detainees were plants.

Mary was there too, but only because she'd been "disrespectful" by answering the phone after being told not to. Peter giggled as he recounted hearing her interrogation. Everyone in the courtyard heard it. She screamed at her questioner about how she was a Christian woman! And how God would strike them all down! And how dare they lay a hand on her! And how they should fear the Almighty's vengeance for the wrongs they had committed that day! They released her the next day, much to Peter's relief because he thought they'd cut her head off if she kept it up.

In the evenings, they were locked in cells that backed onto the Atlantic coast. A beautiful view, but that wasn't the point. The windows were covered in bars and nothing else, so the sea breeze easily made its way inside. It was warm by European or North American standards, but if you were a Gambian, or if you'd acclimatized, a sea breeze was pneumonia waiting to happen. When Peter mentioned it, I involuntarily shivered. My friends and I — the ones who'd been there longest — couldn't hang out by the beach at night during the rainy season without sweaters and hoodies.[160]

---

160 Temperature could be used in all kinds of devious ways. We used to frequent a certain hotel on the weekends for poolside lounging. We visited enough to note a marked increase in the number of well-to-do Gambians using the pool. One Sunday, Abai and I went for a dip, diving in without checking the water temperature. It was so cold, we both turned underwater like synchronized swimmers, using our dive momentum to push us back to the edge. It was like diving through slushy. We were in and out in seconds. The Europeans and North Americans didn't notice it at all. The hotel was a client, and shortly after, while there on business, I made the accusation to

They'd let Peter out because he'd convinced them we didn't use Skype or similar services. This was true, but we didn't avoid voice over IP out of respect for the government's financial issues, but because we felt it used up way too much bandwidth.

So that was Peter's story. We sat in silence for a few minutes and then I went to grab a coffee, after which we started discussing the future. He still had to report to NIA twice every day and they had his passport as well as his wife's. We had no idea when we'd be able to get back into the office. In the meantime, I was to maintain the status quo.

And I did. I was still worried about roadblocks, but slowly things swung toward normal. After about another week we had access to the office again. It didn't look any different. Everything was still there except for the VSAT and its attendant hardware. My passport was still locked in Peter's desk. Mary came back to work, she and I sharing a big, sincere hug. The servers were still going but were in desperate need of maintenance. A month after the raid, I was on my way to Guinea-Bissau on behalf of the orphanage client. Two months later and Mary and I were at each other's throats again.

---

the hotel manager: "Silva! You guys dropped the temperature in the pool to scare away the locals. Deny it!" "Why would I do that?" he answered with a grin. I asked if he was denying the act or refusing to deny the act and so admitting it. He walked away smiling.

Delirium Tremens

Sometime being too long on the job.

I got in the habit of taking dinner in a little restaurant about a block away from work, The Public House. Two Germans ran it, catering to the expat crew. It was an older crowd, more experienced; no fresh-faced interns chattering about power outages or drum circles. People there didn't want to be bothered. Only a block from work/home, I was soon established as a regular. I'd walk in, nod to the waiter, and like magic a glass of wine and a clean ashtray would land at my favourite table even before I did. It was a small, open-air patio stuffed with palm trees, and a high wall segregated it from the street. My preferred spot was near the wall, far from the entrance and shrouded in shadow. Even when the waiter approached, I couldn't see the silhouette of this face until he bent close and caught the glow of the table candle. People I knew walked right past without a hint of recognition. I liked it that way. By this point, I generally preferred the company of wine and cigarettes after a workday. My habit was to end dinner with a bottle (a box, actually) or two, smoke cigs, and think about the day and things in general.

Antisocial perhaps, but things had changed since the breakup of the Brusubi crew. Those of us remaining had serious jobs now. Abais' job had always been serious, and now Roz was working at the local UN secretariat and basically running it because her boss spent more time out of the country than at his desk. We had real jobs. We had real stress. We still went out on the occasional Saturday night, down to Sanity usually, and we made new friends and acquaintances with the newest crop of interns, but their wide-eyed culture shock rankled. How many times can you hear outrage over blackouts? Their attitude rankled too. Most of the new interns — with a few wonderful exceptions — were there to pad their CVs or to fuck off for six months. I've never understood the notion of travelling as sport, seeing how many places you can visit in two weeks or a year or whatever. Whoever lands in the most countries wins! Travel-as-pub-crawl essentially

Work was wearing me thin, stealing every bit of idealistic enthusiasm my 20-odd years of education had stuffed into me. It hadn't taken long either. My firsthand experience of development work had left me pretty disillusioned; starting the first night I'd shared a drink with the human rights defenders in Senegambia and witnessed their treatment of the locals. The litter in Banjul: a problem that didn't require the World Bank to fix, weighed on my mind too, just as so many other problems of that type did. So did our abortive trip to Jufureh where we'd essentially had to fight to add money to the local economy. Naturally, all of the above paled in comparison to the problem we'd had over our VSAT, but I was feeling the full weight of my time there. I was getting jaded and I knew it, which was why I took my meals hiding in the dark. All in all, the dream job hadn't turned out exactly as I'd expected. Optimism had kept me at it, but as time went by, decisive progress felt farther and farther away. Pessimism was setting in. Indulging in drink didn't help.

Often I pondered those NetCorps warnings about people not wanting to hear about your overseas exploits. If they were right, and I was just staying to develop cocktail party repartee, I was being pretty stupid. I was becoming schizophrenic. On one hand I'd gotten used to a level of stress that was callousing over as a "whatever" attitude. I knew it wouldn't endear back in youthfully optimist North America. To the contrary, it would likely make my working life back home difficult. I'd be labelled "negative," one of the most damning judgements a person can attract. On the other hand, the beast Frustration was gnawing at me. I could turn on people in a second with a level of venom that shocked me. I still had it under control, these impulses were still contained, but I wondered for how long? Every time something happened I didn't like there was this agonizing moment when I was torn between shrugging and not giving a damn, tearing someone in half or doing the correct professional thing. Should I leave now and cut my loses? Get back home before the civility of home was an alien custom?

Eventually, my thoughts would wander to the situation in the office. The last month hadn't been much better than the first day at CompCorp. The guys no longer threatened to quit *every day*, but they still cast stones when it suited them. The bonding that occurred during the episode with the president's men had waned. I still couldn't get them to follow basic procedures and requests; I never knew who would show up at a site and what might happen there. Mary still lorded over us, and we still had a hell of a time trying to get things done. I'd try to make sense of things, coming up with strategies to solve the problems once and for all, but all my hypotheses would fall apart when I ran into the biggest problem of all: the incredible unpredictability of the place. The variables were flying so fast and loosely, you were always being blindsided by something. Just as you'd come up with a reasonable solution to some issue, the secret police kidnapped your boss.

I was in "forest for the trees" territory. So many things were going on, it was impossible to see anything beyond the immediate task. I was working as hard as I could, but nothing ever got better. I remember one time we did a job and encountered a private-exchange telephone junction. Back in the late 1980s and early '90s, the Gambia boasted one of the most advanced telecommunications networks anywhere, paid for by the French government.[161] Looking at it then — a little more than a decade later — rusted through, its containment box half-filled with rainwater, felt like history slapping me in the face. What had created that sad ruin? Was it the way foreign aid worked, like economists said? One big capital investment, but without any long-term cash injections for maintenance? That made sense, and yet Gamtel seemed to keep things going when they felt like it. Sure, they weren't AT&T, but considering their challenges, they had enough staff to keep things going well enough to make stationing an NGO in the Gambia a viable option. Couldn't they afford a waterproof box?

The night after I'd seen that exchange, I sat at The Public House and tried to draw lines, like those charts in police dramas linking conspirators with red thread, trying to identify the invisible hand behind it all. I tried to draw connections between things I'd experienced in West Africa, both as an intern and as someone working locally; I linked in my education and its sketch of the West's development. A lot of interconnections, but none led to that swamped ruin. It was almost impossible to conceptualize. There were too many suspects. Maybe it was a political science problem? Poor governance? The money to fix the exchange had been syphoned off by corruption. Maybe a sociological problem? Too much loyalty to the family and tribe undermining the national enterprise. Gamtel workers simply not taking their jobs seriously enough? How much easier our lives at CompCorp would have been had that exchange worked. Trying to build the Internet without a telephone system was brutalizing us, sending us to climb walls and towers without any safety equipment, trying to compensate for infrastructure with main strength and brute force. A robust telecom system

---

161 Why exactly they'd bother, I don't know, but I'd be willing to wager it was in anticipation of unity with Senegal, which was an idea being seriously discussed at the time, going so far as Senegal and the Gambia signing the Treaty of Confederation in 1982. The treaty called for closer ties, economically and militarily between the two countries. In 1989, however, the Gambia walked away.

would have revolutionized our working lives, and to top it all off, one — and a good one — had actually existed. Galling.

More democracy? Less corruption? More loyalty to the state, less to the tribe? Sure, those things all mattered, all were part of the jungle we called "civilization," but there's a gulf between "the big picture" and "right here, right now." I did my best sitting there half drunk to remember the narratives my degree had tattooed onto my mind: the transformation of England from a small, backward little island, dwarfed economically and culturally by European civilizations like the Frankish Empire, into one of world's dominant economies and cultures. The rise of America: from tobacco farmers to world power. *How did that happen?* My mind would grope through what it could remember, having conversations with itself, chasing its intellectual tail and trying to find the one moment or factor that could explain how my own culture had moved from Susanna Moodie's "clearings" to Bay Street, Toronto. Education was supposed to help you make sense of your life, but mine had no purchase on the problems at hand. And that was a problem. I wanted to be useful, and I felt intuitively I was close to being that at CompCorp, but the demands in seeing it through — in terms of personal endurance — were getting the better of me. To keep at it, to keep showing up each day with a positive attitude, to keep trying, I needed some way of measuring success.

Were we helping anyone? Could I look around and say, "Yeah, we made something happen here today"? There were days when I could say that, but there were so many other days where I couldn't. It felt like the difference was pure luck. What were we doing right? What were we doing wrong? What could be done better? Did people *want* things to be better? What was the point? What was the goal? That last question was a sore point. No one said what the final product of "development" was supposed to look like, and that was a massive problem, being on the ground and looking development right in the face. If history books didn't lie, one of the most basic aspects of success was focus. Have a simple, easily defined goal. Napoleon and Caesar never lost sight of their single-minded pursuit of glory; the fate of nations decided by policies as simple as "march to the sound of the guns."[162] But you don't need to read the *Gaulic Wars* to know focus is crucial. No restaurant makeover show is complete without the ritual slashing of the menu, the culinary Jesus focusing the hapless wretch of a proprietor on dishes he can actually master.

So where did that leave me out in the field? *Development* wasn't much of a guide. The traditional war cry of my generation, "change the world!" wasn't much better. Change what exactly? We were definitely changing things at CompCorp on a daily basis, but for better or worse? Back home, I could change the world by cooking a meal: some guy at my local butchery bought his kid dinner with a paycheque that had been, in part, funded by the chicken I bought from him. Some kid whose dad sold that chicken to the butcher was getting school supplies with a cut of the same transaction. In the West, it seemed easy to change the world, but it was a lot more complicated in the Gambia. Did the country really have to be covered in trash? They had everything they needed to get that job done without foreign aid.[163]

---

162 Quite a contrast to the policy folders I've seen at most workplaces, inches thick and the fate of nothing more relevant than travel reimbursements decided.

163 They eventually came up with this plan to clean the streets about halfway through my time there, called Operation Save the Nation. By presidential decree, the population of the land was to stop everything one Saturday each month and clean stuff up. They were to pick up the litter in the streets and do something with it (what exactly was never really clear). This wasn't much of a solution because it meant the streets were clean for about five days of the month. A proper system of waste disposal would have been easy to implement: 50-gallon drums were ubiquitous, the military had the idle manpower and pickup trucks to cart them to the dump and empty them, and there was clearly an impulse to get things cleaned up. Not one Gambian I met liked the litter in the streets, but there was no other option. On the other hand, according to people in the know, Operation Save the Nation was actually about security. One of

259

Frustration fuelled obsession. After dinner I'd usually buy a box of wine from the restaurant and another pack of cigarettes from a vendor in the street and stumble home. I'd go into the office to surf the Internet, tracking down facts I couldn't remember. Between websites, I'd lounge outside with a drink and my cigs, trying to integrate what I'd just learned into the evening's stream of thought. Only when my mind was dripping with red wine would I call a halt. This is how I spent most weeknights.[164]

Clarity came soon, however. My eyes were opened by a German named Helmut. It happened only a couple of weeks after our run-in with the secret cops, and if you remember, that incident began with me on my way to Youth Communities. That meeting had been between the deputy director of the regional operation, Helmut, and myself. It went well, even if the rest of the day (and next couple of weeks) went to hell. Now a month later, the initial turmoil of those days fading, the events of the meeting were coming back into focus. The plan was a go. Come what may, Peter and Helmut weren't going to have their goals derailed by the Gambian secret police. I was about to be shipped off to Guinea-Bissau to help sort the network at the orphanage in Bissau City.

Guinea-Bissau's story was not unlike the Gambia's, with the Portuguese playing the part of the British. In fact, Guinea-Bissau's coastline was once known as the Slave Coast. Their modern history was the same tragic epic shared by many African countries: the nationalistic movements of the 1960s and '70s made tangible by injections of money and weapons

---

the rules was that no one was allowed to drive anywhere, because if you were driving, you weren't cleaning. Apparently, this was the point of the operation: it kept the streets clear for the military in the event of an emergency.

164 I have no idea how much I was drinking at that time, but generally I went to bed drunk every night. Nevertheless, I always made it to work on time. Ragged but on time.

from the Comintern; a successful independence movement throwing off the imperial power, political instability following, the norm ever since.

There had been follow-up meetings and the scope of the trip solidified. I should have been thrilled. I'd be leaving in a few weeks, but the approaching deadline left me unusually pessimistic. A more recent meeting with Peter had left me feeling more tired and hopeless than usual. We were driving around in his car (I can't remember for what) when he started to discuss the "challenges" of my impending trip to Bissau. The first obstacle would be crossing the border. It would be a road trip because flying was too expensive. Since the Gambia was surrounded on three sides by Senegal, we'd have to cross into Senegal first, going south, and then cross into Bissau. The whole notion of crossing the border gave me pause. I remembered my arrival in the Gambia vividly. The high point was being swept into immigration by my fellow passengers, where I needed to fill out a standard form. Unfortunately, I hadn't brought a pen. While trying to decide whom to ask for one, I managed to locate the source of a smell I'd noticed not long after entering the terminal. The smell came from a small man who stood a few inches away in a light-blue button-down, dark-blue trousers and matching beret. No markings on the beret, no shoulder flash, his face intense, knotted up with concentration or disapproval — I couldn't tell which. His odour was fearsome, sour sweat. He radiated "threat." He looked as if I'd stomped on his foot, and he was about to use whatever bureaucratic power his uniform carried to even the score.

Like most people caught by surprise, I focused on basic goals: a pen. He had one. I could see it in his top breast pocket. I asked him if I could borrow it, and he reacted as if I'd just bought him a Cadillac. "Of course, of course!" He pulled the pen out of his breast pocket and held it up as if saying "the missing piece," his face suddenly beaming. I went to work on the paperwork and he adjusted himself to look over my shoulder with a serious curiosity. I couldn't believe how openly intrusive he was, no attempt at subtlety, plus he really smelled. I gave him a big smile and turned my back to him. He tried the other side, I moved again.

"Thank you for your help," I smiled enthusiastically when I was finished, hoping a hearty thanks would settle any score I'd unwittingly incurred. I handed back the pen and made a move toward baggage claim. He jumped in front of me, chest out, and I walked right into him. His interest in my paperwork, the surging crowd of uniforms, the frustrated travellers, general exhaustion and the terrible reek made my head hurt. It had taken me three days to make the direct flight[165] and I was in no mood to put up with any nonsense, so I just shoved the little guy out of the way and headed to customs. That was back when my "entitled North American piss-and-vinegar tank" was still topped up. Now, over two years later, post boss-snatched-off-the-street, I knew his outfit — devoid of any identification — was that of a police officer. Confronted with him now, I'd have calmly wet myself and given him whatever he wanted. The thought of having to cross two borders in rapid succession wasn't setting fire to my youthful enthusiasm at all.

Peter went on: there was an extra "challenge" with the Senegalese border. The area we'd be travelling through — the section of southern Senegal that separated the Gambia from Guinea-Bissau — was currently in a state of revolt. The area was known as Casamance, and it had been fighting for independence since 1982. Peter — finger waving in my face like a parent — said I should stay away from anyone carrying an AK-47 and stick close to anyone carrying an M-16-type rifle. The former was standard issue with

---

165 We'd started at BWI, Baltimore to Banjul direct, the only direct flight to the Republic of the Gambia from anywhere in North America. It looked good: relatively cheap, no connections in Europe, a real bargain. After finding the check-in counter for Ghana Airways, I was told they were having problems with the flight, specifically, they couldn't find a working airplane. Since no one knew how long it would take to find one, my fellow passengers and I spent the next three days holed up in the airport, waiting for them to find a working machine. Finally, Air Canada coughed one up.

the guerrillas, the latter government issue for the security forces. Above all else, I shouldn't — under any circumstances — spend a night in the Casamance countryside. He raised his voice: *Under no circumstances was I to be in Casamance after dark*. Period. All borders into and out of Casamance closed at sundown. "Be across the border before then," insisted Peter. It shouldn't have been a problem, the route was under 140 km, just a couple of hours. Then I remembered our trip to Jufureh.

Peter pressed on. Should all go well, I'd face the final hurdle: there was no way of knowing what the issues were down at the orphanage in Guinea. Communication was sporadic, often limited to text messages. Email rarely worked. The place was a couple hundred kilometres away but might as well have been on the moon. This was why I was going. They had a satellite dish — just like the one the secret police had pulled out of our back lot — but something was wrong.[166] Either it wasn't aligned correctly or the network wasn't sending mail from the office workstations to the transceiver. Without any communication between here and there, I had no idea what to take with me. The obvious solution — take everything — wasn't on the table because Peter wouldn't let me gut the office for this special trip. I had to fill one bag and hope for the best. If it turned out I didn't have what I needed, I was ordered to "improvise."

All the wine in the world couldn't make me feel better that night, or any of the other nights leading up to the big kickoff. Three days before D-Day, Peter took me to Helmut's office for a final briefing. *How could it get worse?* I remember saying to myself on my way there, trying to buck up some optimism. Helmut was an intimidating guy. Always impeccably dressed, usually with a suit and tie or at least a crisp button-down, he carried himself with the dignity of an old world banker. He was austere. I'd seen him several times since our first meeting and I'd never seen him smile once. At this

---

166 Youth Communities only used VSATs where they were legal.

meeting, so close to lift off, he wanted to hammer out the final details. He introduced me to the woman who'd be my official contact while on the road, his secretary, Aminata, who brought me up to speed on the latest from Bissau (which wasn't much) and showed me a map with the proposed route (Birkama, Ziguinchor, Bissau City). I was taking this all in when he came to his final point, saying with his heavy German accent, "Failure *iz* not *un* option!"[167] You see, to help with the satellite dish, I was going to be teaming up with a satellite tech from Nigeria, Sola. Sola worked for a Nigerian affiliate of a U.K. satellite provider, and Sola was expensive. It was costing the orphanage $1,000 USD a day to keep the two of us in the field. That kind of money said "decisive results required" loudly and clearly. Come back carrying your shield or being carried on it.

His point was that I wouldn't just be crossing two frontiers, driving through an insurrection and dealing with the unknown on the other side. I'd be doing it *on a schedule*. And it would be a tight one at that. There were complications as well. After passing the Guinean border, the Rio Cacheu — a large river running roughly parallel to the boarder — needed to be crossed, and there was only one ferry, and it was small and notoriously unreliable.

Helmut said all of this sitting across from me in a leather imported European office chair. He looked comfortable as he slouched low in it, his head bowed as if looking at me over the top of his spectacles. Jesus, another suit. One more damn do-gooder who had no idea what the hell they were talking about. One more damn *expert*. God, I was sick of them. What good were they? Before I left D.C., "the big talk" was Saddam Hussein, specifically what to do about him. Were there weapons of mass destruction or not? Every member of the "chattering class" — politicians, analysts, journalists, generals, pretty much anyone with an advanced degree — was shooting their mouth off about it. Did it help? Did a better result come to

---

167 He actually said that.

pass because of all those PhDs debating ad nauseam? Helmut instantly reminded me of every NGO upper manager I'd ever met. The I've-got-a-degree-in-how-to-hold-empowering-meetings crowd.

I remember being in the offices of a do-gooder agency that will remain nameless, overseeing routine maintenance, when a young lady slammed her hands down on the keyboard and cursed. When I asked her about it, she told me about a project she'd been working on, getting a number of schools built upcountry. It'd been over a year and the job still wasn't finished, and she'd just received an email detailing yet another screw-up. After listening to her, it became clear she'd never actually been to the site, nor had she ever left the coast. She was indignant because her orders — delivered via phone and email — never got anywhere. There was always some excuse why they couldn't get the school built. I asked her if she thought they were lying. I hit a nerve because she answered with a haughty, "Well, the school isn't built yet, is it?" I tried to reason with her, listing many different factors that could've scuppered her plans, including theft of the building materials. It wasn't a welcome set of observations. The underlying problem was that she had no idea how to actually build a school. She was a political scientist and completely dependent on local contractors who were about as honest as Western contractors. She didn't even know enough about building to have a conversation about it, much less notice mistakes or potential dishonesty. She only knew what she wanted, but the key is to know how to get it, and she didn't even know where to begin. Like Helmut, she too dressed well.   So we sat: Helmut staring at me hard, trying to determine what I was making of all this. I could feel my face flush as I forced down the anger. "*Ze* average time, one *vay* is *zeven* hours. You *vill* make it in *zis* time." Balls.

Seven hours? It took four just to get to Dakar and that was an easy run by comparison. I left with a forced smile, and at the end of the day headed back to The Public House. That night, I couldn't shake the fear, the fear of failure. I should have told Helmut no. Instead, I'd taken a job I didn't know I could do. It was a good example of doing something stupid, of not thinking things through. Were my five years of schlepping in D.C. and the Gambian experiences I'd racked up enough to see me through? Should I just leave? The answer to the latter was an emphatic *no*, it felt like quitting, like turning my back. The answer to the former wasn't so clear. The next three nights I spent packing and repacking a single bag, and being pissed off with Peter and Helmut. I wondered how much of that $1,000 a day went into Peter's pocket.

Helmut's Run

D-day.

Helmut sent us a truck and a driver who picked up Sola and then came by the office. It was a beautiful Saturday morning. Sola was a tall, young Nigerian, well-dressed and good-natured, and we hit it off instantly. He helped me shift his satellite stuff, so I could get my gear aboard: tool bag, overnight bag and a box of cable. Comms check: I called and texted Aminata on two different phones to ensure our communications were in order. All good. Peter and Samba waved us off, and we were out the gate and blasting down the highway in minutes.

We were travelling in a large Nissan SUV, very roomy, very comfy. I had shotgun and Sola stretched his six-foot-plus frame out on the backseat. While we bounded out of Kairaba, Sola and I chatted and got to know each other. He was in his late-20s and had studied information technology in the U.K. and back home in Nigeria. He was working for a British satellite provider's regional Nigerian office, and he'd done a couple of jobs for the orphanage already with Peter, so he had Peter stories to swap, which we did happily. I was feeling better; the energy brought by the break in routine overtook my pessimism, and having a good travelling companion — one who shared a lot of the same cultural references — really helped. The last member of our team was Musa, the driver. He was about 50 and as

267

deferential as an English butler. He spoke English well, which was a relief. Once away from the coast, we'd have to rely on him to get us where we needed to be.

Musa was a fast driver. Only 30 minutes after kickoff we raised the Senegalese border. The apprehension of crossing a national frontier started to mount. I'd been across the border a couple of times, going north to Dakar, and it was a long and annoying experience. You took a bush taxi to the border, a long, rambling ride similar to the one we took to Jufureh. There, you would see uniformed officers, blue (police) and brown (customs and immigration), who'd look over your passport and give you a stamp, verifying your departure from the country. After you filed through the long, low concrete building to get your stamps, you pushed your way through the throng of vendors and headed over to the road. The border was marked by a single, rusted swing gate, basically a long pipe with a concrete weight on one end to lift it, and a mob of Senegalese stood on the other side. The mob included donkey-cart drivers. Looking past them, you'd see, outlined in the heat and haze, a similar road gate about a mile down a deserted roadway: Senegal. You crossed by approaching one of the cart drivers, arranging a deal for passage, loading your kit on the flat wooden platform that made up the business end of the cart, and then, legs swinging off the edge, you took your donkey cart to the other side. The mob like disposition of the cart drivers was due to good old-fashioned capitalism. They yelled and screamed, outbidding each other, and sometimes real aggression was needed to do a deal. I crossed it the first time with the Brusubi crew, and Lisa — our best French speaker — actually climbed up on a cart and started taking bids in French, like an auctioneer at a raucous cattle auction, pointing at people and screaming at the top of her lungs, demanding a bid, *"Mille cinq cents? Tu! Tu! Mille quatre? Un mille quatre?"*

"Oui! Mille quatre!"

"Un mille trois cents!"

"*Mille trois! Mille trois? Monsieur, un mille deux?*"

And so it went. Once across, you passed through a somewhat bigger concrete building, got a new set of stamps and then entered a large area similar to a huge, dirt soccer pitch. Hundreds of cars, predominantly Peugeot station wagons, filled the place, and you bought a seat in one to take you wherever. These cars were a kind of long-range taxi call a *sept-place,* "seven seats," which pretty much tells you everything you need to know. The cargo space on the station wagons had been replaced with a second backseat, allowing it to sit seven passengers with their luggage strapped to the roof: six in the back two benches and one beside the driver. Needless to say, riding shotgun would cost you. It was the only seat you could stretch your legs in, and you paid for the privilege. The first time I went I got outbid and spent the four-hour nonstop drive to Dakar in a backseat, hunched over, my knees level with my chest.

All of this was going through my mind as we approached the border. Language was my most pressing anxiety. It probably goes without saying that if your French is poor, trying to cross the border into Senegal by land was tricky at best. Unfortunately, due to a touch of dyslexia, I've never been much of a linguist. I'd made the trip to Dakar on my own once, but I had almost nothing with me and I wasn't on a schedule.

"Hey man, are we closing in on the border?" Sola asked pensively.

"Yup." I looked at Musa for confirmation.

"Wau, 10 minutes, boss."

"You know," said Sola, "the border guards don't take too kindly to IT equipment. Think it's spy gear." I'd never really thought about that. Sola was looking at me expectantly, as if I had an answer. I didn't even have the language skills to find a bathroom if we needed one: "*Mon-sewer touv et moi le sale de bin?*"

Passing through the Gambian side was no problem. Stamps all around and off we went. The Senegalese side of the border was a short stretch up the road, and it was different than the northern frontier. There was no mob of cart-men or vendors trying to sell you water or juice. We slowed as we approached, passing a concrete machine gun emplacement and stopping opposite a tin-roofed shed. As we rolled to a stop, I looked over the soldiers and paramilitary lounging around. Casamance was on the other side of the swing gate, and the local gendarmes were dressing and acting the part. Quiet and serious, none of them flashed the toothy, endearing smile so common in the Gambia. Resigned, I gave a sigh and reached for the door handle but was pulled up short by Musa, "No, Roban! Let me! Passport please! Passport!" I glanced over at Sola and he was already pulling his out. I handed mine over. Musa took them and jumped out.

Sola and I sat obediently in the truck. I checked the time, looked at Musa — who was greeting a surly-looking soldier with a big Gambian smile — and sighed. I rolled down the window and lit a cigarette. How long would this take? Sola had no doubts about how long it would take; he put his feet up, and I could hear him flipping the pages of the book he'd brought along.[168] My impatience was getting the better of me, and I shot peevish glances at Musa every few seconds. Some part of my stressed mind resented anyone who was that pleasant. I finished my cigarette, flicked the butt out the window and was about to start on another when the driver-side door burst open and Musa jumped in. "Alright! We go now, Mr. Roban!" I just sat there with an unlit cigarette hanging off my lip as he started the truck with one hand and gave a quick salute toward the men of the border post with the other.

"How much was it?" I asked, assuming a bribe had been made.

"Oh nothing, Mr. Roban. It has all been arranged by the boss, Mr. Roban." He meant Helmut.

---

168 *Men Are From Mars, Women Are From Venus*. He was getting married soon and was reading it as research.

"Arranged by the boss? How?" As we raced through Senegal, Musa explained things to me. Helmut had a system. As I took it all in, I started to realize that Helmut wasn't some uptight manager with a degree in Theories and Abstractions, but actually some kind of get-it-done god, light years ahead of what I'd seen so far in the Gambia or even back in D.C.

It was pretty simple actually, and it started with HR. Musa told me that all the drivers Helmut hired were ex-military men, retired and with honourable discharges. This was important, Musa explained, not so much because of the personal discipline it implied, but because all border crossings were manned by the military or the paramilitary. Helmut wanted all his drivers to be ex-soldiers simply because it would give them something to talk about with the border guards. Helmut understood the importance of human relationships in that part of the world. After all, most people's first question after greeting a stranger was "where's the family from?" It was a classic icebreaker. People warmed up to each other, swapping stories about their families, trying to work toward a common relative, a common story about someone's aunt or cousin. In another country, the odds that your aunt Fatou knew uncle Sheik's cousin Lamin were remote at best, so Helmut — an ex-soldier himself[169] — countered with the common institutional culture of the military. The drivers could swap old war stories; the pain of a martinet, for example, was a universal bitch. The drivers knew the culture, they knew when to salute, they knew what made soldiers laugh.

That wasn't the end of Helmut's meticulousness, however. Not only were the drivers soldiers, but soldiers who'd worked with the military men they were likely to encounter along a given route. We were passing through Senegal and Guinea-Bissau, and so we were assigned a driver who'd worked closely with the Senegalese and Bissau armed forces during his military

---

169 He'd done his time as a conscript in the Austrian army like every other 18-year-old boy in Austria.

career. He'd been on manoeuvres with them as well as having acted as a liaison on a number of occasions. He knew how they were organised, had friends he could ask after, and knew whom to salute and when. All of this made it easier for him to generate that all important personal relationship with the border patrol. In the event all this familiarity didn't yield an open sesame, Helmut had provided his drivers with other means to leverage a wary customs man. All the drivers had ECOWAS passports.

ECOWAS, the Economic Community of West African States, is an economic union formed by several West African countries in 1975. Countries have come and gone, but current membership is 15 countries, including the Gambia. In addition to its economic responsibilities — the encouragement of trade and stability between the member states — it also provides certain services for citizens of its member states. One of those services is to provide passports. The interesting thing was that there were three levels of passport: an ordinary passport for average folk, an official passport for bureaucrats moving around the region on government business, and finally, the diplomatic passport for diplomats. Somehow, Helmut had managed to get all of his drivers diplomatic passports.

Musa explained that they weren't supposed to flash the passports around. No: "I'm a diplomat, stand aside" nonsense. Drivers were to show them, but put more of their energy into building relationships rather than relying on the letter of the law. I guessed Helmut knew the value of the law at a lonely border post in the middle of the African outback. Even in the West, an immigration official could turn down your request to enter a country even if your papers were in order. As Mustafa chatted, I thought about each time I'd had to renew my work visa in D.C. Every year I had to go to INS[170] to request a renewal, and it was an uncomfortable experience. My papers were always in order, but that didn't mean anything, especially

---

170 Immigration and Naturalization Service.

after 9/11. I remembered reading about a Canadian executive working for a tech company out on the West Coast shortly after the attack. He'd been home in B.C. and was travelling back, but he never made it into the U.S. An angry border guard had denied him entry because he happened to be of Pakistani descent. The executive protested that he was a Canadian citizen, born and raised, and that he had everything he needed to legally enter the country, as he'd done many times before. In reply, the border guard had taken his valid Canadian-government-issued passport and thrown it right into a garbage bin, making sure this guy and everyone else in the line knew what he thought of a legally issued Canadian passport. When people are in a snit, the law's bunk. Helmut was right to focus on relationships, reserving diplomatic rights for emergencies.

Failing all the above, the driver could always call back to HQ. Naturally, Helmut provided his drivers with phones covering all carriers along the entire route. His secretary would be manning the phones 24/7 while such a trip was underway, and she had strict instructions to wake Helmut in the event of an emergency. From his end, he'd pump the juice that had gotten him the diplomatic passports in the first place and pull a solution together.

Quite an operator, our Helmut. Sure enough, we buzzed through every border along the route inside five minutes, a bloody miracle. But staying on schedule was more complicated than that, because the roads were always a big question mark. I asked Musa if Helmut's travel-time estimate was accurate. "Oh yes," Musa replied. Helmut knew how long because he travelled all the routes many times. All new drivers had to travel their routes the first time riding shotgun with an experienced driver behind the wheel and Helmut in the back keeping time. It sounds a little over the top, but driving around the West African outback could be a wild ride. One rainstorm could take you from a Sunday afternoon leisure drive to *The Poseidon Adventure* in 20 minutes flat. In the Gambia, it was actually illegal for foreigners to drive in the countryside, partly to keep Gambians employed, but also to keep white tourists from getting themselves killed. The roads we blasted down in the Gambia were mostly dirt, heavily scarred by water and past traffic. The ruts were so deep even an SUV couldn't simply drive down the road. Instead, one set of wheels rode in a wheel rut while the other rode on the higher outside ridge, or, if the outside ridge disintegrated into a series of potholes (some as large and deep as a wheelbarrow bed), we quickly got the wheels in the rut up on the central ridge and dropped those on the outside ridge into the trench. *Trench* was the right word too. The angles were so extreme I had to hang onto the door to keep from sliding into Mustafa. After one terrible patch that went on for about 20 minutes with the truck at a continuous 40-degree angle, my aching arm had had enough and so I wedged my foot between the door and seat to keep me out of Mustafa's lap. At a sedate 20 to 30 kilometres per hour, roads like that were manageable, but to keep Helmut's schedule Mustafa was charging down them at 50 to 60.

The roads in Senegal and Guinea-Bissau were, thankfully, largely paved, but this brought other problems. There were the ubiquitous animal herds that were always crossing the road at the absolute worst time, but because there was so little traffic on the roads in the countryside, people would use them for all manner of things. I remember driving through Guinea and seeing hundreds of square feet of chopped cassava root lining the highway, leaving only a tiny path down the middle for traffic to pass through. The cassava needed to be dried before it could be pounded into flour for *fufu*,[171] and the flat, hot surface of the highway was the perfect tool for the job.

I should have known that a manager like Helmut would have walked

---

171 *Fufu* is a soft, doughy bread made of cassava flour or any other starchy vegetable. It's quite good.

the ground himself — no armchair management from him. If he'd been in charge of getting that school made, he probably would have been out there pouring the concrete himself. Having made the journey several times, he knew the issues his people faced and could make judgements accordingly. In short, he wouldn't have any of the problems I'd seen other NGO managers suffer from. I thought of a local Gambian manager I knew. We'd done some work for a government agency funded by the World Bank. On completion, Peter and I hoped to pick up a support contract. Unfortunately, the World Bank insisted on hiring "a local Gambian."[172] He was a nice guy, despite a touch of pompousness. I hadn't minded him initially, but as the days and weeks went by, he'd become a pest. He didn't know how to do anything, and he'd call me a dozen times a day to ask silly questions. He was the IT manager for a government agency, and he called me up one day to ask how to update his antivirus software. He'd ordered it to be done, but his technician didn't complete the task, citing some technical detail, and he wanted to know if the tech was lying or if his excuse was legitimate. I asked him how he got his job and he rattled off some professional accounting certification he got while studying in the U.K. Perfect, one more bank manager in over their head.[173]

All this gave me much to think about while we drove along. It seemed pretty clear (as if it wasn't before) that an operator like Helmut wouldn't take no for an answer. I didn't really know what I'd be faced with when we arrived, but I knew I'd better figure out what needed figuring.

Overall, the trip to Bissau was as smooth as you could want it to be. We made the ferry on time and Musa's relief was tangible. He told us if you

---

172 Peter, of course, was a "local Gambian," so I found this curious. Either the fix was in or Peter wasn't the right colour.

173 Talk about cultural imperialism.

got there at lunch, you'd have to sit for a couple of hours while the crew took their break. With the boarders and ferry behind us, it would be smooth sailing to Bissau City. Now it was our turn to feel stress. Sola had ridden in the back the whole way, reading, napping and chatting. But the closer we got to our destination, the more his tone changed. Mine too. Musa had done his bit to deliver us on target and on time, now it fell upon us to finish the job. And what was that job? We only knew the satellite had been out of action for some time. I also had orders to get a new computer lab linked back to the satellite.

Bissau City was not unlike anywhere else in West Africa, low-level concrete buildings predominated, but the streets were generally paved and wide. Many of the buildings were pockmarked, a result of the 1998-1999 Civil War that started when the president ordered the head of the military to step down for allowing some of his soldiers to supply the Casamance rebels. Being the mature professional he was, the latter replied with "make me," or as they put it in the media, "he started a coup." Things looked all right now, save the bullet and shrapnel scarring and the occasional burnt-out armoured vehicle rusting by the side of the road.

Finally, we arrived. Sola and I jumped out of the truck and into the dust cloud kicked up by our skidding stop. We were greeted by the head administrator, João. His English was excellent, and after a quick handshake and "welcome," he asked us if we'd like to see the site before the evening turned to night. We did. Off we went. Unlike anywhere else I'd visited, there were no unnecessary pleasantries, and the common "would you like to drop your bags off and rest for an hour before dinner?" wasn't even proffered. João knew the Helmut way of work.

Sola was even more nervous than I was. The VSAT wasn't working and he had to sort it out in the time allotted. He'd brought spare parts, but the big fear was a problem with the skyline. If someone had built a wall or a low building between the dish and the horizon, there could be problems.

The satellites that Sola's company rented bandwidth on sat low on the horizon, so zero degrees being parallel to the ground and 90 being straight up into the sky, the dish angled only about 30 degrees.[174] To see the horizon, the dish needed to be set up on a pole of a certain height, with 40 metres' clearance between it and any obstacles such as a wall or building. If someone had forgotten these rules and had done some construction, we'd have a big problem. During the drive, Sola mentioned other sites that had gone down for exactly that reason, and the solution — tearing down a brand-new building, or worse, convincing the neighbour to tear down his brand-new building — had made for bad blood.

We half jogged down to where the dish was stationed just outside the admin building. The other parameter controlling dish location was a requirement for it to be within 20 metres of the modem connecting it to the network. We arrived and Sola quickly surveyed the scene. The dish sat on a large steel pole, maybe three metres high and about 10 centimetres in diameter. The poll was set in concrete only a few metres away from the wall of the admin block, the dish pointing in the opposite direction, out over the compound wall and into the twilight sky. Sola looked happy with what he saw, which was a relief. The problem lay elsewhere and we wouldn't have to try to find a new poll, re-site it, find a mason to dig, level and cement it into place, and then move and realign the dish, an almost impossible task to complete in three days. Sola had brought suitcases full of spare parts and he would begin doing diagnostics the next morning.

Next was the computer lab. I asked our host to show it to me, and

---

174 During the drive I made a stupid comment: "But I thought satellites were up there," jabbing my finger at the cab roof, "in space!" Sola, with the frustration of one who's endured the same stupid question too many times, immediately laid into me.

"You *tink de* damn world's flat, man! Let me tell you, Columbus, the damn *ting's* round! Everywhere you see sky, there's space behind. You stand on a cliff and look *down* at the horizon, and so you're looking *down* at space!" Touché.

again we half ran, half walked over to the site, a small building with over a dozen computers crammed in. It looked new and clean, the computers a generation old, but I was assured they worked fine. There was an old hub to connect the computers that led to the instructor's machine, which shared a single 56/6 dialup connection between the rest of the machines. João powered up the instructor's machine and I did likewise with a student workstation. Sola and I could see the problem instantly. The orphanage wanted the students to become computer and information literate; they wanted them to learn how to use a computer and use the Internet, which would give them much better odds of getting a real job when they left. In most of the places I'd been in West Africa, being computer literate was the equivalent of being plain old literate in a bygone Europe. Like the clerks of yesteryear, being computer literate instantly made you middle class in the impoverished parts of the region. Knowing how to run an accounting program could get you a skilled job with an NGO, but even standalone programs needed updating, and since they were almost all built in the West where connectivity was taken for granted, a good Internet connection became necessary just to run a word processor. A good dictionary could be a five- to 10-megabyte download. My back-of-the-envelope calculations implied — at best — the lab machines had barely five kilobits each to access the Internet.[175] Hence the problem. The throughput was so low I could barely load the Yahoo! homepage. Sola tried another computer and never actually loaded it.

---

175 So a 56.6 modem has a theoretical throughput of 56.6 kilobits a second, which, after you account for administrative throughput, gives about 44.8 kilobits a second, which is roughly 5,300 bytes. Because the network was joined by a hub, that amount had to be divided by the number of machines, so about 13 (a dozen student machines and one for the instructor) comes out to about 3520 bytes per machine, or in other words, each machine had about 0.35 megabit connection. The laptop I'm writing this on is connected wirelessly and has a 12-megabit connection. While the orphanage's machines had about 4.2 kilobits to play with, I have 12,288.

There were all kinds of problems: the computers were only connecting to the LAN at 10 MB; they were connected by a hub that caused all kinds of network congestion; the machines were a mess with all kinds of shareware crap weighing them down; and the telephone connection, shared between every machine in the place, was about as reliable as one in the Gambia. None of this bothered me much. Time consuming but easy fixes could right those wrongs. The big issue was distance. To connect the lab to the satellite, I'd have to run a cable from the admin building, and if it wasn't over a hundred metres, it was damn close.[176] You couldn't even see the admin block from the computer lab. As we left, my mind racing over what I'd seen, Sola tugged my arm. He must have known what I was thinking because he was pointing back toward the entrance. The orphanage was big enough to warrant its own water tower, which had been built by the parking lot. We ran over with the middle-aged João right on our heels, his tie flapping over his shoulder. We climbed to the top, only about four stories, but it gave a wonderful view of the orphanage and the surrounding areas.

The orphanage was situated on a huge plot of land inside Bissau City. I'm not sure of the actual size, but it housed over a hundred orphans and included a full school, big enough for hundreds more children from the surrounding community, in addition to the residents. There were workshops where trades were learned, the aforementioned computer lab, administration offices and an infirmary, the latter large enough to serve the surrounding neighbourhood. The children were not housed in a single barrack as you'd imagine, rather, the philosophy of the NGO as I understood it was to try and recreate the family experience as closely as possible. The kids were

---

176 Ethernet — the technology that makes the wired Internet work — has a limit of about 100 meters before the signal strength along the cable weakens to the point of uselessness. I had a set of antennas with me, but they were expensive and so for emergency use only. A wired connection was preferred anyway because it's faster and much more reliable.

divided into groups of 10 and assigned to a house, which were scattered across campus. Each house was headed by a "house mother," who was usually a local woman employed by YC to make dinner, rouse up the kids in the morning and otherwise establish the routines of a "normal" life. If the woman had her own kids, they could stay in the house with the orphans and attend the school for free. The school and trades workshops were generally considered the best in the city (as they were in the Gambia) and so the position was much sought after by local women.

The entire campus was clean, well cared for, with neat concrete paths snaking over the cropped grass, connecting the various buildings. Flowerbeds were trim. The contrast between it and the dusty street outside was stark. All around the orphanage was a sea of low concrete walls and sheet-metal roofs. From above, it literally looked like a rolling sea of corrugated iron with a fleet of antennas riding on it. The litter was visible even from four stories up and through the dust clouds coming from the cars running up and down the side streets. In terms of the job, I could see what had to be done, and so with great relief Sola and I descended and were shown to our quarters.

Our guest quarters were well kept and comfortable. We had an YC mother taking care of us, and João had stocked the fridge in the little bungalow generously with Super Bock, a popular Portuguese beer. After an excellent dinner of rice and chicken, we downed a couple, smoked a few cigs on the balcony, discussed our plan of attack in the morning and turned in early.

We were up before the sun and got to work immediately. In the end, it wasn't a big deal. All the problems were well within the reach of our skills, tools and equipment. Sola discovered that the modem the VSAT was talking to had malfunctioned. Since it was plugged into the mains, we weren't surprised. He replaced it with the spare he'd brought along, added a surge protector (we brought several) and looked into acquiring a UPS.[177] From the top of the water tower, I saw a way to get the connection where it needed to be. I simply ran a cable from the admin building out about 80 metres to one of the children's bungalows, took the hub from the lab and connected the cable to one of its ports. I ran another cable the rest of the distance (about 20 metres) to the lab and replaced the missing hub with a switch I'd brought with me. Some connection tests told me I'd brought about 300 kilobits into the room — quite an improvement over the 48 from the modem — and it was reliable. The connection wasn't dropping every five minutes. The switch was an improvement over the hub because it didn't subdivide the connection, meaning each machine had access to about 300 kilobits all the time.[178] I re-headed all the cables to move them from 10 to 100 megabits, and reformatted all the machines to clean the viruses and shareware off, which increased the capacity of the network by 30 percent.[179] I pulled the machines apart and cleaned them physically as well. While doing this, Sola was polishing up the satellite rig and occasionally helping me out.

It was all pretty mundane stuff, barring the first morning after our arrival. João called us from our work to the parking lot where we were

---

177 Death by power spike was a common cause of death for networking equipment all over the region. The UPS (uninterruptible power supply) was just a big battery in a box that charged from the mains. The modem would draw power from the battery, and the battery was connected to the mains via the surge protector. If there was a power spike, the surge protector would take the majority of the blow. Since almost all surge protectors let some of the spike through before they blow, the rest of the surge would be soaked up by the UPS. In addition to being more able to handle a surge than the modem, both the UPS and surge protector were also cheaper and easier to replace.

178 It might seem like I should divide the 300 kilobits by 13, leaving each machine with about 23 kilobits, but because of the stateless design of the Internet Protocol and the internal workings of the switch, each computer could use a lot more of the 300 kilobits than a mere 23.

179 In other words, there was so much shareware and other crap on the network that nearly one-third of the capacity was being used by crap running in the background.

greeted by everyone — orphans, staff and administrators — singing the "Welcome Song." Although I don't remember the lyrics, it was a conflicting moment. On one hand, you were touched by their faith in you, on the other, you really hadn't done anything to justify that trust except show up. Floating in the background of those feelings, an uncomfortable thought flopped around: it was only the Internet, we were only going to do what any satellite and networking tech would do. Back home, you'd probably bitch about us coming to your house because it would mean you'd have to stay home all morning waiting for us to show up.

Cleaning up the lab and fixing whatever else was wrong with any computers across the campus was an 18-hour day, broken up only by the afternoon meal. João or his aid would take us to a little café made out of a shipping container with a window cut in the side like a food truck. The evening we spent drinking and sleeping. On our last night, we decided to hit the town and went to a well-recommended barbeque chicken joint. We ate and drank to ridiculous excess, prodded on by an indescribable sense of relief. We decided to end the night by crashing the African Commission on Human Rights, which I knew from Abai was in town conducting hearings and he'd be there.. The compliant but worried Musa found the hotel it was being held at and we stumbled in, narrowly avoiding a disaster when Sola almost fell into the open sewer by the side of the road. The sewers in most of the city consisted of two concrete trenches, one running down each side of the major roads. About three metres deep and about as wide, they were completely open, so you had to find a concrete overpass or else you'd fall right in. Going for lunch one afternoon, we saw the back end of a car pointed straight up to the sky, the front buried in the sewer. I grabbed Sola's arm and yanked him back at the last second. We stumbled up to the front desk, where we were eyed with aristocratic disgust by the man behind the counter. I was too drunk to make my intentions clear, so we never did find Abai or the commission. Probably for the best. The relieved Musa returned us to the orphanage, where we pondered using Sola's talents and tools to re-align the VSAT so we could get soccer on our laptops, but again thought better of it. Instead, we drank more and congratulated ourselves on a job well done. We'd been lucky and we knew it.

Unfortunately, our luck folded almost as soon as we started back. We rolled out of bed a bit later than usual, feeling content with a job well done, but about 20 minutes outside Bissau City an important part of the SVU dropped off. I couldn't get a clear answer from Musa as to what exactly it was, but it stopped us dead in our tracks. A few calls back to the orphanage solved the problem: the head of the orphanage would send us his SUV, but first it would have to be fuelled and a second car found to return the driver. Eventually, it arrived, we transferred to the new car and were off, but we were now very much behind schedule. Mustafa was driving like a madman, blasting down the paved but poorly maintained road at 70 km/h, barely slowing below 50 as we winged through villages.

As I said before, in this part of West Africa there were very few cars on the countryside roadways, so people used the flat, warm pavement for any manner of uses, including a place to keep their children out of trouble. This might seem strange, but a flat, open space — devoid of the brush that poisonous snakes, insects and other creepy-crawlies like to hide in — was perfect to keep kids safe. As we came around the corner of one small village at about 55 km/h, I saw a woman drop a basket and charge at the road ahead. Following her direction with my eyes, I saw an infant sitting there, legs spread, back straight, eyes wide. I instinctively grabbed the dash and yelled, "Musa!" He hunched low over the wheel and expertly swerved wide. Looking back through the window, I saw the woman snatch her child up, squeezing it to her breast and running off the road like the devil himself were chasing her. She shot me a look that can only be described as pure, refined hate, which I've never forgotten.

I told Musa to slow down in the villages. I was shaken and angry about almost killing a child, but it was a lukewarm rebuke. I knew what was on his mind, and it was on Sola's and mine as well. It was almost 10 a.m., and if we didn't hurry, we'd never make the ferry before lunch. Two hours wasted in the morning and two hours wasted at the ferry meant an uncomfortable evening: we'd be trapped in Casamance, stuck in rebel territory during the night. Unfortunately, we showed up right when the crew kicked their feet up. We pulled over like everyone else and Musa ran off to find the crew to see if he could entice them away from their lunch. Sola and I walked down to the small shantytown of lean-tos that serviced people waiting for the ferry and downed about four beer each for lunch. Musa came back without any success. After he'd eaten, I sent him back, this time with my wallet. The crew decided that for a small 20,000 CFA[180] deposit, they'd cut their lunch to an hour. Deal. With an hour back on the clock, we crossed and raced back toward the Gambia.

We were fast at the checkpoints, and Musa's focus never faltered on the road. It was down to the last couple of miles to the border and we only had about 10 minutes before closing time. I thought we were going to make it, provided their watches kept the same time as mine, when Musa suddenly hit the brakes and slowed us down. Dozens of armed men appeared along both sides of the road. They were in full camouflage, their helmets and kit covered in the same tall grass the highway cut through. Slowing down, we gave them a good looking over as we passed, and they did the same to us. There must have been 30 or 40 of them; their faces painted green and black, which made them even more intimidating. They were carrying M-16s and a

---

180 CFA, or more formally: the West African Communauté Financière d'Afrique ("Financial Community of Africa") franc, was the common currency used by most of the French and Portuguese speaking countries in West Africa. The currency is backed by the BCEAO (Banque Centrale des États de l'Afrique de l'Ouest, "Central Bank of the West African States") which is located in Senegal. Most people simply referred to it CFA (pronounced "sefa"). At that time 20,000 CFA was about 30 – 40 USD.

lot of hand grenades, but I heard Musa chuckle: "Senegalese army! They must be heading back to the barrack after their patrol." Sure enough, they didn't pay us any attention. They looked exhausted marching along the side of the road, heading in the same direction we were, toward the border. We made it bang on at 5 p.m., closing time for border crossings into and out of Casamance.

Both Peter and Helmut were thrilled with the outcome. During the debrief with the latter, I told him — perhaps with a bit too much fervour — he was the best leader I'd seen in the Gambia, and I meant it. Watching his operation in action had really inspired me. He curtly waved away the compliment and told me leadership was just that: the ability to get people to follow, nothing more. In Helmut's opinion, leadership was about charisma. You didn't even need to be competent, and he pointed to the disastrous and evil career of "the deplorable Austrian"[181] as an example of someone who could get an entire nation to follow him — straight into the abyss. No, he was no leader, he insisted. The willingness of his staff to follow came from generous paycheques and a belief in what they were doing. He was only a manager and his sole responsibility was to keep things running so no one lost faith in the organization as a whole. No matter how much people believed in the mission of the orphanage, if things didn't get done properly, if people started to feel like the place was a disorganized mess, the place would fall apart. His talent was keeping the trains running on time. That's what he gave back; that's how he made the world a better place.

---

181 Helmut's euphemism for fellow countryman Adolf Hitler.

Lazare Carnot

Helmut had given me a lot to think about. According to him, you were one of two people, assuming you were in management. You're either a *leader* or you're a *manager*. There are some people who are equally competent at both roles, and I think everyone's got bits of both in them, but at the end of the day, you're more one than the other. Neither is good at the extreme. That's when leadership tends towards fantasy and management becomes the worst kind of closed-minded bureaucracy. There were only leaders and managers, Helmut said, and when I showed up at CompCorp, I wanted to be a leader because leaders are always the heroes. Kids want to be the hero because heroes get attention. They're remembered; they're known; they're made into action figures. Everyone's heard of Napoleon. You might not know much about him, but there's still some brand-name recognition there. How about George S. Patton? Or Julius Caesar? Or Mother Teresa? How about Lazare Carnot?

Carnot might not be a designer label, but he was a pivotal figure of the French Revolution. He managed to save France from the reactionary armies of the First Coalition bent on stamping out the fledgling French Republic. A mathematician of some renown, Carnot reorganized and stabilized the Revolutionary Army, expanded its size and stiffened its discipline. The army he raised saved revolutionary France, defending it from attacks by Austria, Great Britain, Spain and internal guerrilla uprisings.

286

All good news for a young, plucky Lieutenant-Colonel Napoleon Bonaparte, still pretty much a nobody in 1793.[182] It was Carnot's army Napoleon marched into Italy with, and from there to fame and fortune as the Man of Destiny. Carnot marched into history too. He got his nickname by some member of the National Convention who tagged him the Organizer of Victory. Doesn't have quite the same ring, does it?[183] No one wants to be the Organizer of Victory, not when they could be the Iron Duke.[184] I wanted to be a general, not a secretary, but the more I talked to Helmut, the more I realized I was the latter. It went down rather hard, but it didn't matter. If I really meant to help people — really make a difference in the world — I had to discard my dreams and follow my skills. I endorse the abandonment of dreams. Dreams are so focused they're kind of boring. There's something to be said for letting the wind have its way with you. It's a more creative path. At the end of the day you'll see more of the world. At the time, though, giving up my dreams was a difficult decision.

The experience of having worked with Helmut gave me a whole new series of questions to consider over dinner at The Public House. I ate there as before, but now I mulled over different experiences and doctrines from my working past and from my education. I thought I knew something about leaders. I'd been ensnared by enough of them over my working career to have had some thoughts on the subject. It goes without saying that history was full of them too.[185] The more I thought about it, the more I agreed with Helmut. Being a leader wasn't something you could learn. "Natural born

---

182 He was working his way up the ladder at this point, his performance at the Siege of Toulon getting him his first real notice among his contemporaries.
183 I sometimes wonder if Napoleon, after gaining the consulship, ever sent Carnot a gift for his contribution to the successful conclusion of the Revolutionary Wars. An inkwell, perhaps, with *World's Greatest Secretary* engraved on it, or a paperweight with "I know you'll put this to good use" etched across the top.
184 One of the Duke of Wellington's sobriquets.
185 Full of *them*, not *it*, although there is a good amount of the latter too.

leaders" were the only kind. If leadership could be easily defined and taught, we'd all be leaders. But it's not a skill. Thinking about the leaders I've known, as well as history's long march of generals, politicians, humanitarians and bandits, all I could really say about them was that they led; their ultimate measure of success being whether or not people followed. You can't declare yourself the leader or force people to support or align themselves with you. Sure, your door might say CEO, but that doesn't mean people follow you. They obey because they don't want to lose their jobs. That's not leadership. People are attracted to the leaders they follow. Leaders have charisma. Competence is nice too, if you can get it, but not really a requirement. I'd worked for bosses who were walking, talking calamities, yet their employees stayed loyal long past the dictates of common sense, myself included. They say love is the strongest bond between people, and competence doesn't factor into affection. Attraction's a mystery. Having a "goal" or a "vision" or a "passion" adds to a person's attractiveness because it speaks to sincerity and honesty. This person knows what they want and isn't afraid to say it — or even shout it — to the world. Having a vision implies a lack of agenda; it implies authenticity. At least I suppose so. Discussing charisma is like discussing love. Why one human falls into orbit around another isn't predictable. The only certainty we have about love and charisma is that they exist and can make otherwise normal, rational people do some pretty shocking things.

Take "the unfortunate Austrian," for instance. His official title was the Leader,[186] and his charisma was legendary. It was all he really had. No one can claim he had sense: common, elevated or otherwise. Nevertheless, even as the world around them turned to dust, enough Germans followed him — fanatically — to make his reign of terror viable to the end. Even the

---

186 The word *führer* means *leader* in German. "Das Führer" literally means "the Leader."

attempt on his life brought cries of sympathy from the population at large.[187]

I've never enjoyed this level of charisma; I'm much too introverted. Peter had it, though. We'd work through rainstorms for that guy. I remember being sent out in the back of an open truck with some of the guys to "get something — anything — done." We huddled behind the cab of the truck, not to stay dry, that was totally impossible; we huddled because the torrents slashed our face like a sandblaster as we sped along at 50 km/h. We were angry. We cursed Peter the whole way there and back, but we still did his bidding, we still followed him. We even followed him when he'd come into the office with about 40 minutes left on the clock and sent us out to do a wireless install. Outside of the fact that a smooth install was potentially hours of work, minus travel time and equipment scavenging, the sites themselves could be appalling. I remember one where we had to mount a 10-metre pole on the side of a two-story building. There was only about five feet between the building and the compound wall, which was covered with broken glass.[188] I'll never forget standing on a creaking ladder, body contorted to try and help support a 30-pound pole waving around over our heads. The broken bottles seemed to be looking up at us, waiting. I remember another time being on the roof of a hotel to align an antenna. Grabbing hold of the metal pole, I could feel the surge of current through my arms like a thousand ants chewing at my sinews. Peter was on-site, and I called to tell him the work site wasn't safe because the pole was carrying current. He cursed into the phone, hung up and a few seconds later a piece of dirty canvas came flying up onto the roof. Thanks, boss. He used to curse

---

187 Ian Kershaw's *The End* detailing the last months of Hitler's Reich gives plenty of information on this. True, there was a lot of oppression to keep things running, but that only says powerful things about Hitler's leadership abilities: someone had to do the oppressing on his behalf.

188 It was normal to cement broken glass into the top of compound walls to keep people out.

us up and down almost every day for not getting enough work done. Through it all we stayed. Why? God knows. Part of it was for our own reasons, but part of it was for him. Working for him was like being invited to the big party everyone was talking about. He just had that certain something that made you believe in where he was going.

But where was he going? Not surprisingly, Peter's vision was pretty much about making Peter rich. Not very noble, but it worked on some level. There was a reassuring simplicity to it that made decisions and therefore life in general simple. It took me a long time to appreciate the importance of this. In a complex world, people gravitate instinctively to simplicity. I do, anyway. It's what initially made Google famous. One single search box on a blank page. It was shocking when I first saw it. The competition — services like AltaVista, HotBot and Yahoo! — had the world splashed across them: news feeds, celebrity updates; you could barely find the search box. Faced with hundreds of decisions a day, Peter's vision was like the Google search page. When I got back to Canada and was working for a major hospital in Toronto, I happened to be chatting with my boss, a surgeon who also taught at the University of Toronto. In his spare time he also ran a small NGO dedicated to bringing modern surgical practices to other parts of the world. We were chatting about a meeting that hadn't gone well, and he made the comment that academics didn't make good leaders because they're trained to see both sides of an issue, which robbed them of decisiveness. Listening to him in the elevator, I thought of Peter.

Peter had focus, which was a godsend for his staff, but there was more to it: we respected his audacity. Everyone wants to be rich,[189] but not too many would look at the Gambia and say, "I can make it here." Peter could have worked in the U.K. if he'd wanted to, but he *chose* to work in the

---

[189] Or "comfortable" I guess is the new socially conscious way of expressing the sentiment.

Gambia. He had a wife and wanted a son.[190] He wanted that son educated in the best Western schools, and his wife to have the nicest things, and he decided he could make all that happen in one of the poorest countries in the world. He had balls. He really believed in the place, believed a Gambian could make it, right there in the Gambia. Even when the guys were angry at him, they'd give him the benefit of the doubt.

The guys who'd worked there with Hafeez – the one-man wireless superhero Peter had told me about over dinner with his mom — and who'd seen Peter fire him, made sure every new guy heard the story. The guys thought this was an act of outright cruelty, not to mention a mind-boggling feat of self-sabotage. In their opinion, Hafeez was the best there ever was, and doing him in was a heartless act of lunacy, a statement of utter selfishness. Nevertheless, their resentment was tempered by awe. Far from repelling the staff, its lunacy and cruelty helped turn Peter into a legend. At a certain level, I think they all wanted to be him, the Alpha Dog, the devil-could-care hero. For my part, I found his determination and the "lost cause" aspect of the whole venture completely enthralling.

It wasn't just us who were taken in by him either. Even the clients — Europeans and Americans — were in thrall of him. After one bad patch of problems at a certain NGO, the director of the place was in a raging fit, pronouncing us incompetent and demanding his support contract be terminated. For about two weeks Peter wouldn't take his calls. He just let the guy stew. Instead, this raging Irishman vented his frustrations on my staff and me almost every day. This guy's temperature was just about to break the thermometer when Peter finally made his move. He marched into the guy's office and when he came out, about 40 minutes later, not only did we have a support contract, Peter had him sign a new year-long, all-inclusive

---

190 He would get that son about a year into my time there. Mary nicknamed the kid "Baby CompCorp," and it stuck so tenaciously, I can't even remember his real name.

support agreement. How'd he do it? I haven't a clue, and it doesn't matter anyway. What mattered was the result: Peter walked into the lion's den and walked out with an armful of jerky. Leadership's celebrity, and Peter was a local legend. So I was the manager — like it or not. It was a bit of a relief to finally have a role; a role I felt I could do. My performance during Peter's incarceration was my finest hour in the almost four years I spent in the Gambia, but also one of the most stressful, and not just because of the police. It almost killed me to radiate enough positive vibes to keep everyone's hopes up, both the guys and the clients. I was happy to use Helmut's wisdom as an excuse to stop trying to be the celebrity in charge. I found all that glad-handing exhausting. When I was a kid, my favourite things on *Sesame Street* were the glimpses they'd show you of a factory at work. To a kid still trying to master tying his shoes, frustrated at the impossibility of getting all the loops and ends exactly the same length, those machines revolving seamlessly through their work looked like a miracle. Systems have fascinated me ever since. I wasn't Peter and I never would be. I was an introvert who found creativity in thinking about systems and variables. As Helmut pointed out, that was useful, and I was good at it, at least as far as I was concerned. While charisma was a mystery to me, I understood what management was about.

The manager's job is to make sure the trains run on time. Peter pointed the way and I "made it so." A good manager lives and dies by their problem-solving skills. Everything's a problem: the scheduling's a problem because someone's sick, the truck's a problem because it doesn't have fuel, the equipment's a problem because some of it's missing, the client's a problem because things aren't going fast enough, the weather's a problem because it's threatening rain or worse, and the leader's a problem because he has no idea what he's talking about. Even when all these things are working perfectly, they're still problems. If the weather's great for an install, you have to wonder what it'll be like in an hour. It's a problem that could change at any time, and if it does, then what? The truck's in good working order? Great, but how long will that last? How much gas has it got? Do we have money to refuel it? Will we even be close enough to a gas station to fill it? Do we need to roll out this morning with a stack of jerry cans?

Such is the life of the manager. Management is playing chess with the world. You spend your days trying to outwit fate. You move resources around on the table and hope they're in the right place at the right time. Chess is a useful metaphor, but that's all it is. Chess is a fun game, but it doesn't teach anything useful except to think ahead, which is useful, but ultimately, it's a closed system with tightly controlled variables. When you move your knight, you don't need to worry about a rainstorm whipping out the route between D4 and E6.

One of the problems highlighted by Helmut as well as other effective managers I'd met and known over the years was the way managers were trained in the Western world. The case method is a popular way to teach management. It's been around for a long time and was introduced at Harvard Business School as soon as the doors were opened 1908. The idea is to take a real-life event, reduce it to about a 15- to 20-page summary and give it to students to discuss. With any luck, they'll arrive at the correct conclusion.

Case method is used pretty heavily in legal education as well, which in my mind tends to show its very weakness. The law is highly regimented. What can be called a "fact" is stringently regulated, and there's a lot of control over variables. The regulated facts are analysed against arbitrary laws, and even the act of discussion follows procedures. Like chess, the law is a closed system. The variables are limited and tightly controlled. In other words, it's foreign to everyday life. The distinction is clear when you realize you need to hire a person fluent in the language and customs of the legal world whenever you need to visit the place. In such a regulated environment, case method can work. Reducing day-to-day life — the stuff business people and policy wonks deal with — to standard rules is a very different thing. In day-to-day life, markets can rise and fall because Oprah Winfrey takes a liking to someone's lifestyle choices. Life has a lot of drunk, footloose, freewheeling variables.

Despite this problem, you can argue that professional schools and case methodology have gotten the Western world pretty far, and I won't deny that, but there are caveats. Our high standard of living has to be weighed against catastrophic financial collapses like the housing crisis. Drawing from my history training, I think our successes come down to the fact that we live in one of the most engineered civilizations the world has ever seen. In the Western world, rainstorms are small talk. Only in exceptional circumstances will it make the news. Generally, no one needs to worry about a washed-out route between D4 and E6 because the route between D4 and E6 has been covered — slathered thick — with engineering: sewers scientifically designed to carry water and gases away safely without blockages,[191] a surface designed in a laboratory to carry the weight of traffic, be pliable enough to stretch and contract as the seasons change, and be applied to the street quickly and cheaply. Even the gradient of the street outside your house has been designed. The subtle curvature of the street, which most people don't even notice, is planned and executed down to the millimetre using state-of-the-art machinery and tools. A far cry from a road repair system based on a dirt path patched occasionally by a guy with a shovel working for tips.[192] Western-style management works as well

---

191 Carrying away gas is an important part of a well-designed sewer. Methane gas naturally builds up in sewers, but the trouble really starts when other explosive gases leak in as well. If the sewer isn't designed well enough to handle the gases, disasters can happen. Both Louisville, Kentucky, and Ottawa, Ontario, had serious sewer explosions resulting in millions of dollars in damages, hundreds of injuries and at least one death.

192 That's how some streets in the Gambia were maintained. Guys would fill potholes in with rocks and sand, and when a vehicle came by, they'd ask for tips like a squeegee

as it does because our scientists and engineers have made huge strides in bringing nature to heal: to turn the wilderness into a chessboard. The problem in Africa was that there were no straight lines to anywhere.

According to Helmut, my job was to mitigate this lack of infrastructure, to grease the wheels, to fend off "friction" or anything that might erode the revolutionary fervour instilled in the troops by The Leader. Friction begets frustration, and frustration is the workplace plague. To that end, I put a lot of effort into trying to get a sense of our office's heartbeat. It's all about people, after all, and a good manager rises and falls on their ability to sense how people are feeling. Leaders don't really need to care. If they're good leaders, people will follow regardless of how they feel — to a point. Unfortunately, empathy isn't teachable. I think I did all right, but it took some time for me to find the pulse. Initially, I'd made the mistake of relying on abstractions instead of awareness. I guess it's normal to assume people are like us and respond to the same abstractions, the same "isms" we do. In school, we're taught they're universal, and I guess I believe that too. It's just so hard to tell which "ism" is at play at a given time with a given person.

Empowerment's a big deal here in the West, and I assumed my staff would be into it as well, but they had no use for it. None. I'd wasted a lot of time asking their opinions on things: "How should we go about doing this next install, guys?" That sort of thing. They weren't having any of it, and one of my biggest regrets is that it took me so long to figure it out. From their point of view, I was exhibiting weakness by soliciting an opinion. I was in charge, so I should know what to do. I talked; they listened. Such was the order of things. They'd been raised in an environment where the patricians gave orders and the plebes followed them. Public schooling was by rote.[193]

---

kid.

193 According to the guys, schooling was very much by rote. The emphasis we put on

Bosses and teachers existed to tell you right from wrong and didn't suffer fools lightly. They were experts, the source of knowledge, and whoa to the idiot who questioned the wisdom and will of the master. Bosses were supposed to be larger-than-life characters like Peter: loud, forceful, willful. Quiet, thoughtful and attentive traits were seen as unmanly and unworthy. It took me awhile to realize I was actually undermining their morale by showing concern for their sense of empowerment. It just didn't make any sense to them. From their point of view, they were out in the field dealing with physical danger and hostile clients, and the helmsman seeing them through it all had a limp wrist.

Their other problem was a simple one, one I could completely relate to. Empowerment and all it implied — problem solving and such — was above their pay grade. Empowerment is a nice idea on paper, but in real life lends itself to abuse. When I got back and was working at that hospital in Toronto, I had a boss who exploited us in the name of "empowerment." Serious problems or new projects were usually met with a meeting she'd convene of all the younger contractors and interns. She'd give a long speech telling us how much she believed in empowerment, how much she valued our creative problem solving, how much our opinions *mattered*. How one of the great benefits of working at that hospital was the chance to work with young, energetic people with different outlooks.

Following the speech, she'd state the problem and invite us to weigh in. She'd nod her head up and down with a sympathetic "I *hear* you" plastered across her face. After about 15 minutes, she'd make an excuse about another meeting or a phone call and leave us to carry on by ourselves, and "Oh, Robin, when you're done, can you summarize everything in an

---

problem solving was simply nonexistent. On the other hand, their memories were razor sharp; they could memorize entire software serial numbers, 20 to 25 characters long, and many of them. I never saw anyone add a number to his cellphone or write it down. They didn't need to.

email?" And so we would, and then I would. Invariably, our solution would appear later as an email to everyone — under her name.

As you can imagine, this didn't make us very happy. We were flattered at first and licked up her empowerment spittle down to the drop. But it soured quickly. After awhile she didn't bother with the speech. Eventually, she just sent an email outlining the problem and a date by which we needed to produce an answer. Empowerment: the opiate of whatever generation is coming up the pipe. If she'd really wanted to empower us, she should have kept our names on the email, at least given us a mention. Or if she didn't want to do that, she should've just let us do our jobs without interruption.

Some might see this as the prerogative all bosses have to delegate to their underlings. But as one of my fellow hospital colleagues pointed out, "If we're doing her job, why don't we get a cut of her paycheque?" It was a fair question. Pretty much every opinion she offered to her boss was ours, and she made a lot more money than us. She had a downtown condo and an expensive car, while we could barely make rent. Our regular work and deadlines weren't adjusted to make up for the time we spent doing her work either. Do managers get paid to pillage and ransack the work of their underlings? My dad once told me that good managers had a simple relationship with their staff: "If things go right, you tell the world you had nothing to do with it. It was because of your 'superb staff,' and when things go wrong, you tell people it's your fault and yours alone." The guys at CompCorp certainly had no doubts about what managers were there to do. Managers came up with the plan, told you your part and took it on the chin if it all went wrong. The captain's authority was unquestioned, but if the ship hit a reef, the captain slept with the fishes.[194] In other words, the guys didn't

---

194 I can appreciate a CEO making a lot of money, the caveat being that they pay the piper if it goes wrong. The idea of a CEO or CFO washing the life savings of

want anything to do with the decision-making process. That was my domain, full stop. They wanted to be told what to do, work their shift and go home at a reasonable time.

Once I understood the guys cared less about abstractions like "empowerment" and more about simple, straightforward tasks and getting home at a reasonable hour, things started moving forward. I added momentum by taking advantage of my disaffected feelings. I polished up my sense of "whatever" into a full-blown aloofness, which I trotted out at will. I also learned to strap on my inner Blackbeard, and let him out whenever I felt it was necessary. By the end of my time there, I'd perfected my "welcome to CompCorp" speech for new employees. Peter would hire them and bring them around, doing the whole leader thing. He managed to make them feel like the success of the whole company rested on them and their unique abilities. They'd come bouncing in, thrilled to have a job and to be our saviour. Peter would introduce the kid to me and I'd look them over with a leaden eye.

"OK, my name is Robin and I'll be your manager during your time here at CompCorp. I don't put up with any shit. Peter hired you, but I decide if we keep you. Don't do *exactly* as I say and you're done. Mess with the guys and you're done. Fuck off and you're done. Basically, piss me off in any way and you're done. You need this job? Good. So, we understand each other?" They always understood.

Sounds rough, I know, but I had a few reasons for doing it. First, not having Peter's charm or legend, I knew I couldn't command their respect, at least initially, so fear had to do. Second, the guys didn't like rookies filled with the hot air Peter pumped them full of. They expected

---

thousands of families down the drain, and then getting away with probation and time served is nauseating. You shouldn't be able to walk away from an epic disaster with stock options.

rookies to be scared and humble. Deflating them was in their own best interest in terms of their interaction with the older hands. Third, it established real consequences for failure, clearly and squarely. Being a jackass meant trouble. Being new, they didn't really know Peter was the final arbitrator of their continued employment, but that hardly mattered. By the time they figured that out, they'd be broken in. Finally, it made the leader happy. Peter could be the good cop, the benevolent granddad to my disciplinarian father figure. All leaders like to bask in the joy of their flock.[195]

New recruits had to accept their place, which was the very bottom of the CompCorp universe. That was their first test. If they bridled, I'd start moving to get rid of them. It meant they weren't a team player. I made it clear that their status would improve with good work, and that I had to suck up Peter's crap, so it should be no problem for them to tug their forelock in front of the veterans. It was a fast way to identify whiners and malcontents. Initially, they caddied for the experienced staff while trying to learn something from them. Picking up skills and generally being useful was their second test. It wasn't just picking up skills that mattered, but I needed to see if they could pick up a variety of skills. In a place where the variables flew fast and furiously, and resources were slim, I needed renaissance people. One-trick ponies need not apply. If things went well and I saw some ability, I'd gather the staff together at the end of a day, say two or three weeks after they were hired. I'd announce with a certain amount of ceremony that so-and-so had shown real distinction on this-and-this occasion, and so, from that point forward, he would no longer be the staff peon. He didn't have to fetch tools anymore and no one could push him around except me. After my pronouncement, I could tell instantly if the kid fit in. If the

---

195 Peter, of course, knew he was causing problems with the rest of the staff by overpraising the untried recruits, but he wanted everyone to think they had a special relationship with him, the leader. Again, as the manager, it was my job to grease the friction he caused.

announcement wasn't greeted with good-humoured ribbing and backslaps, it meant they'd failed the third and last test. In our small group — under tremendous pressure to perform — infighting was the highest crime. Anyone guilty of it I declared a pariah and moved hard to get rid of them.

It took awhile, but when I finally hit on this system of apprenticeship, it didn't take long to produce results. It kept the rookies humble and the veterans proud of their mentoring abilities. It also established a hierarchy, which people love, no matter what the union equity officer says. The old hands loved being the old hands, and the rookies — although not in love with their status — did like striving for a goal. Nothing gets more out of a kid than giving them a chance to prove their mettle. Finally, when we had enough staff, I enhanced the system by breaking the guys into two teams and drumming up some competition. It sounds ridiculous, but they were actually tripping over themselves to get things done.[196] Competition mocks common sense.

I never relied on passion for the job to get things done. They didn't care about developing the Gambia. Sure, they wanted to be Peter; they all wanted to have a car like his, but "passion to make the world a better place" had limited appeal. The guys were practical. All of the truly idealistic thinkers I met over there were religious. Religion was the only sanctioned excuse one could have for thinking about issues outside of day-to-day living. Wasting time with a book was just that. People lived in the moment, which was another reason the guys detested overtime. Paid or not, for them life happened at home. It was eating with their friends and family, finding a girl and going dancing. They worked to live. The idea of living to work, of trying to climb to "the top" — wherever that was — for a payoff years away, made no sense to them at all. They were practical guys. Life happened right here, right now, not "when you retired." Care for your immortal soul was the only

---

196 Sometimes with disastrous results.

exception, the one far-off goal worth working toward. Most of the seriously religious people I met tended to see some virtue in mulling over ideals, but there were limits. Peter hired one kid who was all fired up to make a better world for his people. He wasn't incompetent, but his religious convictions — the source of his great feeling for change — annoyed the others. They were religious too, but that kid took himself way too seriously.[197] He didn't fit in, and he constantly needed time off to attend events and do-gooder meetings. After two weeks I got rid of him.

Passion's a limited tool. It's too much about the individual and too intolerant. Speaking to the first point, I remember volunteering for the Red Cross in D.C. and overhearing a conversation between a volunteer and the guy in charge of the shelter-building drill we were engaged in. The volunteer, a young woman with a background in social work, wanted to be the shelter's counselor.[198] This woman was explaining again and again how *passionate* she was about children and *helping people*. She completely ignored the boss who kept saying the position was already filled and what the shelter really needed was someone to help set up cots. Unfortunately for anyone who might have needed a dry bed that night, she wasn't *passionate* about setting up cots. She left, never to be seen again. Good solutions aren't driven by what you like.

Intolerance isn't usually something people associate with passion, but passion is fanaticism's distant cousin. Passion's emotion, emotion's personal, and no one likes their person criticized. As I get older, I've noticed the old adage "let's agree to disagree" carrying less and less weight. When ideas are personal, you can't criticize the idea without pissing on the person, and that just isn't helpful. A good team doesn't walk on eggshells. At one of the jobs I worked when I returned to Canada, the social fabric had been torn

---

197 Passionate people usually do. God help you if you don't think much of whatever it is that moves them. In my experience they're not far off being clerics.
198 Every shelter was supposed to have a counselor to help people through the loss of their home or other difficult issues.

to shreds because the old guard was too attached to their achievements. Younger staff wanted changes, but the older hands couldn't bear to see the end of the systems they'd created and did everything they could to prevent change. Their conservative attitude was purely a function of the strong feelings they had about the order they'd created and nurtured. I admired them because they did what they had to at the time, and it was a great success. But it was a new day. They needed to let their children go. I guess it's the destiny of every passionate revolutionary to become an entrenched bureaucrat.

After passion, there's discipline, and for Helmut, discipline was to loyalty what salt was to stew: a little makes a huge difference, but if it's all anyone can taste, you've ruined the stew. It's necessary in any group, either self-imposed (ideally) or enforced from the top. The guys — like most people — had an ingrained sense of justice, which manifested itself as a complete distaste for anyone not pulling their weight. Slackers made more work for everyone and needed a kick in the ass, and if they didn't straighten up, they got the sack, no excuses. As a result, they appreciated discipline, at least when it was pointed at someone else. It was important to get ahead of problems. If I didn't nip stupidity in the bud, the law of the jungle would take over. At least once, I was too late and had to break up a fight.

My biggest problem enforcing discipline was the leader. Peter liked to do dismissals himself, in theory, on my recommendation. But the leader could be fickle. To prevent undermining my own authority, I needed to step carefully. Because of Peter's unpredictability, I couldn't really threaten anyone with their job, and they knew it. If I made the threat, Peter might overrule me later. More than once I stood in front of the guys with my phone pressed to my ear and saying terrible things to Peter about their performance. The phone usually wasn't on, but they never really figured that out, and I got the reaction I wanted anyway. Maintaining the discipline of your staff is one thing, maintaining the discipline or the leader is another thing altogether.

Managers sit below the leader, but your responsibility is to get the work done, which means keeping a system of workflow running. Unpredictability's the enemy, and the leader can be pretty damn unpredictable. I tried to keep Peter in line by letting him think my plans were really his. It's a distasteful thing: you won't get the credit you deserve for individual ideas, but your ultimate measure as a manager is keeping the system running, and if that means feeding an ego, so be it. You can pitch concepts to staff or your clients, but leaders generally feel they ought to be coming up with the vision themselves. Good leaders do come up with ideas, but generally, due to their exalted position, a lot of their ideas are suspect. They're just too far removed from day-to-day reality to know what's possible and what isn't.

Sometimes I'd couch my idea as a product of Peter's insight: "Remember what you said the other day? It really got me thinking." From there, I'd dovetail his observation with my thought. Making the two match could take some creative reasoning, but he never seemed to notice. Sometimes I took advantage of my familiarity with him. In our morning meetings I'd lay out problems and wait for Peter's input. Having worked with him awhile, I had a good idea of his go-to solutions to certain problems, and I'd be ready for them with a quick excuse about why it wouldn't work.[199] I'd keep giving excuses until Peter landed on the answer I wanted, which didn't work every time. Sometimes I'd have to go back to the guys with a less than optimal answer, but as time went by, I got better at reading him.

---

199 His solution might be fine. I just didn't like it for whatever reason. He might want to fire someone I actually had some faith in, so I'd make something up, like a certain important client likes him for example. With an excuse like that, I'd be sure the important client was someone who liked me enough to do a favour for me, and I'd ask him to put in a good word for the kid, because I knew invariably Peter would check up on things.

Peter could intimidate with his temper, but I found flatly saying no wasn't as big a deal if I phrased it in a way he could appreciate. Telling him I wouldn't do a wireless install because it was 10 minutes to closing and it would piss the staff off was just stupid. Telling him we weren't ready and so might irritate the client enough to make them walk, damaging our bottom line, made more sense. He still wasn't happy; I could hear the clenched jaw through the silence of the telephone, but he had to trust me. I was his manager. And what's a leader without a manager? Still, telling Peter no was one of my biggest problems. Often he'd insist and yell at me over the phone. If I still got my way, he'd find a way to get his back. If the sniping got bad enough, I'd again change the way I phrased things and let my anger do the talking. I hated getting that angry, especially with Peter because he had so much control over me: he was my banker and landlord, after all, but sometimes yelling oaths, slamming doors and throwing tools are worth a thousand words. Peter's unwillingness to keep me in the loop came to a head one afternoon when he called me at 4:30 p.m. and told me to get the boys together for a wireless job. Goaded on by his obtuseness and having lost face in front of my staff (I'd promised them we weren't going to do last-minute Wi-Fi scrambles anymore), I lost it. Completely. I started yelling at him through the phone, holding it about two feet in front of me so I could use my whole body to scream into the speaker. I ended with a threat: "Where the fuck are you?! The office? I'll be there in five. Don't fucking move!" All in front of the guys, who seemed struck dumb by my fury. By the time I got to the office, Peter was gone, but the next morning he was more subdued. He kept me in the loop after that.

Both discipline and passion are useless if the staff doesn't see some self-interest in the enterprise. The guys had to believe the ship was taking them somewhere they wanted to go. "What's in it for me?" was the all-important question. Why should they suffer to make Peter rich? There was no clear answer to this when I started, and morale was on the floor as a result. When I first started the job, theft of tools and equipment was so bad that Peter would keep everything useful in his office. In other words, to get work done, Mary — the secretary — took the call from the client and wrote a report of the problem. Based on Mary's verbal report of the issue, Peter would dole out tools and equipment to deal with the specific problem. After fixing the problem, the tech had to come back to the office and account to Mary for every tool and snip of wire. Peter would usually leave the office by 10 a.m., complicating things even more. This meant I'd often have to wait for him or chase him in the truck to get access to equipment.

A bigger mess you couldn't imagine. Mary — a non-technical person — lorded over everyone, including me. She was no leader and the staff loathed her. She wasn't a manager either. She hadn't a clue what the rank and file did for a living. A good manager should be able to do their job and everyone else's too. Even if you can't do it as well as they can, you should be able to at least carry on a conversation with anyone who reports to you. I once asked my uncle, a high-ranking accountant, what management was all about and he said, "Managers are translators. Their job is to call meetings and make sure the IT guy and accountant actually understood each other." Mary's reign of terror had to end.

I tried to isolate Mary from the technical staff. I dealt with her crap directly and wouldn't let her hand out work assignments. I'd no problem giving her hell for doing stupid things either, much to the glee of my staff. She'd immediately complain to Peter about my attitude, which was exactly what I wanted her to do. I wanted her to complain because I knew eventually Peter would register it as whining. I'd explain myself to Peter in a way I knew he'd appreciate. I'd heavily imply Mary was costing him money because of her poor IT knowledge, and with my grasp of technology, I had no problem convincing the boss she was making mistakes. For example, she'd routinely downplay email problems. It wasn't hard to convince Peter of the importance of electronic mail for an NGO sector working in a place without any real paper mail at all. I had endless anecdotes from the centre to draw from.

There was no trust between Peter and the IT staff, but as I started to bring the boom down on the guys, as I started to crack the whip, as I started to let go of Western notions of office etiquette, Peter started to trust me. I was an outsider with a professional background. To my face, he'd dismiss my rants about Mary, but as his trust in me grew, I noticed him subtly checking up on her. A typical scenario would be Mary heading out to pick up payments. After much pestering, I'd get her to write me a list of stops she was planning to make. She did it just to shut me up. Then she'd vanish for a couple of hours, and I'd call Peter and tell him his whole business was practically frozen in place because we only had one truck and no driver. Normally, he'd call Mary on her cell and she'd say she was just getting to so-and-so's place, taking her word for it. But now I had a list of places she was *supposed* to be at. Peter would call them up and confirm how many she'd visited. Since Mary spent most of her time shopping, it was hard for her to explain why it'd taken her an hour to pick up two payments.

In the meantime, I worked the guys like a tyrant. We had to prove to Peter we could get work done. If Mary was raising the leader's blood pressure, then the IT staff would be the ones lowering it. It was a hard time for the guys because work had to get done faster than ever before, but Peter was still micromanaging everything and Mary was still vanishing with the driver. I paid for taxis out of my own pocket to get them where they needed to be, ran interference with the more demanding customers, paid them overtime bonuses out of my own pocket, appealed to their sense of challenge to get them moving faster, and vented my bile all over them when they were slow. I cracked down on them when they left a site because they'd made a personal promise to another client. I started demanding they call me from the site's landline when one was available, allowing me to verify from the phone number that they were at the correct site. It didn't stop them from leaving in the middle of something, but at least I knew they'd arrived. I also started following up on them by calling every 20 minutes to see what kind of progress they were making. I broke them into teams and let their natural competitiveness boost them to higher levels of productivity. I did everything short of putting a lit slow match under my hat to get more work out of them.

The turning point came when Peter decided to take a vacation, his first since starting the company. He left Mary and me in charge — co-consuls — giving us an impassioned "try to get along" speech before leaving for the U.K. with his wife. It was great news. I knew his vacation was a vote of confidence in my management abilities, and the instant he was out the door, I immediately took control of the truck and driver, making it my mobile HQ. With me riding shotgun, it'd be almost impossible for Mary to call the driver on his cell and nab that vehicle. Samba drove the other one, so I had no worries there. With Peter gone, I'd be the public face of CompCorp. Clients would see me, not Mary. Maintaining good relations with the clients was a critical piece of strategy. More than once I had them call Peter to sing my praises or the guys' praises. Sometimes I'd have them corroborate something I told Peter.

I told Mary I'd collect the invoices while Peter was away, giving her no reason to be out of the office. Without a truck, she had no choice anyway. Although this meant more work for me, I didn't care. Work stress didn't come from the amount of work, but rather trying to get work done in a broken system. It was like running against the tide. Peter had finally left me in charge of the tools, and with those advantages, I started pushing the guys harder than ever. With control of the equipment as well as our direct access to the customers, it was our time to overachieve. Things went well, except for the day I pushed too hard and my youngest staffer freaked out in front of a client. He stamped his feet, called me all kinds of names and walked off the job. He showed up at the office early the next day and we both quietly apologized to each other.

When Peter returned, things changed. We'd earned his trust. He'd left his company in our care and we hadn't ripped him off. To the contrary, we'd brought in more money than he thought we would. Any hard feelings I'd engendered with the technical staff during my dictatorship vanished in the face of Peter's newfound generosity. Small kindnesses were performed. One night I had my phone stolen. One of the guys thought they knew the guy who'd done it, and without me asking, reported the next day that he'd mobilized his neighbourhood into a posse and tracked the guy down. He escaped, but they'd chased him through two blocks of Banjul on my behalf. Another time, we were driving slowly through the streets of Bakau when a man in the street stood up, pointed at me sitting in the back of the truck and started screaming. People stopped to look, a crowd gathered. Suddenly, the truck came to a halt and the guys jumped out. They grabbed hold of this guy and started pushing him around. I jumped out of the back of the truck and freed the guy from their clutches, ordering them back in the truck — fucking immediately. I was furious. They'd almost started a riot. When I asked what had happened, they told me the guy didn't like white people and had called me some terrible names (they wouldn't tell me what), so they intervened on my behalf. With trust came raises, actual staff meetings and a tiny amount of respect.

Best Moment

It was a Saturday, 11 a.m., and I was running through the streets of Banjul. I'd just left a site and was running as fast as I could to another. It was hot; dust covered me head to toe; sand crunched between my teeth. The only thing on my mind was time.

When I started at CompCorp, we could only do one wireless job a day. With the improvements in the office, two a day had become the norm, and we could get them done during working hours. No more unpaid overtime for the guys. It made for a hell of a day, but the guys liked to quit on time, and the clients liked it because it meant we were on schedule, no promises of work to be done on Monday only to have it pushed back to Thursday. Peter liked it because the clients liked it, and the guys liked it because Peter liked it. Even Mary liked it. She'd learned to prefer having me collect the money; she missed her outings but not squeezing money out of jerks. I liked it because I'd made a series of successful changes and enjoyed feeling effective.

We were getting a reputation for getting things done. The crew felt like IT supermen. They were proud of their jobs and recently we'd had an upsurge in potential recruits because their friends wanted in on the action. It wasn't all cream and honey. We'd fired a few bad apples and there were still days we never got off the ground. Well, honestly, we spent whole weeks chasing our tails, but in general there was an overall feeling of improvement in the office, so naturally, Peter decided to up the ante. He arranged for us to do three wireless jobs in one day. Just to keep things interesting, he arranged for them all on a Saturday. Saturday was our shortest day, theoretically only a half-day. Why Peter would try to sabotage us, I don't know. At first I was angry. One more attempt to undermine progress, that's how it looked, but I also think he just wanted to see how far it could go, to explore the possibilities. He appreciated the progress, but he still couldn't resist testing it. I knew the instant he suggested it, when I felt the lurch in my stomach, that too much of my self-esteem was wrapped up in "getting things done." In hindsight, I should have pushed back and convinced Peter to stagger the jobs, and I did try to make a half-hearted argument to that effect. But in the end, I just wanted to show him up. I wanted to show him that we could rise to his challenges.

Peter gave me a week's advanced warning. The first site was an importer's office, the catch being they'd purchased their own antennas and transceivers. We'd never worked with that vendor's products before, but Peter was confident it would work out. The second site was a few blocks away, an agricultural NGO, their office on the second floor of a six-story building. We'd have to set a pole up on top of the building, and somehow run a cable down the side of the building and into their offices. The situation at the last site was similar, but the client was at the top of a five-story building. The guys were angry I hadn't protested the installs. I insisted they could get it done, all three, without working overtime. Over the course of the week I'd brought them out to the sites, and they complained to no end about climbing the five or six stories to the top, but my enthusiasm to rise to Peter's challenge was contagious, and they were ready to go by Saturday. It was great to see their confidence. They were ready to take Peter on, and Saturday morning they were actually happy to be there, or at least looked that way.

We informally referred to the sites in the order we encountered them when driving into Banjul. The plan was for me to do the first site because during the week I'd made myself familiar with the new system. The guys were to head to the second site, the NGO, and assuming we'd be done at the same time, we'd regroup at the third site. We'd only use one truck, the sites being close together and because the bed of the new truck was too short to make carrying six-metre poles practical. Abdu would drop me off with the guys at the second site because the door to the roof was locked up, but I'd gotten a key from management earlier in the week. Abdu would then drop me at the first site and rejoin the guys at the second. I figured if something was likely to go wrong, it would be at the NGO site, so having the truck there, ready to run and fetch, made sense. The truck was just a backup. Experience is the best teacher, and during the week I'd used any free time between other calls to get the sites ready to go.

The locked roof was an advantage. We could leave what we needed in preparation for the big day. Getting a six-metre pipe onto the roof was the first problem, but thankfully, the building was equipped with a generous central staircase. There were no inside walls to the stairwell, so we could carry the pole up the stairs, spanned over the central atrium between the flights. It was tricky work, but we managed to get it up to the roof without skewering anyone passing through the lobby below. The wire required more thought. Our clients were on the second floor, four stories below the roof, and like all buildings in Banjul, it was solid concrete, no internal cable runs anywhere. Dropping it off the roof was the most likely option, but we had to do something to keep it from blowing all over the place. If it wasn't secure, the wind would eventually flap it into shreds. During one trip, Jean Baptiste (J.B.)[200] noticed that the windows running down the side of the building were single-paned. In other words, they all opened in one direction,

200 J.B. was one of our newer recruits, although he was well past the probation period. His family was originally from Senegal, hence the French name.

311

unlike double windows where one pane opened left, the other right. We could open them and get our hands on the wall next to the window. Looking at our support tickets for that week, I noticed that I'd have two guys with me in Banjul on Wednesday afternoon, and so I made sure there was a box of cable, hammers and concrete anchors in the truck. The guys lowered a length of cable down the side of the building while I went door to door asking permission for us to use the windows. Being upper stories, there were no bars, and in half an hour we had a length of cable, well anchored every five metres or so, running straight and taut down the side of the building with a coil of surplus at the top and bottom, ready for the day.

I packed the bags that Friday night. I'd spent the week gathering tools and testing equipment, convincing Peter to give me the antennas, transceivers and routers before the big day, so I could spend time each evening assembling and testing them. Power over Ethernet adapters, all tested, were in each bag; so too were French and British power plugs, backups in the event the power over Ethernet failed. A decent drill and two sets of quality crimpers — purchased by Peter now that staff theft was under control — were all packed and ready, along with three hammers, screwdrivers, concrete drill bits, wrench sets, cable tacks, waterproof tape, one cable tester, a crossover cable, two factory-made patch cables, and all the other bits and pieces required to get the job done. Waterproof boxes had been purchased and prepared. A box of cat 5 computer cable and a 30-metre spool of electrical cable were also on hand, just in case something went wrong.[201]

I wanted to ensure they took everything up in a single trip because

---

201 It might seem strange to have three hammers in each bag, but one of the most time-consuming things at any site was securing the cable. It was slow, finicky work and since a cable run could be anywhere from 2 to 100 meters, it could really take time. An average run was about 20 meters, so there was space for a couple of guys to work at once, hence the 3 hammers.

running up and down the stairs wasted time. One source of friction I'd identified was the time it took to move tools around on a large site, and I knew that because these sites were on top of a storied building, carrying everything in one go would be critical. All the buildings were about the same height, and I figured it was about two minutes to come down and about three to go back up, a five-minute trip assuming you weren't tired. Those numbers increased dramatically if you were. It sounds like nothing, but if they forgot three things, and you factored in time to search for each item in the truck, say another two or three minutes, that would mean 20 to 25 minutes gone, and I knew from past experience that 20 minutes was decisive. You might think they could simply bring all three things up in one go, but the problem is that you don't realize you forgot something until you get to that point of the procedure. You notice the missing waterproof tape when it comes to securing the waterproof box. You notice that you forgot the power over Ethernet device 20 minutes later when it comes time to plug it in. Constantly running around for tools also leaves people full of adrenaline, limiting focus.

Saturday.

Peter took his time that morning. He kept us about a half-hour longer than he would have normally. No matter, we hit the road, and everyone got serious. We pulled into Banjul in record time and headed to the NGO. We charged up to the sixth floor, two steps at a time, the guys lugging everything they'd need. With the guys on the roof, I slammed down the stairs as fast as I could and headed off to the first site. I had Abdu slow down and I jumped out of the truck with my bag of equipment. No need for a pole there. I'd been by during the week with a GPS and figured their office balcony could do the job; I'd only need to strap it to the railings, which I could do alone. As Abdu sped off to rejoin the guys, I lunged across the sidewalk, threw my shoulder against the glass door and bounced off it and into the gutter. It must have looked like a Charlie Chaplin pratfall. My arms were covered in a sticky, indeterminate liquid, my tools spilled across the sidewalk when the bag hit the ground and my shoulder hurt like hell, but at least no one saw me, and the door didn't shatter. Small mercies. I pulled myself together and wondered why the door was closed. It was supposed to be open. That was the arrangement. Dammit.

When I'd spoken to the owners, I'd taken the precaution of getting their phone numbers in the event of catastrophe. They'd passed me off to the office manager, my contact for the duration, so I called him. It took me a few tries, but I got him on the phone. "Hadn't I found the watchman?" he asked with surprise. He'd left instructions for the watchman to be there at the appointed time. No, he had no idea where the watchman might be. Would he come and open the door? Silence. I asked if his boss would come and open the door. He decided he'd come and open the door. When I'd first met him, I made sure he knew I had his boss' number to ensure a level of enthusiasm, and yet it would be at least 20 minutes before his arrival. We got to Banjul by about 9:20 a.m. It was 9:40 now and we only had until noon. A 20-minute delay would leave only two hours on the clock, and I hadn't even started.

I gave it 10 minutes and called Samba to see how they were doing. "Good, Robs, good! We should start aligning in a few minutes." Some good news, but it didn't help my mood any. Alignment was the hardest part of a wireless install. Once the antenna was up on its pole, we had to aim it at its counterpart on the mast back at the office. Aligning wasn't for the impatient. You're trying to aim an antenna about the size of a coffee table book at another coffee table book strapped 45 metres in the air and so far away you can't even see the tower it's on, much less the actual antenna.

Most wireless jobs fell apart with the alignment issue. Sometimes you got lucky and a simple twist of the pole would put you on the mark. The real problem was the azimuth — the up-down angle of the antenna. That meant pulling the entire assembly down, pole and all, adjusting the antenna to point a centimetre or two toward the sky or the ground, re-hoisting the pole, and trying again. This could take hours. I had tried to mitigate the risk by going to each site with a GPS unit and doing a plot with a map. That sorted out (I dearly hoped) the bearing — the left-right angle of the antenna — but the azimuth was a different problem altogether. Because the mast was so far away, it wasn't simply a matter of measuring heights. The curvature of the earth also had to be accounted for. An antenna mounted 36 metres in the air might actually be looking *down* at an antenna mounted on a 45-metre mast if the mast was far enough away.[202] After doing some research regarding antenna alignment, measuring the exact distance of each site from our HQ and the approximate height of the antennas, I'd worked out a probable bearing and azimuth for each antenna. Now it was time to try and see.

Finally, the office manager arrived, exiting his car, all apologies. It wasn't quite 10 a.m. yet and I bounded up the stairs like a hare. The antenna was strapped to the iron railings of the balcony, cable was unspooled, and I dove under desks and clambered over chairs to feed it along the wall to where the router was to be set up. I did my best to be neat, but I knocked over a pencil holder and had a keyboard land on my back while I twisted under a desk. Pain shot through my bruised arm while I strained against two heavy filing cabinets, trying to get an inch of clearance behind them. I quickly cut and crimped the cable, and in 15 minutes I had the transceiver, router and LAN computers all wired together. Sitting at one, I tested the connection. Were my antenna calculations correct? I was practically hyperventilating while the machine booted up. I tried connecting the

---

202 Just as a ship disappears over the horizon bottom to top, only the very top of a 45 meter mast will be visible to an observer standing a certain distance away. The result is that it's completely possible to be on top of a tall building and have to look down at the horizon to see the top of a distant mast.

machine to our office from the command line. Nothing. The computer I was sitting at couldn't touch our servers back at the office. I wasn't frantic, almost nothing worked the first time, and with tense focus I checked my work. It didn't take long to find the problem: the cable I'd run and crimped wasn't working — no light on the router. I tested it with my cable tester — no go. After squeezing it in the crimpers with all my might, to no avail, I ended up cutting the head off and re-crimping both ends.

Crimping is the process of putting a head — that plastic thing you snap into your computer's Ethernet port — onto a cable. A category 5 cable has eight tiny wires inside, twisted into four pairs. Some are white with a coloured line on them, some are a solid colour, all are less than a millimetre wide. The process is simple: you expose the twisted pairs by cutting off an inch of sheath, untwist the wires and straighten each so they'll fit into the slots inside the plastic head, which, like the wires, are all less than a millimetre wide. To make it more interesting, you need to get the order right: you start on the left with the white wire with the orange stripe, followed by orange, then white-green, blue, white-blue, green, white-brown and finally brown. You straighten each, pinch it between your fingers, straighten the next, and when you're done, you clip them all to the same length. Then, gingerly, you push them into the head, praying they don't separate, not even by a fraction of a millimetre. If they do separate, they won't fit. One will bend, and since you've trimmed them short enough to fit inside the head, it'll be almost impossible to straighten it. You'll have to start again by removing more sheath. If all goes well, you take the head, slot it into your crimper, squeeze and the crimper crunches the head so the wires won't slide out while simultaneously pushing extremely tiny contacts — the pins — down into each of the eight wires. It still amazes me that a major piece of the connectivity revolution is based on such a primitive handicraft. What created the Internet? Opposable thumbs.

I re-headed both ends and tried again to connect, and again I got nothing. What the hell? Could the cable be bad? Did I stretch it while pulling it around the room? Should I yank it out from under all that furniture and run another length? Time was of the essence. Other than my familiarity with the new antennas, I was at that site because this was the easiest antenna to align. If my initial calculations where wrong, this antenna — situated comfortably at waist height — was easiest to adjust. Once we figured the angles here, adjusting the others would be a lot easier.

Fuck it. I got down on my stomach and yanked the cable out. It was hard work, the cable straining against table legs and snagging around corners. Finally, I just cut it into pieces and pulled each out. I ran a new length and crimped it. Again, nothing. Was the whole box faulty? It wouldn't have been the first time we'd been sold a box of bad cat 5. I cut myself a short length, crimped both ends and tested it. Dead. Could the tester be faulty? I tested it on a short, factory-crimped cable I had in my bag. It was fine. Dammit. We only had one other box and the guys were using it. My mind raced through possibilities, panic mounting. I grabbed the box, flipped open my phone and was making for the street when common sense broke through: the box was light. We'd used this box on several jobs already, and no one had reported a problem. I grabbed a couple of the heads I'd cut off, took them to the window and studied them up close without my glasses. There it was: one pin wasn't pushed into its appropriate wire. All the heads were the same. I examined the crimpers. The crimpers were crap. I'd checked all the crimpers during the week and we'd been using them without any incidents. Maybe they'd been damaged when my bag hit the ground?

I called Samba. The first thing out of his mouth after "*na'nga def*" was to ask me if I had a connection. The guys were ready, but they didn't want to hoist until I'd gotten a connection, so they could make necessary adjustments before straining to get the pole up. I filled him in, and asked him to send me a set of crimpers, post haste. I also told him to hoist and try. Silence filled the line. Pulling poles up and down to tweak them was morale

317

destroying, but we had to try if we were going to make the schedule. I promised to start the alignment using my laptop, and I'd get back to him as soon as I had a good connection. Samba hung up, resigned.

Despite Samba's reluctant agreement, I fully expected them to wait for me to call with the angles before moving. It was an annoying thought because it would take all of them to mount the pole, meaning I couldn't dispatch anyone to the last site until they were done there. In other words, the third site couldn't start until the second sight was finished, but the second site was going to wait for the first site before trying to finish. It was the worst possible situation: four guys in the field doing no work with the clock ticking. I didn't blame them because I knew it was my fault. If I'd just started with my laptop, I wouldn't have wasted nearly 40 minutes running cable and shifting furniture. The price of overconfidence. Cabling was a menial task and I wanted to get it out of the way before tackling the alignment. If the cabling worked, as it usually did, then an initial alignment test with the laptop would have been unnecessary and therefore a waste of time. How had the plan come apart? A miscommunication with a watchman had led to a locked door; the locked door had led to a damaged crimper; the damaged crimper had led to 40 minutes of chaos and panic; the chaos and panic had led to a complete work stoppage. What a hell of a way to make a living.

Shaking off the defeatism as well as I could, I pulled out my laptop, connected it straight to the transceiver with the short factory cable and went to work aligning. I set the timer on my phone for six minutes before starting. Figuring it would take eight minutes to get the crimper to my building, the two-minute difference allowed me to get to the street to meet them. No more wasted time.

It turned out my alignment calculations weren't half bad. I got a heartbeat almost instantly, but it was faint. I sat there cross-legged, nudging the antenna a centimetre left and right, and up and down. The alarm went

318

off, I sprang up and jumped down the stairs. Just as I ran outside, Abdu turned into the street. His arm was out the driver-side window and he was waving a crimper. I ran into the street, grabbed it as he passed and ran inside as he rounded the corner. The handoff was perfect. It filled me with hope. A long-running criticism I had of the whole crew was the lackadaisical way they passed tools around. This was an important issue considering how few tools we had, so I came down hard whenever I found out so-and-so had to dismount and go room-to-room at a site to get a hammer from such-and-such.

Back upstairs, luck was turning my way. In 10 minutes I had a good, strong connection back to the office. I called Samba and gave him the instructions, but it wasn't necessary: Peter had arrived and had made them hoist the pole and start aligning. They'd locked in and were clearing up and moving to the next site. He asked if I wanted the truck to come and get me. No, just get to the last site! I could hear the excitement in his voice. We were going to make it!

I ran my third cable of the day, crimped it, connected it, and all was well. I called the office manager to come and lock up, and in the 15 minutes it took him to get there, I'd finished with their network and was packing up. I took stock as I left the building. We were running late, but the last site promised to be much easier since we already had a good idea of how to align it. It was just a matter of pushing hard to get it done. Halfway down the block, Samba called. He wanted to know where the rope was. The rope? Wasn't it in the truck?

There was no lock on the roof of this site, so we hadn't left the pole there. The cable had been run, which hadn't been a problem since the client was on the top floor. The client only had a few computers and they were mercifully modern and new, so connecting the network together wouldn't be a trial. The bracket had already been installed during the week, so all that was left was to get our setup on the roof. The stairwell of the building, like

319

most in Banjul, was open air, running up the outside of the wall with a landing on each floor. It was too narrow to manoeuvre a pole up, so I figured we'd use a rope and pull it up. To that end, I'd borrowed a long spool of cheap nylon rope. We'd just run it through the pipe, tie it off and haul it onto the roof. I was certain I'd thrown it in the truck that morning, but the guys couldn't find it anywhere. There just wasn't time to go back and try and find it. I told Samba to hang on, no point in sending the truck, I was halfway there. With that, I broke into a flat-out run, my bag flapping to one side like an oversized briefcase, the box of cable flapping to the other.

So there I was running like a maniac and sick to my stomach for letting the guys down. I'd put a week of planning in, but it wasn't enough. I remembered the old army maxim that "no plan survives implementation," and this was a wonderful case study for anyone who cared to debate its truth. I arrived to find the guys slumped by the truck, wondering what I'd have them do next. Peter was gone, off to an appointment. I knew I'd hear about this on Monday, but I'd had a thought on my way over. Dropping my stuff in a clatter, I had J.B. and Abba[203] lift the pole up vertically on the sidewalk, leaning it against the side of the staircase. After studying the pole closely, I told Samba and Edi to run up to the third-floor landing, and I made for the second floor. When I got there, I reached over the banister and yelled down to the guys to push the pole as high up as they could. Stretched over the banister, with my tiptoes brushing the floor of the landing, I could just reach the top of the pole with one hand. Next, while holding on with my good arm, I started kicking my legs to try and slide back off the ledge, and so get my feet back firmly on the landing. For one terrible moment I thought I might slide the wrong way and go headfirst over the side, but slowly my body weight pulled me down onto the landing. Soon, both hands were around the top and I started pulling the pole straight up, hand over hand.

---

203 Our newest guy, currently the office lackey.

It wasn't terribly heavy, maybe 10 to 15 kilograms, but the problem with hoisting poles was trying to manage the weight from the bottom end. Leverage was a bitch. By pulling the pole straight up, held tight against the sides of the staircase, it was much easier to handle. The test would come when most of its length was over my head, but not enough length for Samba to catch it on the third-floor landing. The moment arrived, and with it came great pain and panic. Suddenly, I really regretted having rammed my arm into that door. I also regretted wrenching it without mercy to move the furniture, and finally, I regretted jarring it on the run over with a heavy bag of equipment. Instantly, I broke out in a sweat and I felt the pole slide through my fingers. Gripping for all I was worth, I yelled down to J.B. and Abba to get up to the fourth floor double quick, so he could take the top of the pole as Samba passed it up. Being no fool, J.B. ignored me and stopped at my landing, immediately grabbing the pole. Our most athletic guy, J.B. easily heaved it up to Samba and Edi, so both of them had hands on it. I took Abba to the fourth floor as fast as possible so Samba and Edi wouldn't have to hold it too long. We got a hold of it, Edi feeding it up to us, and in seconds J.B. and Samba rushed past on their way to the roof. It worked. The pole was on the roof with 35 minutes remaining.

Everything was on the roof and everyone leaped into action. There was none of the usual chatter or ribbing. Everyone knew their task and focused on it. In about 10 minutes everything was strapped to the pole, we raised it into the sky and carried it over to the brackets, which were anchored to the concrete wall of a utility shed on the roof. With a massive amount of effort, the pole was pushed up and lowered onto the bottom bracket's spigot, and bolted loosely into the upper bracket's clamp, which was about a metre above the lower arm. Now we aligned. I was already at a computer in the client's office with a walky-talky giving the guys orders like, "swing it two degrees left." In no time, we had a good strong connection to the office.

In the end, we missed the deadline because of the cleanup and the

321

necessity of driving back to the office, but no one seemed to care. The Saturday workday usually ended at noon and it was getting close to 1 p.m. when we returned to the office, but everyone felt great. I was with them in the back of the pickup truck as we bombed down the highway going probably way too fast. The camaraderie was visceral, backslapping and bro bumps all around. I remember thinking what a silly thing it was for us to be so ridiculously happy about. In the end, all we'd done is prove to a local businessman that we could make him more money. All we were doing was connecting computers together. We hadn't hit the beaches of Normandy or saved a child from a burning building. Had we made the world a better place? Who knew? Either way, our day in Banjul wasn't going to make the history books. Nevertheless, I knew some part of me had settled down that day. An itch had been scratched.

One for the Road

It was a race to the airport. My flight left around midnight, and Rosaleen and Abai agreed to drive me. I'd been in West Africa for over three years and my baggage consisted of a duffel bag and a laptop case. I was 34 years old and their contents were, barring an Ikea table and two captain's chairs stored with my sister, everything I owned. I'd shown up at about 8 p.m. because of the inevitable hassle at the airport, more prosaically called "security and customs." I was tired, practically sleepwalking, and it wasn't due to a restless night either. It was the final sum of the last year or so.

Sitting in the back of Abai's car, I was lost in thought. I'd never see this sliver of the world again. I'd already decided that I'd never come back. There were so many other places in the world it would be impossible to justify another trip to West Africa. I knew it was time to leave, but I was bothered by something. Was the trip a success? Certainly I'd seen things. As we turned up the main road leading to the airport — its lights clearly visible in the distance — I caught a glimpse of the dark wall of Yundum barracks, which took me back to a memory from the last year.

I was leaving a friend's place in the morning after a long night of drinking. On my way to work, I noticed through the alcohol haze that the streets were deserted. I went back and asked my buddy what he thought was up. He blanched. He'd worked in the NGO sector a long while and he knew the drill. He dragged me back inside, locked all the doors and started dialling numbers. Between calls, he got out a radio and tried to get some local news. That's how you know the government's malfunctioned, he explained: no one's in the street. Sure enough, as calls were returned, the news came in that there had been a coup. Was it successful? No one seemed to know. I called Peter but couldn't get through. By about midafternoon things started returning to normal, and over the next week or two, as the trials began, the facts — as the government understood them — emerged.

The government understood that president Yahya Jammeh was in Mauritania when members of his cabinet and the military tried to depose him. When he found out, the president called the commander of Yundum garrison, sitting as it did conveniently and probably not accidentally beside the airport.[204] The commander, declaring his undying loyalty, prompted Yahya to fly back to the Gambia, rally his loyal troops in Yundum, and move on Banjul. The coup collapsed literally overnight. About a half-dozen formerly loyal members of the regime were found guilty and carted off to a prison far upcountry. I saw the convoy leave the Kairaba area myself: a dozen Land Rovers filled with paramilitary, assault rifles all around. But it turned out the prisoners never made it to the prison. They escaped, all of them. I was blown away when I heard and guffawed about the truly heroic level of incompetence on the part of the authorities. In response to my brazen laughter, Peter quietly mentioned that "escaped" was a euphemism for "dead." It went like this: if the prisoners "escaped," the government had a ready excuse for being unable to produce any remains so no autopsies. On the other hand, if corpses were found, the government had plausible deniability. How do you prove any misadventure was caused by the

---

204 Although it was called Banjul International Airport in the tour guides, locally it was called Yundum Airport. The fact that one of the largest garrisons in the country sat a kilometre from the only major airport I found hard to believe was coincidental.

government if the departed weren't in government custody? If they'd been beaten, it could have happened after the escape, bandits perhaps, or angry farmers venting their outrage at the attack on their beloved president. A thin excuse but hard as hell to disprove, and a huge improvement over "he fell in the shower." One of the guys knew the family of a defendant. On hearing he'd "escaped," they organized a funeral. Yeah, the Gambia had given me stories to tell.

I made my goodbyes and jumped into the airport chaos, worry and adrenaline flowing. In a country where the government couldn't manage street addresses or SIN numbers, only a fool would assume a booking made two weeks earlier would be on file. Was the information on my booking even accurate? Was the flight time correct? And if so, was it expressed in local time or destination time? Between us, my friends and I had pretty much suffered all the travel mishaps the questions above implied and more. Flying was always trauma. I was there hours early, but people were already cued up; it could take 40 minutes to get through a line of 10 when you considered the arguments about luggage weight, computer problems and booking mishaps. And that was just check-in. Security was the real pain.

Security was there to pick your pocket one last time before you left. Every time I'd passed through, my bags came out light. I was extremely nervous this time because my net worth was in my pocket. About $900 USD, the sum total of my time at CompCorp, minus weekly withdraws for drinking, eating and drinking. I knew damn well they'd search my wallet because it was standard procedure, so I had the wad — mostly twenties and fifties — divided between my pockets, with some hidden in the clothes in my bag. I was also nervous because I knew I wasn't in a good frame of mind. My mind had been trained over the last three-plus years to expect anything, anything at all, at any time, and the stress of living with the unknown around every corner had taken its toll.

325

What kept me sane during my first six months as an irresponsible intern was flexibility: that "go with the flow" attitude people without a care in the world could afford. If you have no passionate attachments anywhere, then flowing around makes good sense. See as much as you can, the more possibilities the better. Who cares if you miss a flight? You might meet someone interesting waiting in the bar. But as a grown-up, trying to do right by a local business, making the hypothetical flight was a lot more important than a chance meeting. Sure, the possibilities intrigued. Sure, it might turn out to be the love of my life, but I knew from experience it'd probably just be another travelling alcoholic.

Having goals meant the possibilities became a source of stress, a delayed flight, an impromptu thunderstorm or a corrupt cop could keep you from your destination — and your destination mattered more than a chance encounter in a bar. I'd been playing chess with the world for a long time, and felt I'd won enough games to say I had done something useful, but no matter how many games I won, the fear life would checkmate me in the next match always lingered. The endless questions: Would we be raided again? Would someone be detained? Would someone be electrocuted? Would a client pick a fight with us? Would Peter pick a fight with a client? Would war with Senegal break out? Despite our success, as time went by and the number of disasters and near misses increased, I found it hard to sleep at night. I'd been waking with images of what *might* have happened when the bracket came out of the wall three stories up with one of my guys on it. My eyes would flick open and I'd lay there immobilized with panic, questioning what was true and what wasn't.

"Did that really happen? Did someone get hurt today?"

"No, we didn't even put a bracket up today. No. That was from a week ago, and J.B. managed to jump onto the top of the ladder. No one was hurt. Right. No one was hurt — there was some damage to the client's property — but no one was hurt."

326

"Did I deal with the client? I can't remember. When's the next installation?"

"Friday, pretty sure Friday. I gotta get more control over that site, so we don't have any accidents. I'll go over there tomorrow — no wait, I can't tomorrow — OK, the next day. Is that possible? Will I have time?"

These conversations with myself would normally end with me rationalizing why the next time wouldn't be so bad. Lightening doesn't strike twice, or at least it doesn't strike twice often. Once I was calm, I'd drift off again. As time went on, I began to feel that lightening could strike as many times as it felt like. Waiting to go through security, I couldn't make myself believe it wouldn't strike right then, just as I was leaving the country. Exhausted, I practically twitched with nervous energy, my eyes darting at the people around me. At that time, they still preferred the personal touch at Yundum Airport, and despite the metal detector, they still inspected your baggage by hand. I moseyed over to the table when it was my turn, threw my bags up and offered my wallet. He took the wallet first, ran a thumb over the bills, gave a suspicious glance and handed it back. "*Anyting* in your pocket?"

"No, sir." He rifled through my bags, pulling out a CD of music a friend had brought me from Canada awhile back. He put it aside. Satisfied, he let me go.

The gate area looked right out of the 1950s: high ceilings with slow, sweeping fans. The seats looked as if they dated from the same time. There was no teleprompter listing flight status — you just had to listen and watch. You'd hear something over the PA which was usually indecipherable but served as a cue to start looking for a lineup. You'd grab all your stuff and go ask whoever seemed to be in charge if this was the right line to be in. It wasn't a great system and necessitated staying awake. More than one friend had missed a flight because they nodded off or weren't paying enough attention or got the wrong answer from an airport employee. I had to stay awake, I knew that, but I couldn't help going over to the refreshment stand and grabbing one for the road, my last Joyful JulBrew.

I sipped it and thought about my last month. CompCorp was doing great. Peter had expanded and built a brand-new office on the top floor of his brother's warehouse. It wasn't finished when I left, but enough was in place to imagine the finished product. The whole space was more than twice the size of the old office *and* my quarters *combined*. I'd have had my own office, twice the size of Peter's old one, and it had windows. Peter wanted me to stay, offering me a rent-free apartment in the new space, a third of which was for high-end apartments he could rent out to NGO and World Bank consultant types. He gave me a hard time about the money, all kinds of excuses about how long it would take to gather the cash in American funds. He asked me to wait until he'd found a replacement, but he never really tried, as far as I could tell. His charm was still appealing to me, and I didn't want to leave on bad terms. In the end, I lied and told him my mother was ill, knowing he'd never get between a guy and his mother. It worked. He took me to dinner and we had a great time. It was Peter at his best, with the inside jokes just between the two of us, his stories of the glory days when some of his code had actually been included in a Windows release, reminiscing about his incarceration. Pugnacious Peter, the guy who'd take on the Gambia and come out on top. I was sure of it.

Sitting there in the airport, I had nothing to do but mull things over. Why was I leaving? I tapped a couple of pockets to ensure my hundreds were still safe and remembered a phone call from a few months back. It was a Sunday, and I was walking home from the beach when my cell rang. It was Ken. We'd met in university and both gone into librarianship. I hadn't seen or heard from him in nearly 10 years, barring a two-day trip to Chicago six years back.[205] The connection was terrible, but we managed to exchange email addresses.

He was doing well, personally and professionally. He had a wife and a young daughter, and he was also about to become the head of his own academic library, making him essentially a dean at the age of 34. It gave me pause. I caught myself daydreaming about being back in Canada, where I wouldn't have to fight with foreign governments, African or American, or search the crowd for people who understood my sense of humour. Back in Canada, I wouldn't have to fight against my own foreignness. The more I thought about it, sitting in the dark at The Public House, the better it sounded. I had it all worked out: my experience in the Gambia would be worth something: proof of my ability to triumph over adversity, my ability to cut through bullshit and kick asses. Who didn't want that? I'd get a good job, meet a girl. I'd be around people I shared common points of reference with — things like pop culture and books. I didn't want to be confined to a beach somewhere for the rest of my days, eating the same food, looking at the same trees, talking to the same small group of expats and djembe players.

They finally let us on an actual plane bound for England. From there, I'd connect to Toronto. We piled aboard, exhausted. I closed my eyes and pretended to sleep in order to discourage any conversation, preferring to be lost in my own thoughts. Before I really did fall to sleep, I overheard two English tourists in the seat ahead of me chatting about returning to work. One hated her boss, and her blood pressure was going up knowing she'd have to face him on Monday. The man was rude. *The heartless bastard*, I thought. Rude! How dare he? His rudeness created a terrible working environment for everyone else. It was hostile. It was stressful. Listening to her, I remembered a moment when I had to climb a mast about the height

---

205 We'd graduated a year apart, and while I went to Washington, D.C., to work, Ken had gone to Chicago.

of a telephone pole to adjust an antenna. I had a belt, but the antenna was on a rod strapped to the top of the mast. To reach it, I had to undo my safety belt and stand on top of the mast, which was only wide enough for one of my feet. The whole thing swung back and forth as I stood ramrod straight, one foot dangling over nothing, one hand on the rod, the other loosening the antenna by feel, shifting it around and tightening it when it faced the correct direction. Rude? I was left confused; I couldn't even imagine how that could be a problem. It didn't add up. If you weren't in physical danger did it really matter? Sure people occasionally snapped at each other, just like every other animal on the planet, but if you finished your shift without anyone getting hurt and made something happen into the bargain, wasn't that a good day?

The other one bemoaned having to leave paradise for the rat race back in England. People back home were so structured and uptight. She offered up an anecdote from her vacation where she and her friend had missed some tour they'd signed on for. Undeterred, they let their sense of adventure run wild, walked up the street and found a small bar where they spent the afternoon drinking and dancing with the locals. She'd had a more "real experience" than the ones who made it to the tour bus on time, she reckoned. Back home, people just got angry when the schedule hiccupped. They were so uptight.

Her story reminded me of my own anecdote from about a year before, concerning an intern I got to know, a man from Kenya named Fred. He'd met Abai, and through Abai, the rest of us. He'd brought his very pregnant wife with him on his internship,[206] and I'd met them once or twice. Fred was a pudgy guy, full of life and smiles, always laughing. His wife was quiet and thoughtful. The thing I remember most about her was her placid

---

206 Although in North America we tend to think of interns as young, a lot of the African interns I met were in their late 20s and early 30s. Fred was in this group.

smile.

When the baby was on its way they were driven down to the local clinic, calls were made, and we all gathered there to wait for the good news. I can't remember how it went down exactly, the specific order of events. I remember arriving and being told things hadn't gone well. The next image I remember was Fred holding a blanket and cooing into it: "My sweet little girl, my sweet little girl." I remember the numbed awkwardness we all shared silently as we watched him walking around the corridors of the clinic with his bundle. In whispers, people discussed how to get the baby away from him. Someone had to, because she was dead. His little girl had died during birth, but Fred couldn't accept it. There we were — colleagues, interns, friends — wandering around the clinic trying to comfort, but mostly just standing in silence trying to figure out what to say. Finally, his wife demanded to see Fred. A couple of us were in the corridor outside her room, and I remember her saying quietly but firmly that the baby was dead and it was time to move on. She told him that he'd had an hour to mourn, and now he had to be a man. He had to pull himself together, which he did. Immediately after the death, one of Fred's colleagues had made a call and left, returning later with several white towels, a small white linen sheet, thumbtacks and a box. The latter was a small plywood coffin that a friend of his had managed to put together quickly over the last couple of hours. We watched as he took the baby from Fred, put her down on a gurney in the hallway, wrapped her carefully in the towels and put her in the tiny coffin. The white linen was draped over the coffin and pinned in place with the thumbtacks. He created a small cross on the top with the rest of the tacks. We immediately drove off to one of the few Christian graveyards in the country where a small hole had been dug, and we laid her to rest. Fred and a few of his co-workers went back to the clinic to comfort Fred's wife, and the rest of us went to get drunk. That's when I found out. Over drinks it was explained that the baby had been born alive and healthy, except that

331

the umbilical cord had been wrapped around her neck. But there was no doctor. The delivery had started about 9 a.m., he wasn't scheduled to work until 11, and he refused to come early; this was his time off and he had to live his life after all. The nurses attending were instructed to never take the initiative, only to follow orders, and so without any instructions, they let nature take its course. Paradise killed that baby. Good old follow-your-feelings-take-it-easy-don't-rush-or-get-uptight paradise killed that baby. A sudden surge of respect washed through me for every disciplinarian and martinet I'd ever heard of. I fancied the baby would have survived had Peter had been running that hospital. I crossed my arms and legs and rolled over toward the window, trying to shut their chatter out, waiting for sleep.

London. I'd slept but stumbled off the plane without really waking up. It would be about six hours before my connection, and I wandered around looking for a drink. I found a little place with a view of the tarmac, vodka and a non-judgmental bartender. I slugged a few down to pass the time and studied the wireless kit installed around the airport outside. It frightened me. I knew they were similar in principle to what I'd worked on back in the Gambia, but I also knew there were depths to them I couldn't even begin to fathom, despite my experience. Could I really make a go of it back in Canada? I shook it off.

I'd moved along to another place without windows. I was finishing a beer and upended the bottle to get the last bits. The place filled with tourists just in from some tropical clime: corn-rolled hair, tans and burns, European languages. I resented them. I resented them because I knew they'd spent more on their vacation than I had to show for the last three years of work. I shook it off. I caught a girl — maybe 10 — watching me jiggle the empty bottle to gather any remaining foam in the bottom for one last quaff. She wore a look of concern, the kind kids show the first time they see a homeless person outside the grocery store. I chased her off with a glare. At least I still had my stories.

Toronto. Early evening, dark and freezing. The bus to my hometown was taking forever to get there, and I was so scared I thought I'd cry. Blasting down the highway with other cars and trucks so close. I hadn't gone that fast in a vehicle in years. Images of fiery wrecks flashed through my mind and my rationale's attempts to smother them couldn't keep them away. Just as I'd convince myself the driver was a skilled and experienced professional, the bus rocked and weaved in its lane, and for a moment I could have touched the side of the transport screaming along beside us. The traffic was too close, too fast. I clenched my seat so hard I bent a nail back. Passengers were reading — didn't they understand the peril we were all in? Tons of steel hurtling along, sliding in and out and around one another with only the abilities of people — flawed, silly, clueless people — to keep disaster at bay. I just wanted to talk to someone; to vent the strain, to get some reassurance from my fellow commuters, but one look at them and I knew they wouldn't even understand my desperation. I knew immediately NetCorp was right. None of these people wanted to hear what I had to say or to know where I'd been. My doubts would be understood as hysteria. Maybe it was.

Home. I shrugged up the stairs, exhausted, and tried the door. It was open. Hugs all around. Mum asked if I was hungry, and without waiting for my answer, off to the kitchen to warm up the leftovers. Man, the house looked small and crowded.

"How was it?" my sister asked from the TV room directly off the kitchen.

"Hmmm, I dunno. Hard to say."

"Well, I just got back from Thailand. Two weeks!"

"Cool. You know, there was this funny moment when we went to this local wedding and —"

"We went scuba-diving! It was cool — you could get certified right there!"

"Neat. So this wedding..."

"We rented a moped and drove all over the place. By the way, did you know that Debbie is about to get a divorce?"

"No, I didn't know that."

"What? Who told you that?" Mum demanded from the kitchen.

"I heard it from Jennie. Yeah, they're done."

"Serves him right. He was lazy. Robin, is chicken alright?"

"Sure."

"He was lazy..."

I grabbed my bags and dropped them in my old bedroom and came back downstairs. I rummaged around for some beer, but luck was with me and I found some scotch instead. I poured a glass, dropped on the couch, grabbed the remote and flicked the channels to see what was on.

THE END